PLATO'S
METHOD OF DIALECTIC

PLATO'S
METHOD OF DIALECTIC

BY

JULIUS STENZEL

TRANSLATED AND EDITED BY

D. J. ALLAN

New York
RUSSELL & RUSSELL
1964

FIRST PUBLISHED IN 1940
REISSUED, 1964, BY RUSSELL & RUSSELL, INC.
L. C. CATALOG CARD NO: 64—11848

PRINTED IN THE UNITED STATES OF AMERICA

PREFACE

THE following translation of Stenzel's dissertation on the Literary Form and Content of Plato's Dialogues and of his studies in the development of Plato's Dialectic, was made from the second German edition of 1931. In my Introduction I have attempted to make clear to English readers the purpose and value of these works, and have limited myself to that task. A complete survey of Stenzel's contribution to our understanding of ancient philosophy would naturally have to include his *Zahl und Gestalt* (1933, edn. 2), his *Platon der Erzieher* (1928), and his *Metaphysik des Altertums* (1931)—a far wider undertaking then I here had in mind.

The sense of such words as ἰδέα, δόξα, and διαίρεσις, with those nuances which they possess in Greek, but not in any modern language, is often the main subject of discussion in these studies, and in the German edition single terms were often quoted in Greek or transliterated, and nearly all quotations from the Dialogues were given in the original. In translating so technical a book, I myself have not hesitated to make a liberal use of Greek phrases; but I have ventured to give an English equivalent in a few places where it did not appear that the argument would suffer; and I have reproduced all longer quotations in the version of Jowett. For permission to use this I am obliged to the Jowett Copyright Trustees.

The spirit of these studies is, as the author himself emphasizes, one of historical criticism, as opposed to what it was then fashionable to call 'systematic' exposition. Nevertheless, more use is made of the technical language of philosophy than we are accustomed to find in English works on Plato; and the word 'concept' (*Begriff*) is in a special way fundamental to the thesis of the book, which tells the story of Plato's progress towards clarity as regards the distinction between individual and universal. The word *Begriff* is widely used by German logicians and in a fairly stabilized sense, owing to the influence of Kant and Hegel, but its English equivalent 'concept' (preferable,

I think, to 'notion' or 'essence') is much less familiar and may be a source of suspicion. Let it be said, then, that this term is used here with no metaphysical implications, and is intended to denote something which any logical doctrine must acknow-ledge. The 'concept' is that which we comprehend when we know a definition; it is contrasted with visible form, with the thing perceived by the senses, with the individual; it is what Berkeley called a 'notion', and Aristotle τὸ τί ἦν εἶναι; what Antisthenes, in his famous dispute with Plato, called ἱππότης and professed himself unable to see. The word does not *necessarily* denote something which could not exist apart from a mind: Zeller held that the Ideas of Plato were concepts which somehow existed in their own right, and Stenzel himself agrees that this was the position in the later Dialogues, though he denies that it was so at the outset. The terms 'conceptualism' and 'realism', invented under different circumstances at a time when Latin was in normal use, are here misleading: in the sense of the German *Begriff*, both schools recognized the existence of the concept, but the conceptualist held that it was only a thought, whereas the realist held that it existed *in natura rerum*.

I must express my deep indebtedness to Frau Dr. Berta Stenzel, who has offered me just and helpful criticism, and saved me from many mistranslations.

D. J. A.

INTRODUCTION

Julius Stenzel, who taught as a professor of philosophy at Kiel and afterwards at Halle, and died in 1935, was one of the most original and industrious Platonic scholars of his time.

The signs of a powerful and adaptable mind will be obvious throughout the following pages. Stenzel is primarily a faithful and observant student of the text of his author; but he is also extremely skilful at summing up a long and tortuous argument. Sometimes he devotes a chapter to the dissection of one crucial sentence; sometimes he surveys two or three Dialogues in a paragraph. But these obvious virtues of Stenzel's work do not help to make it more lucid, and the translator feels it to be his duty to say something of the problems which Stenzel had to face, and of his success in finding a solution.

Two distinct works are included in this translation: an essay on the literary form and philosophical content of the Dialogues, and some studies on Plato's Dialectic. The essay was read to a society in 1916, and the studies were written during the following year; when they came to be published, the essay was used by the author as an introduction to them, and we have followed his example. In the essay he shows how certain changes in the Dialogue form, used as a guide to the thought, tell us something which we could not otherwise ascertain. Plato does not appear in person in any Dialogue, yet he is able to show whether he agrees with a particular assertion, or how seriously he means it to be taken. From the formal point of view, it is natural to divide the Dialogues into two classes, according as Socrates is or is not the chief speaker. Now Socrates' leadership begins to waver in the *Parmenides*, where, to say the least of it, he is no longer triumphant; in the *Sophist*, *Statesman*, and *Timaeus* he is present simply as a witness; in the *Laws* he vanishes altogether. These are the Dialogues which, by stylistic tests, we should assign to Plato's old age. The facts, therefore, at first seem to lend themselves to a simple chronological interpretation. How familiar, and how empty of true information, this interpretation is! Plato adopted the Socratic Dialogue because he wished to give to the world a true picture of his master; retained it, after he had begun to have a philosophy of his own, because the mask was not yet inconvenient to him; eventually lost his interest in popular and descriptive writing, turned to more abstruse philosophical questions, and came before his audience in cap and gown.

If it is a fact that in the earlier series of Dialogues Plato himself always remains behind the scenes; if he presents Socrates as a man of unvarying mood; if he does not resume the Socratic Dialogue in old age, but steadily forgets his master, and if his last Dialogues are a pure exposition of doctrine—then this is a plausible view. But not one of these things is true. In the *Phaedrus* and *Philebus*, of which the second at least is very late, Plato resumes the Socratic form. In the earlier Dialogues, i.e. the Socratic Dialogues proper, he presents his master sometimes as devoid of knowledge, sometimes as a reporter of sublime doctrines. And there is a strong tradition, which all scholars now accept, that the later Dialogues do not reveal, and are not meant to reveal, the real teaching of Plato. This was reserved for oral exposition.

Stenzel's essay, then, is designed to show that the familiar view of Plato's development is too simple, and that the truth will only appear if we make a joint study of form and content. What does this mean? Not simply that Plato is at once a supreme writer and a great philosopher. This statement would be true, but could make no pretence to novelty. The suggestion is that it suits Plato's temperament to insinuate part of his meaning by artistic, or formal, devices. His whole meaning is not always conveyed in plain words, as it is with a thinker who regards expression as a secondary matter.

It follows from this that it cannot be the task of one student to criticize the philosophy of Plato's Dialogues, whilst another, careless of their meaning and truth, goes into transports of enthusiasm over the beauty of form and felicity of style. Yet this, or something like it, is the course normally ordained in our universities. The whole philosophy of Plato, it may be said, is hostile to specialization. How, then, can specialization ever bring us nearer to his meaning? Of this difficulty Stenzel had become deeply aware. He saw the interpretation of Plato's meaning consigned beyond recall to the faculty of philosophy, whilst the linguistic scholar, content to have a province of his own, surrendered himself to the soothing influence of style, tracked down topical allusions in the Dialogues, compiled statistics of Plato's vocabulary. In one classroom the form of the Dialogues counted for nothing; interpreted as treatises like those of Kant and Hegel, wrenched into the moulds of modern philosophy, they lost much of their original meaning. In the neighbouring room the quest of theoretical truth was not a primary consideration; one read Plato as one would listen to an eloquent sermon.

Thus in emphasizing the interrelation of form and content, Stenzel was trying to attract his fellow Platonists to a new method of study, and to show that existing methods were fruitless. His own early training was that of a philologist; but he had gone on to read Kant and Husserl until he was able to debate with philosophers in their own language. He soon found himself alone in his judgement of Plato. To 'philosophical' writers— Natorp, Cohen, and others—he acknowledged a great debt. Again and again they had explained passages of Plato which remained a mystery to their classical colleagues. But he was convinced that, in the version they gave, a vital part of Plato's philosophy had evaporated. He dissented entirely, as we shall see at a later stage, from their version of the theory of Ideas; he assumed that when Plato distinguished two *worlds*, the intelligible and the sensible, and passionately insisted on this contrast, he meant what he said, and meant it *as a philosopher*.

We can now approach the argument of the essay. The first point is that, in the early Dialogues, Plato sometimes peeps over the shoulder of Socrates. Thus, in the *Meno*, Socrates shows by his own method of argument that whatever knowledge is, it is not entirely derived from experience—it is latent in the soul, and learning is 'reminiscence'. Then he tells how he had once heard from 'priests and priestesses' that the soul has really pre-existed —that it comes for a time into the body and will depart again.

In the *Symposium*, he is able to show by his own methods what Love is *not*. But when he begins to describe what it really *is*, namely a progress away from the visible world towards the intelligible, he begins to report a discourse which he had heard from the priestess Diotima, and not properly understood.

But this, it may be said, is not necessarily a hint of Plato's own belief; it might, for instance, be meant to indicate that there are certain limits to intellectual apprehension. Where it suits Plato to ascribe metaphysical doctrines to his master, he does so. Thus, throughout the *Phaedo* Socrates discourses on the immortality of the soul. In the *Parmenides*, he propounds the belief in Ideas as his own, insisting upon their separateness from the world of sense. The whole of the *Republic* is an excursion into an ideal realm where change and imperfection do not exist. The whole fabric depends upon knowledge of a sublime and abstract, but to the philosopher supremely real, Idea. How can it be maintained that Socrates has only rare and fleeting glimpses of knowledge?

Stenzel strives to meet this objection by a comparison of the *Phaedo* with the *Republic*. It is true that Socrates, throughout the *Phaedo*, is a metaphysician; but the state which he is in is not his normal state. Within a few hours he is to die, and he faces death with a serene confidence. We find him still under the influence of a singular dream which has exhorted him to write poetry. He is like a swan, which sings once before it dies; and the swan-song is his final proof of the immortality of the soul (84 E). Now it is precisely this proof which involves the doctrine of Ideas.

But the *Phaedo* itself contains evidence that Socrates had not really maintained the belief in Ideas as a settled doctrine. This is in the famous autobiographical passage. He had begun, he says, as a student of nature, but could find no satisfaction in the usual explanations of the world; they were all, except that of Anaxagoras, in terms of matter alone. The notions of intelligence, design, purpose, good, are necessary to a full explanation of the world, or of any fact within it, such as his sitting here in this prison. But Socrates confesses himself unable to state 'the highest kind of cause'. He had, however, been accustomed in his arguments to discover a second kind of cause, which was obvious in argument (ἐν λόγοις), though, without the first, it could not be proved to be real. Here the theory of Ideas is stated in an unusually tentative way. Wherever many like things existed, it is necessary to postulate an Idea—e.g. the Idea of Beauty, that which is beautiful 'in and by itself'. The Idea is a *hypothesis*; and nothing more is said here than that it causes what we perceive. But we are shown how hypotheses can be examined, if it should ever occur to us to doubt them: we would have to find another hypothesis, from which the first one followed, and continue this process until we had attained 'something adequate'—i.e. either a self-evident truth, or a hypothesis which all disputants agreed to be satisfactory.

The Idea, then, is a hypothesis used as a premiss to a particular argument, or assumed to explain a particular set of facts. Nothing is said of its independent reality. Nor is it said that all such hypotheses are necessarily connected with each other, or again that they may all be deduced from any single self-evident truth. It is only said that when a hypothesis is questioned, it is necessary to re-establish it by connecting it with 'something adequate', whatever that may be.

What is most remarkable in the *Phaedo* is that Socrates, though he personally feels this method to be satisfactory, describes it as the *second best*. He knows that it is defective because the hypotheses are not related to the Good, without which no explanation of causes can be complete. In the metaphysical part of the *Republic*, Socrates is made to foresee much more definitely the character of the ideal explanation; and in the *Timaeus*, when another speaker has taken over the leading part, that explanation is actually attempted. We are here concerned with the *Republic* alone. Socrates, it is true, professes the greatest hesitation before he begins to speak about the Good; and he will only consent to delineate its visible image. However, his difficulty is not so much that he himself does not know the Good from experience, as that such an experience cannot be adequately described in words. His first image, that of the Sun, emphasizes that the Good is not a postulate of the mind, is not brought into existence by thought. The sun not only illuminates the world, but causes

things in it to live and grow. Similarly, the Good is the source not
only of true explanation, but of real existence. In the next simile,
two stages of knowledge are contrasted, νόησις and Διάνοια, which
represent human thought with and without the Idea of the Good.
In Διάνοια certain 'hypotheses' are taken for granted; from these
the mind proceeds to conclusions which have a kind of provisional truth. Though the parallel is perhaps not exact, this is
what Socrates in the *Phaedo* had called the second best method.
In νόησις the hypotheses themselves are tested and, if possible,
justified; the mind does not rest until it has reached a truth
which is unconditionally true. And the goal is no longer the vague
τι ἱκανόν of the *Phaedo* (which suggests that the mind can rest
where it wants); it is a point firmly fixed in the nature of things.

We shall mention later that there are certain interpreters for
whom Plato's Ideas are not entities existing in their own right,
but mere rules of scientific explanation. For these critics the
statement of the theory in the *Phaedo*, whereby the Ideas are
hypotheses, shows it in its true colours, whereas in Book VI
of the *Republic* it appears in a festive dress. Stenzel opposes
this interpretation. The effect of the two passages, he thinks,
is to show Plato's relation to Socrates, although the latter never
relinquishes the role of chief speaker. Socrates sees the promised
land, and is allowed, in the *Republic*, to make an imaginative
excursion over it; but he never really crossed its borders. The
passage from the *Phaedo* gives an accurate picture of Socrates'
philosophy, because, until the Good is known, no Idea is more
than a hypothesis. In the *Republic*, together with more positive
information about the Good, we receive an assurance that the
Ideas are real. Plato does not need to appear on the scene; yet
he shows that he has answered, in the spirit of Socrates, a problem
set by Socrates. It is scarcely necessary to say how essential is
the difference on this point between Stenzel and his opponents;
for them, the real existence of Ideas is a mere fancy, not to be
dwelt upon in a critical spirit; for him, it is a step forward taken
in real earnest, and proudly viewed by Plato as a culmination
to his master's lifelong pursuit of truth.[1]

[1] Stenzel does not ignore the possibility that Plato himself had acquired a more

After the *Republic* Plato's doctrine undergoes a material change, and, corresponding to this, there is a gradual transition to a new form of Dialogue wherein Socrates plays no active part. No longer is everything seen in the light of moral goodness, no longer are there a few select Ideas. The theory of Ideas itself is either passed over in silence, or put forward in a tentative spirit. A time of reckoning has plainly come. Meanwhile, Socrates has lost the inspiration which had guided him in the *Phaedo* and the *Republic*. In the *Theaetetus* he reappears in his least positive mood, criticizing all beliefs and asserting none. In the *Parmenides* Plato finds it convenient to show him amid the hesitation of youth.

The criticism of the Ideas in the first part of the *Parmenides* is not particularly mysterious, once we realize that there was bound to come a time in Plato's life when he turned a critical eye upon the whole Socratic philosophy which he had inherited. This criticism is to be viewed as a revelation of Plato's state of mind when he wrote, not as an essay on the state of philosophy in the time of Socrates' youth. The second part of the Dialogue is of interest to an observer of literary form, since here for the first time a speaker other than Socrates is allowed to assume control. Stenzel, in his essay, has unfortunately omitted to give any special interpretation of this change, and, in his work on Plato's Dialectic, he similarly omits to compare the Dialectic exercised by Parmenides in the Dialogue so named with that exercised by the Stranger in the *Sophist*. But it is clear what his view on these points must be. Having formulated his difficulties, Plato sees that it is by Dialectic that he must solve them. Notice that this is Parmenides' final injunction to Socrates:

Πρῷ γάρ, εἰπεῖν, πρὶν γυμνασθῆναι, ὦ Σώκρατες, ὁρίζεσθαι ἐπιχειρεῖς καλόν τέ τι καὶ Δίκαιον καὶ ἀγαθὸν καὶ ἓν ἕκαστον τῶν εἰδῶν. ἐνενόησα γὰρ καὶ πρῴην σου ἀκούων Διαλεγομένου ἐνθάδε 'Αριστοτέλει τῷΔε. καλὴ μὲν οὖν καὶ θεία, εὖ ἴσθι, ἡ ὁρμὴ ἣν ὁρμᾷς ἐπὶ τοὺς λόγους· ἕλκυσον Δὲ σαυτὸν καὶ γύμνασαι μᾶλλον Διὰ τῆς Δοκούσης ἀχρήστου εἶναι καὶ καλουμένης ὑπὸ τῶν πολλῶν ἀΔολεσχίας, ἕως ἔτι νέος εἶ· εἰ Δὲ μή, σὲ Διαφεύξεται ἡ ἀλήθεια.

positive belief about the Ideas during the interval between the *Phaedo* and the *Republic*. In this case the contrast would not be between himself and Socrates, but between successive stages in his own development. But in twe Dialogues which are otherwise so closely similar, is it not more natural to suppose that they were to some extent both planned in advance, and that during the *Phaedo* something was held in reserve?

But the method of Dialectic has never yet assumed a definite shape: Plato sees two alternative forms of it, and conducts a long experiment in each, assigning the chief parts to Parmenides and the Eleatic Stranger in order to indicate in what direction he had found most help.

To come next to the *Theaetetus*: if in time of writing it is roughly contemporary with the *Parmenides*, it is externally linked up with the *Sophist* and *Statesman*. With them, it forms a dramatic trilogy, to which some think that a fourth Dialogue, on 'the Philosopher', was to have been appended. Has the *Theaetetus* any philosophical claim to belong to this group? On the one hand, it is hard to think that the dramatic sequence is a mere fancy without further significance. And some questions are undoubtedly common to the *Theaetetus* and *Sophist*, the latter being dogmatic where the former is critical. On the other hand, the earlier part of the *Theaetetus* preserves the 'moral orientation' of the *Republic*; and the statistics of style and vocabulary seem to demand an interval of composition between it and the *Sophist*. With the evidence at our disposal, it is not easy to decide whether Plato really shared the doubt ascribed to his master in the *Theaetetus*, or whether he set out in systematic fashion to state the questions before he gave the answers. Taking the latter alternative, Stenzel rests his case on two convincing grounds: firstly, on the aptness of the answers themselves, and secondly, on the fact that in the *Theaetetus* there is too much profession of mere criticism: 'Socrates' is too impeccably himself. Most of the examples are carefully chosen from the moral sphere, rather than from science. Socrates makes a great show of his μαιευτικὴ τέχνη. He helps Theaetetus to discover that Knowledge does not consist in sensation, but searches in vain for a more satisfactory definition, and does not openly bring in the theory of Ideas. Here is an interesting point of literary form: while Plato himself was really in the Socratic mood, he permitted Socrates to become momentarily 'above himself' and foresee a solution to his perplexities. Now, he apparently has to strive to recapture the Socratic frame of mind.

A suspicion being thus formed, we begin to look for a pattern in the discussion of these two Dialogues.[1] The *Theaetetus* is entirely devoted to the question, What is Knowledge? It is naturally divisible, however, into two parts. In Part I we learn that sensation, though no doubt an element in knowledge, is not knowledge itself; neither is it true, especially in morals and politics, that things really are as they appear. Plato develops for the first time an account of the mechanism of sense-perception; he emphasizes that the senses cannot perform acts of comparison and judgement, since each has its special work to do; he begins the terminology which has become customary. (184 D: ψυχὴν... ᾗ διὰ τούτων οἷον ὀργάνων αἰσθανόμεθα ὅσα αἰσθητά.) Part II is also negative in its result. Can knowledge be defined as the possession or exercise of δόξα? This word has now to be taken in a broader sense than before. Even in the *Republic* δόξα had been mere opinion or belief, essentially contrasted with ἐπιστήμη, and any suggestion that it *was* knowledge, or could be intensified so as to become knowledge, would have been *ipso facto* ridiculous. There is a new emphasis on the activity of the mind—on the endeavour to form δόξα, rather than the possession of it as a permanent state; a new interest in the psychology of knowing, and a decline of interest in its metaphysical implications. But an unexpected obstacle arises to defeat the suggestion that 'true judgement' is Knowledge: what is false judgement? and if we cannot tell, how can we say which judgements are true? As a last resource, it may be said that Knowledge is true judgement 'accompanied by reasoning', μετὰ λόγου. This would have been full of meaning at an earlier stage in Plato's thought, since he would have defined λόγος simply as the apprehension of the Ideas by the mind. Now even λόγος is included in the general scepticism. The word may indicate three things: (a) speech or vocal expression, as contrasted with the inner speech of the mind, (b) the complete description of a thing by an enumeration of its elements, (c) the definition of a thing by discovery of its distinctive nature, διαφορότης. The third of these meanings seems at first to promise a positive criterion of Knowledge. But look more

[1] Here, for convenience' sake, I anticipate the argument of Stenzel in the third chapter of the longer work.

closely: it is not the thing's Διαφορότης, but *knowledge* of its Διαφορότης which will constitute Knowledge; and this is circular. Such is the argument of the *Theaetetus*: Part II follows naturally upon Part I—but Part II is deeply interwoven with the positive sequel in the *Sophist*.

Next day the friends of Socrates return by appointment, bringing with them an Eleatic Stranger who is courteously introduced. A problem is soon stated, and a method of inquiry selected, in a more formal fashion than ever before. Socrates fears that the new arrival may be no Stranger, but a God, come to spy out and refute unskilful reasoners (φαύλους ὄντας ἡμᾶς ἐν τοῖς λόγοις ἐποψόμενός τε καὶ ἐλέγξων). Theodorus has described him as a philosopher: will he tell the company whether he thinks the philosopher to be identical in nature with the statesman and the sophist? Or are there three distinct characters, as there are three names? Let him not trouble about the method, for they are ready to listen to him either in a Dialogue or in an uninterrupted talk. The Stranger, no doubt as a compliment to Socrates, selects the Dialogue; but it is made clear that this no longer implies any genuine resistance on the part of the respondent. Socrates quotes as an instance of Dialogue, not his contest with Thrasymachus or Protagoras, but his juvenile debate with Parmenides—in which the replies he gave were never more than mere formulae of agreement!

Turning to the question proposed, the Stranger is not slow to profit by the freedom granted to him. He employs a peculiar new technique of definition, having first illustrated it to his hearers by some examples, because it will be strange to them. This is the technique of division into classes, τὸ κατ᾽ εἴδη Διαιρεῖσθαι. By dividing a class exhaustively into sub-classes, generally two at a time, the inquirer proceeds until he reaches a class which coincides with the notion to be defined. This, in its simplest form, is Διαίρεσις. It may not be obvious without previous inquiry which major class should be chosen for division; in this case there will be need for a reverse process of 'collection', τὸ συνάγειν εἰς ἕν, which begins with particular species (not sensible particulars) and decides on their natural arrangement. In these two operations is summed up the work of the dialectician, according to Plato's later theory. But even with the new method the definition of the Sophist does not follow an easy course. He belongs to the class of those who make what is illusory or unreal. But is there any class of the unreal, τὸ μὴ ὄν? The Stranger had not been present at the previous day's discussion, when Socrates had asked how it was possible to think or state 'what is not'. Nevertheless he now answers that question, among others, as though he had known all about it. A theory of Being is wanted to give the clue to the nature of Not-Being. The Stranger has a theory, which he offers as a compromise. There are some who believe only in what they can see and touch, others who admit the reality only of Ideas:[1] if we define the real as that which has the power (Δύναμις) of acting or being acted upon, both may be satisfied. Some maintain the unity, others the multiplicity of the real: what if there are many real forms united in one system, so that their interrelation can be accurately defined? Each form will then 'be', but it will 'not be' in the sense that it is not some other form. This disposes of the paradox both of false judgement and of negative statement. Both seem to involve a declaration about 'what is not'. The new theory maintains that whatever is, also is not, since it is other than many other things. Not-Being may therefore be said to be, without the absurdity of supposing it to be a department of reality. From this follow various conclusions, which are all answers to problems raised in the *Theaetetus*. Knowledge is the power, which the philosopher alone fully possesses, to judge truly about the interrelation of forms. Judgement (Δόξα) is the act of uniting a predicative expression (ῥῆμα) to a noun or subject (ὄνομα): its truth or falsehood depends on whether or not it faithfully represents the union of Ideas. As to λόγος, it means the audible speech in which judgement is imparted by one person to another. Thus, by examining what is taught in these two Dialogues, we see why Plato forms them into a dramatic sequence, and why he makes Socrates hand over his part to the Stranger; conversely, the dramatic situation

---

[1] i.e. the earlier Plato and his followers, whose theory, viewed by the Stranger, now appears as partial and inadequate.

contains the essential key to what Plato has to say, and the degree
of confidence with which he says it. The form is fitted to the
content, the content to the form.[1]

One more question remains. May it be assumed that, after
the retirement of Socrates, Plato speaks without disguise, and
coincides entirely with the new leaders of the discussion, such
as Parmenides and Timaeus? No, we are obliged to reply, for
although Plato deposes Socrates, he preserves the Dialogue form,
and the Dialogue is literature. What does Plato say of literature
in the *Phaedrus*? He claims, still using Socrates as his exponent,
that books are entirely unsuitable for philosophical teaching.
They can serve only for amusement, when a philosopher chooses
to write on some subject which is not nearest to his heart, or as
notes to remind a man in old age of the true knowledge which he
has received by some other means (276 A–D). Earlier scholars[2]
were inclined to assume either that Plato was here making
Socrates speak in character, or that he was joking. But Jaeger
entered on a new path with his inquiry into the origin of Aristotle's *Metaphysics*, published in 1913. He found that, whereas
Plato's Dialogues were designed for publication, more or less
in the modern sense, the treatises of Aristotle were the records
of his oral teaching. In so far as the prevailing opinion of Aristotle as a stylist is founded on a comparison between his treatises
and the Platonic Dialogues (and it is so, to a greater extent than
many care to admit), it is absurdly wrong. And it is wrong,
again, to assume that Plato's teaching in the Academy necessarily resembled his Dialogues, even the later ones, either in
manner or in substance. Aristotle mentions 'unwritten doctrines' of Plato, and when dealing with the doctrine of Ideas,

[1] Stenzel stresses the exact correspondence between the problems in the *Theaetetus* and their answers in the *Sophist*, and seems definitely to take the view that the
plan was prearranged, so that the Socratic 'criticism' in the *Theaetetus* is insincere.
But (1) he himself does not deny that Plato did pass through an interval of doubt
between his two stages of positive assertion; (2) he perhaps goes too far in arguing
that the answers are perfectly adapted to the questions. The questions raised were
psychological—what happens in the mind when we are said to know, or to judge
falsely. The answer given is metaphysical. And in regard to λόγος, the 'answer'
is little more than a play on its double meaning of 'rational discourse' and 'speech'.
[2] e.g. Bruns in his work on *Das literarische Porträt der Griechen.*

refers mainly to his recollection of these, and very little to the Dialogues. Both he and his master were therefore faithful to the precept given in the *Phaedrus*; and there was no reason why a pupil who had heard the inner doctrine should refer to the published version. The only difference in their practices was that Plato kept no notes of his lectures, whilst Aristotle wrote very full notes; and these have accidentally survived, when by an irony of fate the literary works for which he was once famous have perished.

This knowledge perhaps gives little help to the modern student, who is obliged to know Plato through his Dialogues. But it makes it easier to understand his meaning in the *Phaedrus*, and also in the *Statesman* where he insists that no written and codified law is necessary if living and adaptable knowledge, the knowledge of a wise *man*, can be obtained. And the later Dialogues, as a whole, will be better estimated when we think of them as containing what Plato himself considered to be the mere outer husk of his teaching.

It remains to say something of the *Phaedrus* and *Philebus*. The form of these Dialogues is peculiar, inasmuch as they present Socrates once more in the leading part, although there are many manifest signs of late composition, both stylistic and philosophical. Stenzel does not deal separately with the *Philebus*. He would not, I think, agree that it couples the Socratic form with a non-Socratic type of thought; he would deny that the form is truly Socratic. The opening theme is, indeed, an old one—Philebus maintains that the Good is pleasure or enjoyment, Socrates that it is thought or knowledge. Philebus and Protarchus are young disciples of Gorgias. We can almost imagine Socrates meeting them in the gymnasium, and compelling them to have their beliefs criticized—until we discover to our astonishment that it is they who have come to him with a special request for an 'audience' (συνουσία, 19 c). He has graciously consented; but they fear that he may slip away, and threaten to detain him by force until he has put a 'satisfactory conclusion' to the argument. The scene somehow recalls the visit of Odysseus to the underworld to consult Teiresias. And the ghostly Socrates brings with him, not a firm persuasion of his own ignorance, but a sheaf of Pythagorean speculations. The old problem of the one and the many is a childish game. There is, indeed, a new problem— but that too, fortunately, can be solved by the heaven-sent method of 'division'. All truth depends on numbers and proportions; the purest pleasures are those aroused in the mind by the sight of regular geometrical figures; the good life itself is not so much a compound of pleasure and knowledge as a kind of ratio in which these elements are mixed. The whole world is an animate being, inhabited by a rational world-soul.

The mystery of the *Phaedrus* is so well described by Stenzel in two passages (pp. 17, 149) that little need be said here. Because of its enthusiasm and exuberant beauty, its numerous stories and passages of myth, it was once classed as a juvenile work—the earliest Dialogue, said Schleiermacher, in which Plato, at the outset of his writing, gave a presentiment of the whole (*Ahnung des Ganzen*). As the later Dialogues have been sorted out and their characteristics defined, it has become increasingly clear that the *Phaedrus* belongs with them; and this conclusion is, on the whole, reinforced by the statistics of style. The fact remains that the speaker is Socrates, and that the problems dealt with— love, rhetoric, the soul, the Ideas—are Socratic problems. Stenzel correctly observes that the whole personality of Socrates is transformed; he speaks as one inspired. Moreover (the content corresponding as usual to the form), he shows a prophetic insight into the methods of a later generation; as in the *Philebus*, he expounds the method of Division, and confesses himself its 'lover'. Thus the *Phaedrus* ceases to be a problem, and is claimed by Stenzel as a crowning illustration of the thesis of his essay. Plato prepares us admirably for a change in Socrates' character. He shows Socrates meeting Phaedrus at the city wall, and being lured into the country by the book which he carries concealed beneath his cloak, like a hungry animal by a branch; he shows him reclining, in the noonday heat, under a plane-tree beside the Ilissus. No occasion could be more favourable for a prophetic glimpse into the future. And Socrates—we are not quite sure whether he is awake or asleep—proceeds to foretell how his successor Plato will found a school in which his memory is kept alive, and invent methods to set his doubts at rest. The writing of such a Dialogue would be attractive to Plato, because it would enable him to show how his thought, in every fresh form which it assumed, was inspired by Socrates. He could make fun of the readers, of his own or a later day, who wished to inflict upon him 'stages of development'.

From the point of vantage attained in his essay, it was possible for Stenzel to follow either of two roads.

He could attempt to give, perhaps for the first time in the history of scholarship, a complete picture of Plato's later philosophy, a picture which would include on the one side his oral teaching, as reported by Aristotle and some of his neo-Platonist commentators, and on the other side the later Dialogues. To this hazardous undertaking Stenzel devoted his *Number and Form in Plato and Aristotle* (1924; 2nd edition, 1933). Here he made a great contribution to the history both of mathematics and of philosophy. He concluded that it was principally the notion of Διαίρεσις, division, which served as a link between the literary and oral branches of Plato's philosophy. In the Dialogues he deals with the division of physical substances and the division of Ideas; for in the *Timaeus* he stated an idealistic atomic theory, in deliberate antithesis to Democritus, and in such Dialogues as the *Sophist* and *Statesman* he expounded a logical division which began and ended in the intelligible world. Finally, in his lectures Plato seems to have discussed the division of Ideas, especially those of numbers, into their elements. Everywhere in nature, but most clearly in the case of numbers, he discovered a formal and a material principle, 'the One' and 'the great and small', or as he calls them in the *Philebus*, 'limit' and 'the unlimited'. (Cf. Aristotle, *Metaphysics* 987^b 18: ἐπεὶ Δ' αἴτια τὰ εἴδη τοῖς ἄλλοις, τἀκείνων στοιχεῖα πάντων ᾠήθη τῶν ὄντων εἶναι στοιχεῖα. ὡς μὲν οὖν ὕλην τὸ μέγα καὶ τὸ μικρὸν εἶναι ἀρχάς, ὡς Δ' οὐσίαν τὸ ἕν· ἐξ ἐκείνων γὰρ κατὰ μέθεξιν τοῦ ἑνὸς εἶναι τοὺς ἀριθμούς.) Stenzel had little patience with the view that Aristotle misunderstood, or purposely misrepresented, this later Platonism. He saw that this speculation about numbers, though it seems strange to us, is not to be dismissed as an idle dream of Plato's dotage. Aristotle criticized the real theory of Ideas, not the popularized version; and this was the natural thing for him to do.

A second course was to follow Plato's philosophical development in the Dialogues, assuming a broad division of them into an earlier and a later group. This is undertaken in the present work, entitled in the original 'Studies in the development of the Platonic Dialectic—Socrates to Aristotle'; there is a sub-title 'Aretê and Diairesis'. This work was written in 1917, whilst the author awaited a summons to military service. He wrote in great haste, and addressed the preface from the battlefield. This must be taken into consideration before a complaint of obscurity is raised. But it is doubtful if a work so planned could have been lucid, even in more favourable circumstances. A concise review of a number of Platonic Dialogues, detailed enough to be useful, yet brief enough to offer a genuine comparison, can never be easy.

It is, therefore, very desirable in reading these studies to have freshly in mind the argument of the *Republic*, *Theaetetus*, and *Sophist*. The English reader needs further to be equipped with some knowledge of the German authorities constantly cited or refuted. In the remainder of this Introduction I shall attempt to explain the polemical intention of the Studies, make clear their argument, and estimate their value. Let it not be thought that the prejudices opposed by Stenzel were local and ephemeral; English scholarship has, unfortunately, been overshadowed by similar misinterpretation.

It has been said that he wished to steer between two extremes, a sentimental literary criticism of the Dialogues, and a forcible adaptation of them to the notions of modern philosophy. As was natural, the book upon first publication was not fully intelligible to either party. The representatives of 'philology' saw its importance; but the majority complained of an overdose of philosophical terms. The philosophers, on the other hand, not only had to listen to a sharp criticism of themselves, but found themselves drawn into a fatiguing analysis of the text. We must begin here by a statement of this 'philosophical' Platonism. There were in fashion two different versions of the theory of Ideas. According to the first of these versions, which was due mainly to Zeller, the Platonic Ideas were substantialized concepts or universals. Plato had learnt from Socrates to distinguish Justice from just actions, redness from red things—and, if we follow certain passages in the *Republic* and *Parmenides*, bedness from beds. Since these concepts were *known*, it followed for Plato that they were *real*. They did not draw their life from the sensible world, but infused life into it. And they were not thoughts. Zeller gave overwhelming proof from the text that the Ideas were never conceived by Plato himself as thoughts of God or man. The theory of Ideas was a theory of Being, in the tradition of the Eleatics. But whereas Parmenides taught that reality must be single, simple, and motionless, Plato discovered, especially after the *Republic*, that distinction, complexity, systematic relationship, and movement were indispensable conditions of both Being and Knowledge. Such was Zeller's exposition. He did not consider too curiously the chronological development of Plato's views; he had no reliable data about the order of the Dialogues, and he did not fully realize their popular and literary character; he regarded them, in fact, from a systematic point of view.

This was, in substance, the account of the theory of Ideas which Aristotle gives in the first book of his *Metaphysics*. It was not obviously untrue; and, coming from a scholar with an unrivalled knowledge of the ancient philosophers, it required no forcible assimilation of ancient Greek to modern European thought—Zeller's view was, however, discarded by the next generation of philosophical critics. Natorp and his associates (the 'Marburg school', as they are termed by Stenzel) were Kantians, convinced that Kant had put an end to disputes about the theory of knowledge, and very anxious to show that Plato had anticipated him. All great philosophers must agree—all must be interpreted through each other—and Kant is the latest and most complete; such were their axioms. Kant's philosophy was first whittled down to a bare theory of knowledge; no notice was taken of the more speculative tendencies of the *Critique of Pure Reason*. It then remained to suppose that Plato's Ideas were the same as the categories of Kant—laws or principles employed by the mind in its explanation of the sensible world. There was one world, not two; the relation between the intelligible and the sensible was that between form and matter. What else is meant by the famous passage in the *Phaedo*, in which Socrates introduces the Ideas as necessary *hypotheses*?—Was there no more? Undoubtedly, for Plato was at the same time a poet, gifted with soaring imagination. So, regardless of logic, he had sometimes described how the dialectician leaves behind him the world of sense, and divests himself of sense-perception to rise to a world of pure forms, 'substance really real, Being colourless and shapeless and intangible'. This, however, was when Plato had put off the academic gown. It was unfortunate that his first disciple and successor had been a person criminally insensitive to the difference between prose and poetry. The whole influence of Platonism down to the time of Kant had been impeded by the Aristotelian interpretation of the Ideas as real substances. The Dialogues do not give the least support to this view, if only we use imagination where it is required, and restrain it where we are invited to restrain it.[1]

One would have thought it necessary, if such a view were to be maintained, to show by quotation from the text that the substantial being of the Ideas is involved only in passages written in a fanciful style, never in passages of logical argument. This has never been shown; and, on the first attempt to show it, the dissection of Plato's personality would stand revealed as quite

---

[1] Among works published in England, Stewart's work *Plato's Doctrine of Ideas* is avowedly an adaptation of Natorp; but Stewart imagines that Plato had anticipated not only Kant, but Bergson, the Pragmatists, and the greater part of modern psychology. (For quotations see A. Diès, *Autour de Platon*, ii. 352.) Bosanquet (*A Companion to Plato's Republic*) borrows from Hegel a curious and disastrous distinction between the Ideas as pictures, and the Ideas as essences. The latter, he thinks, are never viewed by Plato as 'things'; see his notes on Book V. Nettleship (*Lectures on the Republic*, 249–55), though he was too early to have been influenced by Natorp, expounds the Ideas as 'laws of nature'. All these writers are therefore tarred with the philosophical brush.

untenable. It is a complete misunderstanding of the myths to regard them as mere fancies, like Grimm's fairy-tales, or think that they are mere appendices to the arguments which precede them; and, apart from this, the substantial being of the Ideas is constantly implied in passages which are half-mythical, or not mythical at all. The problem is this: the very critics who denounce Aristotle as the villain of the piece, are really in complete agreement with him in so far as they regard the real and separate Being of the Ideas as a flagrant absurdity. But if none of these diverse authorities has correctly apprehended the meaning of Plato, who has? The only avenue which remains to be explored is that of historical criticism. Perhaps the usual account of the *origin* of the Ideal Theory, begun by Aristotle and closely followed by Zeller, stands in need of revision.

Stenzel therefore begins with the remark that scholarship has not elucidated the Theory of Ideas, but only made it more and more mysterious. Wasting no time in negative criticism of his predecessors, he roughly divides the Dialogues into two main groups: on the one hand, all those in which Socrates predominates, with the exception of the *Theaetetus, Phaedrus,* and *Philebus*; on the other, the remainder. The philosophy of the first phase might be termed Socratic. It was marked by 'moral orientation'—the topics chosen, and the examples used, were moral in the broadest sense; the theory of mathematics was indeed discussed, but only because Plato found in it something akin to moral perfection. The second main phase shows us Plato beginning to take a wider interest in the world, extending the range of his Ideas, and consequently baffled by logical problems. He welcomes the method of division, διαίρεσις, as a heaven-sent means of deliverance from his difficulties. Both the problems and their solution seem childish to the modern logician; he is so accustomed to find logical theories of great profundity in *earlier* Dialogues, the *Republic,* for instance, that he is unable to account for this apparent triviality in the later ones. How often have we heard that Plato, in his examples of διαίρεσις, is simply amusing himself and his readers!

After what has been said, it will be clear that Stenzel by no means assumes, *within* these main groups, complete uniformity either of literary form or of doctrine. Neither does he suppose that they are quite discontinuous, and represent two successive philosophies. But he does suggest that Plato's interest, having at first been confined to the sphere of human action, was afterwards widened to include the study of nature, and that we can point to some external influences which might either have caused or have intensified this change.

We may now outline the account of the earlier phase contained in Chapter I. Socrates, though he had made logical distinctions, was not consciously a logician, and Aristotle saw him in a false perspective when he ascribed to him the first theory of definition and inductive argument (*Metaphysics*, 1078^b 17.) Action had been the end of Socrates' philosophy; seeking knowledge passionately as a means to virtue, he did not stop to analyse its nature; yet he gave instinctive and accidental expression to many a logical truth. All this was equally true of Plato in that earlier phase of his thought which culminated in the *Republic*. He inherited from his master no doctrine of 'concepts', no power of treating questions in abstraction from the practical issues involved, but an intense desire to escape from a world where moral distinctions could be altered to suit men's taste or interest, and all knowledge was a mere groping after temporary truths. Founded on this desire, there arose a belief in real and powerful Ideals. Everything was viewed in a practical light. The *meaning* of the world, or of any single thing in it, must be the same as the supreme Good for which it strives. Plato was not yet philosopher enough to contemplate dispassionately the objects around him, and to ask, What is their essence? how can we know them? and what do we mean by knowledge? These same questions occurred to him in practical form, What excellence (ἀρετή) does this thing require? What purpose ought knowledge to serve? The Ideals which this view assumed must necessarily have certain features: they must be few, and confined to the sphere in which the need for improvement seemed to be urgent; they must be real and individual; they must be far enough above the familiar world to fire our imagination.

Evidently such Ideas were not a suitable means for the solution of all-pervading logical difficulties. On the contrary, Plato would be lucky if, when he came to consider those difficulties, he did not find them immeasurably increased by the new world which he had incautiously postulated.

Thus nothing was more remote from Plato's original purpose than the formulation of a theory of knowledge. In a practical sense, knowledge was naturally his main interest, since he followed Socrates in identifying it with virtue. But both now, and to a less extent in his later thought as well, he viewed knowledge simply as an impression made on the mind by the Idea. Upon the 'philosophical' version of his theory, Plato was the forerunner of those modern logicians who regard knowledge as an active process, in which the mind impresses its own forms upon the data provided by the senses. Stenzel, on the other hand, emphasizes the etymological derivation of εἶδος and ἰδέα, 'vision'; as shape and colour are to the eye, so is the Idea to the mind. This, in prose as well as in myth, was Plato's doctrine, and no Greek could have held the complicated modern view, especially at such an early stage: Greek thought was *intuitive* and *objective*. It is true that Plato possessed, almost from the beginning, a marvellous insight into mathematical knowledge. But it is a peculiarity of the mathematical sciences that they can ignore the difference between the individual and the universal; in them, an intuition of one clear instance serves to demonstrate a universal truth. Geometrical proof, especially, depends on illustration. Moreover, in mathematics the imperfection of the sensible world is a familiar fact. The reasoner knows that the triangles which he declares to be triangular, the magnitudes which he declares to be equal merely seem so to the gross perception of his senses. Could Plato ask for a more striking confirmation of the theory which he had previously assumed on moral grounds?

The *Republic* is so clearly the fulfilment of the earlier Dialogues, and so sharply cut off from the first of those which follow (namely, according to the stylistic researchers, the *Parmenides* and *Theaetetus*), that it is natural to treat it as the crowning manifestation of this earlier mode of thought. Already, in the Tenth

Book, there are signs that Plato is wavering in his 'moral orientation', and beginning to consider how it is possible to know objects
which could not conceivably have Ideas in the earlier sense. In
the education prescribed for the guardians every tendency to
empirical observation had been harshly repressed, and yet there
are signs of a more sober and impartial conception of knowledge.
Once Plato's first effort of construction had spent its force, it
was inevitable that he should look back at it in a calmer frame of
mind; and then a crisis would come. The progress of empirical
science in his time, even within the Academy itself, in all probability hastened this crisis. The allusions of comedy show us that
some consideration was given there to animal and plant life;
the interest in biology which was common to Speusippus and
Aristotle probably began in the Academy. Plato, moreover,
began the close association between philosophy and medicine
which Aristotle continued; he himself dealt with physiology, not
entirely in an *a priori* spirit, in the *Timaeus*. Most significant of
all, he proposed to the astronomers a problem which must necessarily involve observation of the planets, and when it was solved
by Eudoxus, completely withdrew his condemnation of empiricism in astronomy (*Republic*, VII. 529 c). His whole attitude to
the visible world was transformed by the discovery that, in one
region at least, changes recurred with unalterable regularity.
At the same time the pungent attacks of Megarian logicians compelled him to attend to the logical problems which he had hitherto taken in his stride. Everything tended to show that his earlier
theory had been too rigid and exclusive. He had made logic
the servant of moral sentiment, and now it seemed that logic
was about to take its revenge on him.

Plato was not content until he had made a full exposition of
his own doubts and weaknesses. This we have in the *Parmenides*. It was neither, as some hold, an indirect hit at his contemporaries, nor, as others hold, a jest, but a frank confession
that his doctrine was in need of revision. And in the *Theaetetus*,
which we have already analysed, he raised afresh the whole
inquiry as to the nature of knowledge, omitting any open mention of Ideas and laying aside his old technical terms. This gives

to these two Dialogues their elementary character. Though Plato had now passed the summit of his career as a writer, he was only beginning his career as a logician; and he began with questions to which he did not yet know the answers.

The arrangement of Stenzel's book is as follows. He enumerates four logical problems which were latent in Plato's theory of Ideas from the start, and goes on to describe how they emerge to view in the two Dialogues just mentioned. The real Being of the Ideas and their separateness from each other, features which had been vital to the older theory, were now a special source of embarrassment. Then, in the *Sophist*, Plato begins to surmount his difficulties. He deposes Socrates from the leading part, brings in an unknown speaker armed with an entirely new technique, and attaches the new Dialogue to the *Theaetetus*.[1] The new developments did not, in Plato's own eyes, amount to a surrender of the theory of Ideas: in *Philebus*, 16 c, for instance, he seems to insist that it is the old problems which have been solved, though perhaps there has been some transformation in the nature of the Ideas. In Chapter VI Stenzel elucidates the new method of Dialectic. In the chapters on δόξα (Chapter VII) and on the metaphysical status of the Ideas (Chapter VIII), he shows how Plato fulfilled to his own satisfaction the self-imposed task of adapting his earlier doctrine to serve the purpose of a general theory of knowledge. The last three chapters have the nature of appendices; that on Democritus, though inadequate as it stands, is especially interesting, for Stenzel has not only shed new light on Plato's physical theory, but shown how the development of his views in this field was parallel to his logical development. Even in the *Phaedo* he had demanded an interpretation of nature which would show how its phenomena were intelligently designed for a good end. But the demand was instinctive and practical, and was prompted mainly by a sense of the defects of earlier science. In the *Timaeus* Plato is not only better informed about Nature, but far clearer in his conception of an explanation of Nature in terms of design.

[1] Or, it may be, plans the two Dialogues together; some vagueness is permissible here.

I propose here to deal only with two essential questions arising from the book: what was the nature (*a*) of Ideas, and (*b*) of judgement, in the later Platonic theory? The former question Plato always meets by an appeal to the technique of Διαίρεσις and συναγωγή which he had introduced in the *Sophist*; and no further progress is possible until we have said something of these processes.

In order to stress the contrast between Ideas and particulars, Plato had at one time implied that each Idea was self-sufficient. Either it had no relation to other Ideas, or it was not vitally affected by such relations as it had. In *Parmenides*, 129 D foll. he had made Socrates throw out a challenge on this point: could it be shown that the Ideas 'participate' in each other, as sensible things participate in them? The challenge was taken up by Parmenides in the latter part of the Dialogue, and still more by the Eleatic Stranger in the *Sophist*. He shows, in some simple examples, how a notion may be defined by including it within a wider class, and 'dividing' the class into its natural components, one of which will be the notion required. In its *simplest* form, such division might be represented by the diagram

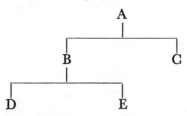

but Plato sometimes appeals to instances which cannot be so represented: e.g. in *Philebus*, 18 B, he mentions the divisions made by the science of grammar: and here there is an original division of φωνή (voice) into the vowels, the semi-vowels, and the consonants or 'mutes', ἄφωνα: now these classes can be subdivided until the various letters of the alphabet (στοιχεῖα) are reached. What distinguishes the grammarian, however, is not the power of making these distinctions, but knowledge of the way in which letters from all three classes must be combined in order to spell words.

However, it will do no harm to concentrate here on the simpler variety; let us observe the following points. (1) The terms εἶδος and ἰδέα are, as we should expect, retained and applied to the classes in the διαίρεσις; whether they preserve the nature, as well as the name, of the old Ideas is the main question which we have to decide. (2) Plato must obviously face the criticism that this is not a method of discovery, but only one of arrangement. This point also cannot be fully discussed at present. But it should be said that the classifications which Plato has in mind are in no sense artificial or capricious. He often advises the philosopher to divide only at natural 'joints', making two or three or more sections, as is appropriate. He thinks, as does the botanist in classifying plants, that in a true classification the human mind traces the course of nature. (3) Every Idea is 'one' in the sense that it gives unity to the subordinate Ideas which it comprehends, 'many' in the sense that its essence is shown to be composite, unless it is the supreme Idea of all, e.g. the essence of D is AB, plus some specific quality. Or this may be reversed: every Idea is 'one' because its essence is a unity composed of diverse elements, and 'many' because it comprehends a variety of lower species. Φαμέν που ταὐτὸν ἓν καὶ πολλὰ ὑπὸ λόγων γιγνόμενα περιτρέχειν πάντη καθ' ἕκαστον τῶν λεγομένων ἀεί, καὶ πάλαι καὶ νῦν, 'the one and the many, reduced to the same thing by discussion, perpetually recur in every sentence that is uttered, both now and of old'.[1] (4) Whether the Ideas dealt with are on the level of common experience, like man or horse, or very abstract like Movement and Sameness, the method remains the same—it is either Division (διαιρεῖν κατ' εἴδη) or Collection (συνάγειν εἰς ἕν). But Plato observes that the commoner εἴδη may be represented to sight or some other sense, whereas the abstract ones must be contemplated by the mind alone without assistance from the imagination. In the former case it is possible to explain the nature of an object without reasoning (χωρὶς λόγου); but the highest Ideas are detached from physical reality, and no image

---

[1] The translation 'this same one and many' cannot be right. The passage then describes the excesses of the young man who, debauched with dialectic, vexes his parents and neighbours, τοτὲ μὲν ἐπὶ θάτερα κυκλῶν καὶ συμφύρων εἰς ἕν, τοτὲ δὲ πάλιν ἀνειλίττων καὶ διαμερίζων. The metaphor is from rolling open a book.

could bear any resemblance to them (τὰ γὰρ ἀσώματα, κάλλιστα ὄντα καὶ μέγιστα, λόγῳ μόνον, ἄλλῳ Δὲ οὐΔενὶ σαφῶς Δείκνυται). The higher the mind is required to ascend, the more difficult becomes the exercise of Dialectic, and training among familiar objects, where the accuracy of one's divisions can be checked by experience, is needed to impart the necessary skill. Plato's discussion of μέγιστα γένη in the *Sophist* is a specimen of this exalted Dialectic. (5) There had always been some hint of degrees of dignity within the world of Ideas (compare, for instance, the gradual ascent towards τὸ καλόν in the *Symposium*, or towards τὸ ἀγαθόν in the *Republic*); but with the extension of Ideas beyond the moral sphere, and the development of the method of Division, these differences of degree are accentuated. The diagram of a Διαίρεσις inevitably suggests that Reality forms a kind of pyramid, with sensible particulars at the base, and the supreme Idea, whatever name be given to it, at the apex. In the main, this impression is a correct one. Even in the *Republic*, the main contrast between the intelligible and the sensible was far more important than any gradation within the intelligible sphere; and there was no attempt to mitigate the suddenness of the mental leap from one sphere to the other. The method of Διαίρεσις appears to indicate a *rapprochement* between the two worlds, not only in the sense that it shows the gradual approach of the intelligible to the fringe of the perceptible, but also in the sense that both alike are analysed and found to reveal the same structure. The imposition of Form upon Matter, πέρας upon the ἄπειρον, is a feature common to *both* worlds.

Nevertheless, Plato insists that it is impossible, by prolonging the division of Ideas, to reach perceptible individuals. It is important to grasp this, since upon it depends his view of the relation between sensation, αἴσθησις, and judgement, Δόξα or λόγος. He always says that, just as there are physical atoms, so there are logical atoms or indivisibles, ἄτομα, ἄτμητα. In defining a concept, it is a mistake to rush straight to one's goal by means of a hurried division without any natural basis; but it is equally a mistake to 'arrive at unity too slowly', i.e. to persist in division beyond the natural limit (*Philebus*, 16 D). There comes a time when one should 'allow the innumerable individuals to fall back into the undetermined', τὸ ἓν ἕκαστον τῶν πάντων εἰς τὸ ἄπειρον μεθέντα χαίρειν ἐᾶν. More simply expressed, this is a warning that we may seek to define man or dog, but not *this* man or *this* dog. Unfortunately Plato deserts us here, and does not bring out explicitly the grounds for his view. Why is there this limit, and why is it not an arbitrary limit, relative to the degree of knowledge one has so far obtained? Plato's reason no doubt is that a limit must come somewhere: the intelligible can never be attenuated step by step into the sensible, and it can never be the same thing to hear a logical formula and to perceive the thing to which it relates. What constitutes an individual, a 'this', is not so much the possession of a private description as the fact that it is in time and space, here and now. In the *Timaeus* Plato does his best to account for individuality on the metaphysical side—and to account for it without using the notion of substance! In the *Philebus* and *Sophist*, he attempts an even more difficult task—to show how our sensory and logical powers assist one another, although, since they operate in different worlds, there can be no real contact between them. The fact of division is common to the physical world and to the world of Ideas; and Plato therefore stresses the divine origin of the method of Division (*Philebus*, 16 c, E, *Phaedrus*, 266 B) and insists that it can remove the problems which had perplexed him in the *Parmenides*.

Plato, then, severely warns the dialectician not to define individuals—not to intrude into the kingdom of the ἄπειρον. He probably perceived the logical truth that individuals are not alternative *specifications* of their class, as classes are specifications of their genus. He likewise realized that sensation is, or at least *begins as*, a physical process—a bodily change, caused by some other bodily change in the neighbourhood. It must always be a mystery how such a process could have the least relevance to knowledge, which is the perception of Ideas by the mind. Here are two mysterious 'separations'—the one between sense and reasoning, the other between sensible individuals and 'atomic forms'. The 'atomic form' is like an outpost of reason in its campaign against the chaos of irrationality. And the method of Division shows that it can communicate directly with the inner citadel of knowledge—unless the outpost itself is unwisely thrust forward into a region which can never be subdued.

Let us now briefly follow Stenzel a stage further in his argument. Late in his career as a writer, Plato undertakes to solve the logical problems which had emerged to perplex him in middle life. In Chapter VII, an obscure but highly original chapter, Stenzel interprets passages from the *Sophist* (261–4) and the *Philebus* (37–40); they show how the mind and the senses, by their alliance with each other, produce δόξα and λόγος. The special problem about *false* δόξα is incidentally solved. From the *Sophist*, *Timaeus*, and *Philebus* we have also to try to understand the metaphysical status of the Ideas in Plato's later thought. Stenzel argues, during the course of the long chapter on δόξα, that the Ideas are still independently real, though in every other respect they are now class-concepts; and he reinforces the proof of this in Chapter VIII. Now the method of Διαίρεσις is Plato's key to all these problems, both epistemological and metaphysical. Those scholars have misunderstood Plato who, because they themselves despise Διαίρεσις as a trivial game, deny that he was deeply attached to it. He is sincere in proclaiming it as 'a gift from the gods to men, thrown down to us by some benevolent Prometheus together with a very luminous sort of fire'. Only a perverse view of Plato's development, whereby he is credited with profound logical insight from the start, has hitherto made it impossible to take him at his word.

Is Plato's instrument adequate to his purpose? That is to say, is he over-optimistic in thinking that his account of knowledge and of the Ideas is no longer threatened by 'separation'? (*a*) As regards knowledge or judgement, his final theory is well seen in the *Philebus* (37–40). The body is subject to movements, some of which 'are extinguished before they reach the soul', whilst some others penetrate to the soul, and 'the communion of soul and body in one feeling and motion may properly be called consciousness' (34 A). Memory is defined as the preservation of consciousness; recollection as the recovery of a former conscious state. From memory and perception springs the act of opining or trying to form a judgement (ἐκ μνήμης τε καὶ αἰσθήσεως δόξα ἡμῖν καὶ τὸ διαδοξάζειν ἐγχειρεῖν γίγνεθ' ἑκάστοτε). Thus, suppose a man indistinctly sees some object at a distance, and wishes to judge about it. His first act is to question himself, 'What is it that appears to be standing beside that rock, beneath a tree?' He may hit on the true answer 'it is a man', or on a false one 'it is a figure made by some shepherds'. When he has formed the judgement (δόξα), he may desire to communicate it by speech to a companion, and it now becomes a spoken proposition (λόγος). To see the difference between truth and falsehood, we have to mention two new faculties. The soul at such a time is like a book: 'memory, coinciding with the sensations, and with the other feelings which accompany them, appears to me, as it were, to write judgements (or speeches) in our souls.' At the same time there is another craftsman at work, a painter, who creates images of the judgements written. (Thus e.g. an image of 'scarecrow' might follow upon the judgement that I had seen a scarecrow.) The images are true or false according to the judgements which they represent. Plato has not tried to say here what more profound cause there may be for the truth and falsehood of judgements.

Here it should especially be noticed, first that Plato has not taken the scientific judgement as his instance, but that of perception, and secondly that he depicts judgement as a *process*, taking time and involving an effort of the mind (notice δόξα καὶ τὸ διαδοξάζειν ἐγχειρεῖν)—not as a passive acquiescence in some object of higher or lower grade.

Perhaps the crucial phrase is 'memory, coinciding with the sensations, appears to write judgements in our souls'. This is very similar to Hume's definition of belief as 'a lively idea accompanied by a present impression'. The sensations result in a mental image (φαντασία or εἰκών), and this, with the help of memory (i.e. memory either of previous images, or of the judgements to which they gave rise), is ascribed to some *class* for which we have a name, 'it is a man', 'it is a scarecrow'. And the survey of classes is the work of Dialectic and pure reason. On the surface, it does indeed seem that this analysis of Δόξα has made possible a transition from the physical act of sensation to the mental one of thinking. But, of course, there remains some mystery about the first stage of all. The φαντασία is presumably of a mental rather than a physical character—in the mind, not in space. How, then, is it the consequence of anything physical? On this, Plato has nothing to say. His analysis *begins* with the φαντασία and shows how, with the help of memory and other faculties, it is referred to the proper Idea—or, if the judgement is false, to an improper one. For this purpose the φαντασία is the limit of analysis, and its relation to the movements below it remains an insoluble problem. Though the analysis remains incomplete in this way, it is interesting that Plato should have condescended to deal with the judgement of perception, and typical of the direction in which his mind moved. But would it be true to say that Plato has abandoned the purely mathematical ideal of knowledge which he upheld in the *Republic*, and made room for a new method in which perception and observation play a large part? Stenzel's answer to this is not quite clear; it will be more convenient to consider it in connexion with the *Philebus*.

(*b*) As regards the Ideas, our question is whether Plato, as a result of his exercises in Διαίρεσις, is any better able to explain their relation to particulars than he had been at the time of the *Parmenides*. It will be remembered that the original Ideas were not class-concepts, but rather Ideals from which human aspiration could derive its force and take its direction. For this reason Plato not only saw no absurdity in giving them an existence *in rerum natura* and making them independent of the mind, but felt obliged to do so. But how did the absolute existence of Ideas fare when the moral point of view was abandoned, and Ideas were freely *postulated* (*Republic*, 596 A), wherever a common name was applied to a group of objects? There are really two questions to consider: firstly, whether Plato withdrew his claim that there were Ideas which did not depend on the mind, or otherwise modified his opinion about them in an essential way; and secondly how, if he held fast to that claim, he supposed that the method of Division could make their separate existence seem more plausible. Now it has been positively maintained by Lutoslawski and others that in Dialogues later than the *Parmenides* the Ideas are nowhere said to have real existence outside the divine or human mind. Plato, it is said, soon retreated from the 'objective idealism' which he had unwisely recommended in the *Phaedrus*, *Phaedo*, and *Symposium*, and in some books of the *Republic*. In Book X a new phase has already opened, for Plato not only introduces God as the maker of Ideas, but says that we (i.e. men) *assume* an Idea wherever we use a general name. Plato's exercises in Διαίρεσις seem at first to confirm this view. When the concept of 'art' or of 'animal' is split up by analysis, and subordinate classes are found in higher and lower ranks, we do not seem to be dealing with entities which could exist apart from the mind. It would appear fantastic to suppose that each Idea in a scheme of classification *really exists*,[1] independently of its parent Ideas and of the knowing mind. Is there not, then, abundant evidence that Plato was only able to escape from his perplexities by changing his earlier theory out of all recognition?

It is not enough, in answer to this question, to point to the passage from the *Parmenides* (132 B) in which Socrates seems to reject the view that the Ideas are 'thoughts' (νοήματα), for he takes this suggestion in a rather different sense. Let us attempt a fuller reply. In the Tenth Book of the *Republic*, we are not told that God creates the Ideas *by thinking* them; he makes them precisely as the human craftsman makes a table, as is clear from the contrasted names φυτουργός and δημιουργός. As to the general question, Plato himself is confident that he has met the difficulties of χωρισμός fairly and squarely (*Philebus*, 15–16); and surely this is not hypocrisy or self-delusion. There is no passage from which it unavoidably follows that the Ideas are mere thoughts; and so important a change, if it were ever made, would surely call for the greatest emphasis. Again, it was the function of the Ideas to be objects of knowledge, and Plato would

---

[1] It is sometimes alleged that the classes displayed by 'divisions' of the type used in the *Sophist* are not Ideas. But cf. *Philebus*, 15 c foll.

hardly be satisfied if they had anything less than an existence in their own right. Even if they were created by the mind of God, a suspicion of unreality would still surround them.

Plato had once stated the principle τὸ παντελῶς ὂν παντελῶς γνωστόν (*Republic*, 477 A). This belief he always retains, even when Dialectic has become classification and the Ideas, to all appearance, mere general notions. The μέγιστα γένη, abstract Ideas which no sensible images can represent, are also τιμιώτατα. Most people would think that a faint gleam of reality is transmitted to these Ideas from the world of life and movement: Plato thinks the reverse. Reality emanates from the Ideas of genera to those of species: it does not emanate from them to sensible particulars, since particulars are *only* real in so far as they are known to belong to an Idea. Neither the word 'emanate', it must be said at once, nor anything similar actually occurs; but Plato evidently finds the secret of the intelligible world in some sort of derivation of complex and inessential notions from simple and all-pervading ones. Did he consider this derivation to be merely logical, or also temporal? Are we meant literally to think of reality as streaming at every moment from the highest Ideas? It is extraordinarily difficult to answer such questions. But perhaps it is fairly certain that Plato always considered knowledge to be an intuition of independently existing objects. And this accounts for Aristotle's impatience with the theory of Ideas. He had not been an eye-witness of the earlier phase, in which it was absolutely necessary that the Ideas should have existence in their own right. Coming to the Academy at about the time when the *Theaetetus* was written, he could only regard the εἴδη as concepts, and their existence 'apart' as a harmful and unnecessary addition.

Stenzel describes the *Philebus* as solving 'the problems stated in the *Parmenides* by the methods of the *Sophist*'. In order to see that this is quite correct, it is enough to compare *Parmenides*, 129 c–e, with *Philebus*, 15–16. Two things become clear in the *Parmenides*: first, that neither of Plato's usual metaphors is sufficient to show how the Idea can retain its singleness, and yet be present in sensible particulars; and secondly, that the main problem for the future is to show how various Ideas can 'be blended and separated' (συγκεράννυσθαι καὶ Διακρίνεσθαι) amongst themselves,—a phenomenon which Plato had at first tried to confine to the sensible things. In *Philebus* (15 B) these problems are briefly summed up: have the Ideas[1] real existence? How can each remain single, though it pervades an infinity of things in the world of Becoming (ἐν τοῖς γιγνομένοις καὶ ἀπείροις)? Then we hear that it is as comforting to know the answer to these questions as it is embarrassing to be without it (ἁπάσης ἀπορίας αἴτια μὴ καλῶς ὁμολογηθέντα καὶ εὐπορίας αὖ καλῶς). And Socrates knows 'a way' which will lead out of the embarrassment, though it is difficult, and he has frequently missed it in the past. (οὐ μὴν ἔστι καλλίων ὁδὸς οὐδ' ἂν γένοιτο ἧς ἐγὼ ἐραστὴς μέν εἰμι ἀεί, πολλάκις Δέ με ἤΔη Διαφυγοῦσα ἔρημον καὶ ἄπορον κατέστησεν.) Its secret is that 'all things which are ever said *to be*, are derived from One and Many, and have finitude and infinity inherent in them'. A procedure which we cannot fail to recognize as that of Division is now described, and its use is illustrated, as in the *Sophist*, from the sciences which deal with letters and sounds. Division reveals the manifold structure of the intelligible world, but constantly reminds us that its variety is not infinite. Only if one is so incautious as to approach the sensible world will 'infinity' be in danger of obtaining the mastery over 'finitude'. τὴν Δὲ τοῦ ἀπείρου ἰΔέαν πρὸς τὸ πλῆθος μὴ προσφέρειν πρὶν ἄν τις τὸν ἀριθμὸν αὐτοῦ πάντα κατίΔῃ τὸν μεταξὺ τοῦ ἀπείρου τε καὶ τοῦ ἑνός, τότε Δ' ἤΔη τὸ ἓν ἕκαστον τῶν πάντων εἰς τὸ ἄπειρον μεθέντα χαίρειν ἐᾶν.

But how does this method mitigate the eventual break between the two realms, the sensible and the intelligible? Or, if Plato does not intend that it should, how is the earlier problem, the problem of the *Parmenides*, answered? Is he telling us that by advancing step by step to the edge of the cliff, we can persuade ourselves that it is not there? We must give this answer: Plato believed now, as he had always believed, that the real was the knowable. His later treatment of Δόξα in the *Philebus* and *Sophist* confirmed him in the belief that the particular, as such, is not

[1] Now denoted by the mathematical term μονάΔες.

knowable. Αἴσθησις is not ἐπιστήμη. But he saw now, what he had ignored before, that αἴσθησις and Διάνοια can meet on common ground and work together. The particular may not be knowable, but the particular considered as belonging to a class, and jointly apprehended by αἴσθησις and Διάνοια, is the starting-point of knowledge. So much for the theory of knowledge. Plato must have thought that he could overcome his metaphysical difficulty by the same approach. 'To be' is to participate in the Idea of Being, and this is the supreme Idea, the apex of Διαίρεσις. By Διαίρεσις it is shown that all true Ideas are ultimately species of Being. And particulars 'are' when they have been subordinated, by the act of judgement, to one of the specific Ideas.

It does not, indeed, seem likely that any one who had been dissatisfied with the earlier theory would be content with it in this modified form. Both as a metaphysical theory and as a theory of knowledge, it involves an utterly mysterious transition —in the former case, from the intelligible to that which is in space and time, and in the latter case, from thought to sense-perception. No solution seems to have been found, no real concessions to have been made; and the profession of respect for empirical science has turned out to be hollow. But here it is essential to grasp the thesis maintained in this book. Stenzel says that Plato was impressed by the growth of empirical science and thereby induced to modify his theory in an interesting way; he does not say that he was overawed by it and obliged to surrender. Plato in fact always remained a Platonist; and to any one who is not a Platonist, his doctrine will always seem to be a *petitio principii*. He had said, or rather had learnt from Socrates to say, that truth can only be found by reasoning, ἐν λόγοις; and it was easy to defend this view as long as the Ideas in which he was interested were those of morals, of mathematics, and of art. Here the theory that we learn by 'reminiscence' seemed to be valid, and too detailed an attention to particulars seemed to be harmful. The consequence was that in his judgement of the sciences in the Seventh Book of the *Republic* Plato went too far, and rejected observation even where it is desirable and necessary. Then the success of empirical methods within the Academy itself widened his interests, and drew his attention to a new class of Ideas which did not entirely share the characteristics of the older ones. Quite late in his life, and *after* the first theory of Ideas had been completed, he 'discovered the concept'. His argument for ἀνάμνησις in the *Symposium* and *Phaedo* had been that no particular in the sensible world is a worthy representation of Beauty or Equality as they are 'in themselves'. No experience, no process of abstraction from particulars, can bring us to the contemplation of such Ideas. But when it came to Ideas like 'horse' or 'fire' it seemed impossible to maintain this any longer. A class-concept is *fully* present in the various species which exemplify it, and by studying them with the method of διαίρεσις and συναγωγή one obtains an exhaustive definition of the class. In this respect the Ideas are brought nearer to particulars, and διαίρεσις appears to some extent as an alternative to ἀνάμνησις (see Stenzel's account of the *Phaedrus*, pp. 17, 149). Nevertheless, it is still reasoning (λόγος) and not sensation which discovers the essence of things; and this is why Plato, in the *Sophist* and *Philebus*, is so proud of his new method. When the horizon of Ideas was first enlarged, he had felt a temporary check, and not known how to proceed. Now it had again been shown that reason was dominant over the whole sphere of Ideas, down to the very fringe of the sensible world. It seemed that, far from having to make concessions to empiricism, he had been able to show the primacy of reason even where it was least expected.

The last two chapters of the book are scarcely convincing as they stand, but are full of brilliant conjecture. Many scholars have wondered how much Plato knew of Democritus. Stenzel points out that in the later Dialogues the lowest Ideas are with curious persistency described as ἄτομα or ἄτμητα. They are logical, not material atoms; and they are separated from each other not by a spatial vacancy, κενόν, but by logical difference, μὴ ὄν. Plato delighted to refute other thinkers in their own terminology; has he transferred the atomism of Democritus to an ideal plane? This suggestion does not go very far, since Democritus' theory was a purely physical one and is not necessarily inconsistent with anything maintained in the *Sophist*,[1] except in a single digression on causation in nature. The real inconsistency is between Plato's teleological account of the world in the *Timaeus*, involving a theory of mathematical atoms, and Democritus' mechanical account wherein there is no design, and the atoms are arranged by chance in innumerable shapes. (In a work published after Stenzel wrote, and referred to on p. 164, Dr. Eva Sachs attempted to show that in the physical theory of the *Timaeus* Plato aims at a refutation of Democritus, with the help of mathematical constructions recently worked out in the Academy.)

The last chapter is designed to show how Aristotle begins his metaphysical inquiry at the point where Plato had ended. The earlier Idea had been an individual, an object of intellectual vision; the later Idea was primarily an essence or definition, which Plato had tried to invest with the substantiality of its predecessor. To Aristotle there are two distinct things: the form (εἶδος or μορφή), which we perceive in sensible individuals, but which is not an object of scientific knowledge; and the logical essence (τὸ τί ἦν εἶναι), which we try to define and know. It is only the first of these, on his view, which is capable of combination with matter; and neither of them has a claim to exist in its own right.

In conclusion I would call attention particularly to two points. (*a*) Stenzel has made it abundantly clear, against Zeller, that Plato did not arrive at his theory of Ideas by giving substantial existence to general notions, and against Natorp, that this theory is something more than the *Critique of Pure Reason* in paint and powder. A more lasting service, he has given a positive interpretation of its meaning and development, which is faithful to all the evidence, and does not require us to tax

[1] Here it is maintained that the works of nature are the products of divine craftsmanship:

ΞΕ. Ζῷα δὴ πάντα θνητά, καὶ δὴ καὶ φυτὰ ὅσα τ' ἐπὶ γῆς ἐκ σπερμάτων καὶ ῥιζῶν φύεται, καὶ ὅσα ἄψυχα ἐν γῇ συνίσταται σώματα τηκτὰ καὶ ἄτηκτα, μῶν ἄλλου τινὸς ἢ θεοῦ δημιουργοῦντος φήσομεν ὕστερον γίγνεσθαι πρότερον οὐκ ὄντα; ἢ τῷ τῶν πολλῶν δόγματι καὶ ῥήματι χρώμενοι—
ΘΕΑΙ. Ποίῳ τῳ;
ΞΕ. Τὴν φύσιν αὐτὰ γεννᾶν ἀπό τινος αἰτίας αὐτομάτης καὶ ἄνευ διανοίας φυούσης, ἢ μετὰ λόγου τε καὶ ἐπιστήμης θείας ἀπὸ θεοῦ γιγνομένης;
ΘΕΑΙ. Ἐγὼ μὲν ἴσως διὰ τὴν ἡλικίαν πολλάκις ἀμφότερα μεταδοξάζω· νῦν μὴν βλέπων εἰς σὲ καὶ ὑπολαμβάνων οἴεσθαί σε κατά γε θεὸν αὐτὰ γίγνεσθαι, ταύτῃ καὶ αὐτὸς νενόμικα. (For a translation see p. 161.)

either Plato or Aristotle with imbecility. (*b*) The method of Division cannot be expunged from Plato's philosophy. It is given a place of honour in the *Sophist, Statesman,* and *Philebus*; it is very conspicuous in the *Philebus* and *Timaeus*; Plato, as we have seen, looks to it for a solution of all his main problems (*Philebus,*15–16) and, under the name of Dialectic, praises it as being more scientific than the sciences. There is evidence that it was known, even to the outside world, as a characteristic of Plato's Academy (Chapter IV). Both Aristotle and Speusippus were influenced by their training in this method, and though the former protests against the exaggerated claim that it is a method of discovery, he remains an incorrigible 'divider'. Yet some scholars refuse to believe that Division was considered to be more than a childish pastime. We find Paul Shorey, after a lifelong study of Plato, acquitting him of any serious interest in it, and denying its influence on the formation of the theory of the syllogism.[1] Always the same argument, 'because the doctrine is puerile, Plato cannot have believed it', inviting the reply 'see it in its historical environment, read the text as an ancient Greek would have read it, and it will no longer seem puerile'. So sure is Stenzel's position on these two points that his work will, I think, stand against other criticisms that have been or will be raised. It will be said that the theory of Ideas was never entirely *practical*; that, in the *Republic* especially, besides the desire to attain the good, Plato manifests his general interest in knowledge, and that his profound and elaborate account of its degrees cannot be entirely instinctive. But any one who maintains this criticism has to explain why Plato relapsed in the succeeding Dialogues into a discussion of elementary questions. And Stenzel, of course, makes no special claim for his division of Plato's thought into two phases. He realizes that all such divisions are artificial. But he tries to show that Dialectic in the *Republic* has not yet the special significance of the analysis of classes into parts, and the reassembly of these parts into a whole; and, above all, that it differs from the later method in being directed to the Good.

[1] In his paper on 'The Origin of the Syllogism', *Classical Philology*, vol. xix, and in 'The Unity of Plato's Thought'.

CONTENTS

THE LITERARY FORM AND PHILOSOPHICAL CONTENT OF THE PLATONIC DIALOGUE

IN any intellectual problem of the more complicated type, a wide survey of all the difficulties must be the first step on the road to certainty, even though it may appear to postpone the possibility of a solution, and to call in question results already secured. Such was the significance of the recent inquiry into the growth of the *Metaphysics* of Aristotle by W. W. Jaeger. The path which he trod was essentially different from that of his predecessors, inasmuch as he supplemented his analysis of the content and meaning by a thorough investigation of the *form* of the treatises of Aristotle—products as they are of a very intricate process of growth. He was then able to formulate the problems in quite a novel way. Inevitably he became aware of a difference in essence between these treatises with their loose style, resembling that of a note-book, and the Platonic Dialogues, which are the acme of literary perfection. Hence he writes:

'We cannot apply to the Dialogues the standard of the Ionian λόγος which had been adopted by the natural philosophers, nor their standard to it. It is Plato's ambition to follow in the succession of great Attic art; in him, the ideal tragic and comic poets mentioned in the *Symposium* are blended in a higher unity. . . . It is a remarkable fact that while Plato thus gave to the world works of art in a new and unexampled prose, the older manner maintained its existence within the peaceful walls of the philosophical school. Here, within the school, was the dwelling of the true philosophy which is heralded by the *Phaedrus* of Plato in such tones of enthusiasm. She never imparted and published her wisdom in the form of Dialogue. We do wrong to forget that it is only in our emergency, and because other sources fail us, that we go to Plato's Dialogues for information on such points as his theories of Ideas or of Numbers. Aristotle, indeed, constantly quoted the *Republic* and the *Laws* for his master's educational and sociological views, but, apart from details, it never occurred to him to appeal to the Sixth Book of the *Republic*, or to the *Symposium*, for the theory of Ideas, and the argument on which it was founded' (p. 140).

In these remarks, although they have a paradoxical sound, a

kernel of genuine fact has found expression, and if only we had a single word from Plato himself in addition to this 'emergency' evidence of the Dialogues, light would have been thrown on the whole Platonic problem, especially upon Aristotle's critical attitude to the theory of Ideas. But in the present state of affairs it is extremely doubtful how far this new knowledge can affect our understanding of the philosophy of Plato. Yet something can be learnt from any line of argument which has been pursued to its logical conclusion.

However little we know of the content of this philosophy which was not included in the Dialogues, the fact *that* such a philosophy existed, side by side with them, must be observed, if we would judge from the correct standpoint the meaning of the doctrines contained in the surviving sources. The two facts especially emphasized by Jaeger: firstly, that Plato's Dialogues are poetical in character, and secondly, that there probably existed, alongside the later Dialogues at least, a set of doctrines which Plato expounded orally or in writing, have, no doubt, never yet been disputed in any detailed way, though there must be many scholars who have not had them present to their minds at all.

Aristotle clearly recognizes that Plato's Dialogues, and the Socratic Dialogue in general, are works of literature. He treats Empedocles' hexameters as prose, and the Socratic conversations, because they are imitative in character and strive to represent reality, as poetry. Here he is in conscious opposition to the current terminology, which recognizes no poetry without verse (*Poetics*, 1447^b 11). The principal subject of this poetic imitation is Socrates. It seems unnecessary to us to-day to emphasize that Plato's Dialogue must soon have gone beyond this original aim. We are coming more and more to suppose that the real content of the Dialogues is the exposition of Plato's own doctrine.

The question of literary style is thus seen to be bound up with that of Socrates' personality; but it will be well at the start to guard against a false impression which may easily be formed, that it is our intention in this discussion to draw the line in the various Dialogues between the historical Socrates and Plato.

This discussion can at the most serve only as the necessary preliminary to a proper estimate of the Dialogues as a source of
Socratic teaching. We are here concerned rather with them as
evidence for Plato's own philosophy. If we leave aside the earliest
writings, which, in view of their richer *mise en scène* and their
failure to reach philosophical results, are, on any hypothesis,
simple descriptions of Socrates, it is customary to expect, without any reservation, that the remaining Dialogues will show the
development of Plato's own philosophy; strenuous efforts are
therefore made to determine their exact sequence, and it is
completely forgotten that Plato through his whole career may
have had some other purpose than to expound his philosophy,
as far as it happened to have advanced. Since this assumption is
made, the further fact that in the end he laid aside the mask of
Socrates tends to appear as an accidental circumstance in the
story of his development. Still, it must cause surprise that no
one has tried to consider the retirement of Socrates in connexion
with the doctrines themselves; for if, when he deprived Socrates
of the leading part, Plato had at the same time wholly given up
the dialogue form—if it were this form which he now found
inconvenient—his motive would be plain to see; we should not
need to bring in questions of doctrine. But the case is actually
not so simple; to the end, in the *Laws*, he is faithful to the dialogue form. Surely we need not remain satisfied here with the
entirely vague and empty assertion that Plato withdrew farther
and farther from Socrates, till at last a point was reached when
he preferred to give the leading part to other persons like
Timaeus, Parmenides or the Eleatic Stranger? What are we to
say, then, of the *Philebus*, where, although the method is closely
related to that of the *Statesman* and *Sophist*, Socrates is suddenly
brought back to the centre of the stage? Such facts compel us to
conclude that, as far, at least, as the early Dialogues are concerned, Plato was always intending to give a picture of Socrates
which should be artistically coherent; and the portrayal of
Socrates remains, to a certain degree, the aim of Plato's imitative art. If this were not so, there was absolutely no necessity
for Socrates ever to be deposed; the artistic unity would already

have been impaired—Platonic touches would already have covered the portrait of Socrates until it was no longer recognizable.

The portrait was not one of the historical Socrates, whom Plato had tried to depict in the *Apology*, but of another Socrates to whom he seems to stand in a varying relation at each phase of his development. Because Socrates had practised the 'maieutic' method, whereby his own knowledge always remained concealed, Plato thought, as he made each new discovery, that he had simply found some new side to the main Socratic question— some other consequence of the critical, yet productive logical method which the master had practised. Yet the different impressions of Socrates sketched by his other disciples must have reminded Plato, if nothing else did, how much was due to his own labour; while his more profound insight into the master's spirit must have prevented him from using Socrates in the uncritical manner of Xenophon as a mouthpiece for any opinion whatsoever which he himself deemed correct. We have, then, a fixed final term, the disappearance of Socrates from the Dialogue; can we not detect any artistic devices whereby Plato before this time was able to expound his own doctrines within the framework provided by the personality of Socrates, as it appeared to him?

To one very transparent method of indicating where the portrait of Socrates ends, it is enough to make a brief allusion, since it has always been understood in this sense: I mean the appeals by Socrates to some kind of higher authority—to priests and seers in the *Meno*, to the priestess Diotima in the *Symposium*. In the latter case Plato frankly states his purpose (209 E): Diotima draws a clear line between what Socrates can at least grasp in parables, and what he cannot grasp at all. She is dubious whether he could follow her in the last stage of the upward climb to knowledge, the vision of the single, self-subsistent Beauty. What is here, by the fiction of the Dialogue, said to transcend Socrates' power of comprehension, must certainly be Plato's own doctrine of Ideas; and for this reason I scarcely expect any one to argue—maintaining to the end his view that Socrates is always identical with Plato—that the heights to which Socrates here 'cannot attain' are meant to be poetical fancies as distinct from the genuine philosophy which the writer wishes to be taken seriously. Only one scholar—Wilamowitz, in a lecture on the *Symposium* of Plato delivered to the Berlin Academy—has tried to insist, even here, on the same equivalence of Plato the philosopher to the Platonic Socrates which is assumed as an axiom everywhere else. Unfortunately only a short report of this lecture has, as far as I know, hitherto appeared. But it is one which leaves no doubt of the main thesis:

'The answers of Socrates', it runs, 'show that Plato definitely does not want the speech of Diotima to be taken as an expression of his own intellectual conviction. The prophetess no more speaks to the point than the doctor and the poet have done. Demonstrative speeches may contain much that is fine and beautiful, but do not lead us to the truth, which is found only through serious Dialectic. If we wish to understand the philosophy in Plato, we must remember that his poetry must be treated as poetry.'

An interpreter of Plato's philosophy is entitled to express some doubt here, for after all it is just the dialectical doctrines, and they alone, which are communicated in the speech of Diotima, no doubt in a tone of enthusiasm. Moreover he can safely invite any one to go ahead and apply such a canon of interpretation to the *Meno*. For if, with no reservation at all, we here take the attitude of Socrates to indicate how much is meant seriously and scientifically by Plato—and this is admittedly the criterion applied by Wilamowitz to the *Symposium*—we find that the entire doctrine of Reminiscence and Immortality falls into the class of what can only be hinted figuratively to Socrates; it thus becomes at the most a 'probable myth'. Nothing remains over but a few suggestions of Socrates' own. I cannot discuss the *Meno* exhaustively from this angle; I will only call attention to the main points. The discussion sets out from the question whether virtue can be taught, and culminates in two problems: Is learning in any form possible? and, Is there any distinction between knowledge and right opinion? Both questions are carefully examined, and answers are found. Learning, especially where one acquires certainty, as contrasted with mere empirical

knowledge, is the recollection by the Soul of its experience before
birth. Thus Plato appears to be establishing logical facts on the
basis of a metaphysical theory of the Soul. Now Meno, and with
him the average naïve reader of the Dialogue, may be entirely
satisfied with this result of the first stage of inquiry; but Socrates
goes on to make two parallel observations which must evidently
reopen the entire dispute. It is as though he suddenly remembered his characteristic ignorance.

'Some things I have said of which I am not altogether confident.
But that we shall be better and braver and less helpless if we think
that we ought to enquire, than we should have been if we indulged
in the idle fancy that there was no knowing, and no use in seeking
to know what we do not know;—that is a theme upon which I am
ready to fight, in word and deed, to the utmost of my power.'
Meno, 86 B (tr. Jowett).

'Knowledge differs from true opinion because it is fastened by a
chain. M. What you are saying, Socrates, seems to be very like the
truth. S. I, too, speak rather in ignorance; I only conjecture. And
yet that knowledge differs from true opinion is no matter of conjecture with me. There are not many things which I profess to know,
but this is most certainly one of them.' (98 A.)

For the *Meno*, therefore, at all events, the main problem of our
Platonic studies to-day: What is meant by the Ideas? coincides
with the question of the present essay: Is Socrates, in this instance,
expressing the final philosophy of Plato? Where he doubts, does
Plato doubt also? Is the modality of the judgements he makes
entirely binding upon Plato? We must not be hasty in our
answer to this momentous question, especially as it would require
an extensive argument to solve the principal difficulty of the
Dialogue, the so-called 'reasoning about the cause' (λογισμὸς
αἰτίας). This, the criterion of knowledge in contrast to right
opinion, is simply identified with Reminiscence.

Let us examine the *Phaedo*. The view that learning is Reminiscence is here so well known that it becomes the foundation of
one proof of the Immortality of the Soul. Socrates here makes
no appeal to priests and priestesses; but it is the hour of death,
and he is himself in an unwonted spiritual state. A dream has

inspired him to write poetry, and he compares his thoughts on immortality to the last song of the swan. There is a long myth proclaiming the joys and sufferings of the departed souls. This is not the Socrates whom we know; here, if anywhere, we hear the note of Orphic piety and mysticism. But although there is this tension caused by the approach of death, Plato has taken care that we may recognize the true Socrates, the dialectician. The version of the theory of Ideas in the *Phaedo* is undoubtedly the one which comes closest to the view of those philosophical interpreters who would have us believe that the Ideas are 'postulates of thought', or judgements (λόγοι) with which we set our seal upon the facts of experience. Since Immortality, the existence of the soul before and after death, is so important in the *Phaedo*, this is a particularly striking fact; for *this* version of the doctrine of Ideas does not need to be founded upon a metaphysical theory of the Soul. In his earlier discussion of Reminiscence, Plato still has such a foundation in mind; but on coming to his theory of the Ideas as hypotheses, he omits it, and it would be difficult to bring it into harmony with the text, since it is his deliberate purpose to forget the objects, and to talk of the judgements made about them (99 E). After he has announced that he will describe his special procedure, Socrates says (100 A): 'I always assume some principle which I judge to be the most reliable, and then I affirm as true whatever seems to me to agree with this, whether relating to the cause or to anything else; whatever does not agree, I regard as untrue.' He explains this by reference to his position, known to all present, that the Beautiful, Good, Great 'in themselves' exist. This procedure of holding fast to the concept which is being examined, so long as is possible without self-contradiction, is in truth no new procedure, but the normal one which Socrates follows elsewhere. In the last resort it does not make much difference whether a particular Idea, such as the Beautiful, is viewed as the ὑπόθεσις, or whether the ὑπόθεσις is the existence of such Ideas in general. But it is an essential point that discussion may cause us to *change* the ὑπόθεσις; for even that 'satisfactory' assumption (ἱκανόν), to which we may ascend in the course of our examination (according to a later passage, 101 D), must in this context be taken to be only relatively final. That which at present 'satisfies' may be fundamentally revised in the course of profounder discussion. At all events the reference here is not to some single ground of all ὑποθέσεις; the text definitely says '*some* satisfactory view' (τι ἱκανόν).[1] It is entirely possible to give a 'philosophical' interpretation of this, holding that the Idea according to this version is meant as the foundation of rational scientific inquiry. Indeed this is necessary; for Plato now (100 c) returns to the λογισμὸς αἰτίας which he had left obscure in the *Meno*; it is now explained as an apparently tautologous argument of the kind: this thing is beautiful because beauty is present in it, or, because it participates in the beautiful. In the light of Plato's earlier argument, this can scarcely mean more than that we judge, or apply a predicative concept to the experienced. And it is a fact that when Natorp wants to determine what an Idea means for the epistemology of other Dialogues, he always takes his bearings from the version of the theory in the *Phaedo*. He cannot deny that in earlier passages of the *Phaedo*, as in the *Meno*, this 'logical method' makes its appearance in connexion with Reminiscence and Immortality, i.e. with a metaphysical psychology; and that even later (100 B foll.) this 'logical method' is made to yield a new proof of Immortality, quite clearly ontological. But it is quite understandable that the 'philosophical' scholars, and not they alone, should not be moved by this to depart from Plato's plain meaning when he calls the Idea an hypothesis. There is a clash between two views, which both beg the question at issue: (1) the 'hypothesis' doctrine is associated with the doctrine of Immortality; therefore it is not meant as a mere principle of logical method. . . .

(2) Since there are these two incompatibles side by side, we ought to conclude that the whole doctrine of Immortality belongs to religion; it is not meant seriously and scientifically by Plato. Owing to the death scene, the element of drama has encroached upon the sphere of philosophical doctrine; Socrates in his last words *as a philosopher* actually repeats the very doubt which we

---

[1] See Ritter, *Platon*, ii. 576.

have heard him express in the *Meno*, though the tone is adapted
to the grave moment at which he speaks:

'A man of sense ought not to say, nor will I be very confident,
that the description which I have given of the soul and her mansions
is exactly true. But I do say that, inasmuch as the soul is shown to
be immortal, he may venture to think, not improperly or unworthily,
that something of the kind is true. The venture is a glorious one,
and he ought to comfort himself with words like these, which is the
reason why I lengthen out the tale. Wherefore I say, let a man be
of good cheer about his soul, who having cast away the pleasures
and ornaments of the body as alien to him and working harm rather
than good, has sought after the pleasures of knowledge; and has
arrayed the soul, not in some foreign attire, but in her own proper
jewels, temperance, and justice, and courage, and nobility, and
truth—in these adorned she is ready to go on her journey to the
world below, when her hour comes. Me already, as a tragic poet
would say, the voice of fate calls' (tr. Jowett).

A closer inspection shows us that Socrates here, as in the *Meno*,
confines himself to postulates; and the culmination of these is
his advice that we should learn, and so attire the Soul in the
adornment which belongs to her. By a faint tone of tragic irony,
everything else is thrown back into uncertainty. And so even
this rapid survey of the *Phaedo* brings us back to our old question,
which must be answered before the theory of Ideas is interpreted: Do Socrates and Plato entirely coincide in their attitude
to this set of problems? Is it Plato's last word, his own real decision which he here voices through the mask of Socrates? Or
was there some remnant of personal opinion, something which
he *could* have expressed even when he wrote the *Phaedo*, if his
sense of the limitations of Socrates' logic had not imposed hesitation and reserve, and even made him withdraw results which
had seemed secure? The latter view is bound to appear highly
improbable from the first to any one who takes the version of the
Ideas as hypotheses to be the purest expression of Plato's theory
(simply because it happens to be most fruitful for the theory
of knowledge), and uses this norm to modify all those other
versions in which the logic is rounded off by metaphysics. The
closer he looks, the more will such a critic find to surprise him.

In the above-mentioned passage from the *Phaedo*, where Plato described the gradual ascent to higher and higher hypotheses, he did not yet appear to have in view any absolute (and consequently metaphysical) single Cause of all hypotheses; but in the *Republic*, Book VI, this is no longer so; Plato there emphasizes that nothing save this ascent to such a single, unhypothetical End of hypotheses can give its proper meaning to the true Dialectic of the philosopher. Only by their relation to the 'unassumed' (ἀνυπόθετον), the Idea of the Good, will our hypotheses be known to be true; reason can then dispense with them, and descend from the Good among pure concepts. There has been no satisfactory inquiry hitherto into the relation between the *Phaedo* and the *Republic*, and I cannot do more than make a few suggestions; but the philosophy of the dialogues is inseparably bound up with their literary form, and neither can be studied without the other. An essential point of comparison between the two passages is this: It may be true that in its logical aspect the Idea of the Good recalls us to the doctrine of method outlined in the *Phaedo*. But in the *Republic* it plainly secures, side by side with this, a metaphysical meaning; the Good is not only the source of knowledge, but also of all being and life (509 B). Is not this a direct indication that its importance is not merely logical? But when we admit a metaphysical aspect of the Good—which is very awkward for many interpreters—it assumes the shape of that very teleological principle for which Socrates had searched in vain. (In his survey of the doctrines of earlier philosophers in the *Phaedo*, he says that, when he failed to find this principle even in Anaxagoras, he at last gave up the search.) Socrates' despair is difficult to understand: for he had made good the vital distinction between a final and a material cause, in a form which Plato retains in all his writings, and still adopts in the *Timaeus*. The position assigned to the material cause is one of complete subordination. Socrates in the *Phaedo* (99 c) had also clearly indicated that the Good was the true cause (αἰτία). In the *Lysis*, which may perhaps be later than the *Phaedo*, but cannot be far distant from it in time, the discussion of these two kinds of causation leads us to the πρῶτον φίλον ('first object of love'), that which is desirable in itself (219 D). This concept is akin to the Beautiful 'in itself' in the *Symposium*, and to the Good in the *Republic*. They are simply three aspects of one fundamental notion, a notion which gradually appears as the central theme of all the Dialogues down to and including the *Republic*. At one time the emphasis is on the moral side, as in the *Gorgias*, at another time on other sides. It cannot, then, be foreign to Plato's thought in the *Phaedo*. Moreover, to see the need for a teleological principle is tantamount to having found it; and Socrates in the *Phaedo* does see this need. Yet it is just here that he breaks off—'And yet this is the principle which I would fain learn if any one would teach me. But as I have failed either to discover for myself, or to learn of any one else, the nature of the best, I will exhibit to you, if you like, what I have found to be the second best mode of inquiring into the cause.' Now follows the doctrine of the Ideas as hypotheses, in which the 'philosophical' scholars are especially attracted by the very feature which makes it unfit to do service as the teleological principle mentioned immediately before—i.e. the fact that no attempt is made to link the hypothesis to any metaphysical entity. But in the *Republic* such an entity, in the shape of the Idea of the Good, is unambiguously demanded as a necessary complement to the 'hypothesis'; since this Idea is the cause, not only of knowledge, but of being.

This is far from being an exhaustive account of the relation between the two Dialogues at this point; but it should have shown that in Plato's opinion it is not the whole nature of Ideas to be hypotheses—they must also have some metaphysical significance. 'Hypothesis' is only one side of the meaning of the Idea, and to Plato not the more essential side; for it lacks the power to satisfy those demands for an End, of which he had given a clear formulation in the *Phaedo*, and elsewhere before that. The same ground serves to exclude another possible explanation: that Plato's thought had developed between the *Phaedo* and the *Republic*, and that in the earlier dialogue he had only worked out his view as far as was there recorded. It is on such an assumption, extended to the Dialogues generally, that some persons have founded a 'genetic' approach to Plato, which tries to fix the sequence of the Dialogues down to the last detail on internal grounds. This view attempts a task which is insoluble, because wrongly propounded; and this general statement applies to the *Phaedo*. Let us then try another view—that Plato is still an artist, and, whatever other motives he may have, regards it as a vital part of his task to portray Socrates. Everything now appears in a new light. If we may assume that from the moment when Plato became conscious of his personal philosophical outlook, he both continued to write works of literary art, and gave expression in his school, either in writing or by word of mouth, to his own teaching, we shall then be able to judge these works in the very spirit of freedom which their author intended.

An important consequence of this is that one Dialogue may be explained by the help of another, as the example of the *Phaedo* and the *Republic* has shown—i.e. we are quite entitled to assume that Plato can already solve problems which are stated by 'Socrates' in his own characteristic way. We saw how Socrates clearly pointed the road to a solution, although he himself ended in doubt. And Plato's view is never in *conflict* with that of Socrates; he had turned away precisely as his master had done from the inadequate 'elements' (ἀρχαί) posited by earlier thinkers towards rational knowledge, and away from πράγματα towards λόγοι (*Phaedo* 99 E–101 E). Again, for Plato also the δεύτερος πλοῦς is beyond question the only right way; but he goes much farther along it than Socrates.

But we have not yet explained to the full the inner connexion between Plato's own philosophy and the imitative Socratic Dialogue. We have left in the background the question whether the historical Socrates can ever be separated from the one whom Plato has drawn, and fortunately the contrast which is to follow does not compel us to attempt such a separation. In the character as presented by Plato there is noticeable a certain inner tension which is confirmed by all that tradition records about Socrates; he is a man who exerts the strongest influence by conversations conducted according to a strict method, yet will not and cannot state any definite doctrine of his own; in his teaching a mere critic of moral problems, to some degree a sceptic, but in action a firm and assured believer. His scepticism, however, does not exclude investigation; for he is represented as searching for that same absolute knowledge which Plato found in religious metaphysics, and claimed to see with increasing clearness. Plato could feel that he and Socrates were kindred spirits, inasmuch as they both sought for a knowledge which pointed beyond all experience. But as for the solution of what *we* call 'criticism'—the philosophy which seeks to ascertain the presuppositions of thinking, and does not hope to overcome them—both definitely passed it by; for its hour had not yet come.[1]

The Pythagoreans had already given philosophical form to the religion of a 'world beyond'. It was here that Plato found a home for his idea of 'absolute being'. (*Meno*, 81 A: 'Those who say so are priests and priestesses, who had studied how they might be able to give a reason of their profession.') It will be found to be an essential *motif* in his philosophy that he calls in the assistance of religious faith in order to complete the Socratic ideal of an absolute knowledge; he gives to mere mythology the dignity of a religious metaphysic, and proves that it is the foundation of that synopsis of the whole of knowledge for which he strives; or rather that it is the foundation of all knowledge whatsoever. To us, the union of metaphysical belief and intellectual thinking is a union of opposites; but to Plato, whose manner of thought was inherently intuitive, it was more natural. Since thinking, to him, was always the intuition of an object, he easily came to believe in an entity whose essence involved existence; but the same fact made it harder for him to obtain a clear view of the simpler discursive thought which finds relations between concepts. It cost him much effort to acquire such a view in the *Sophist* and *Statesman*. Knowledge and faith, then, are to be seen indissolubly united in his individuality; they are opposites which supplement each other, and which he tried to combine in his conception of reason, νόησις. The Socratic Dialogue gave him a suitable form in which to depict this inner antagonism; he could show how thinking of the Socratic type

---

[1] [Stenzel is thinking of 'philosophical' critics who interpret Plato's doctrine in a Kantian sense. He refers to Cohen, *Platons Ideenlehre und die Mathematik*, p. 30.]

was directed towards the Good as he understood it, but was not prolonged until it attained a transcendent object; hence it had always come to a stand in mid-course—had sought, but had not found. Socrates' state of doubt in the *Meno* and *Phaedo*, beyond which we saw that he would not venture, though the goal was near, certainly does not imply that Plato himself is in doubt of the need to attain somehow to a higher world; on the contrary it is his intention to prove that without this final step there can be no demonstration of the main principle of Socrates' life: that Virtue can be taught, so long as it is not a mere opinion about the Good, but knowledge.

Two consequences follow from Plato's choice of this form of exposition: firstly, that we see the Socratic method from the standpoint of a follower who strives for an absolute knowledge of reality—a perspective historically very false, if we may believe the thesis recently maintained by H. Maier; secondly—and for our main theme this is still more important—that when, in spite of everything, the method of Socrates is amplified by the introduction of new and strange doctrines, we see these doctrines in the sceptical perspective of Socrates as the chief speaker; otherwise his true character could not have been retained. Plato at first certainly did not feel that this cramped his artistic purpose. On the contrary some special device was necessary in order that the mystical doctrines might be revealed by Socrates (he had, as it were, to divine from afar their deep connexion with the knowledge which he also had desired); and this gave Plato a welcome opportunity to narrate a myth at full length in poetical style. He would take over all the parts of the traditional story, and there may well have been additions due to his own artistic invention; for all such details he naturally did not wish to claim scientific validity. Now this method made it possible for him to represent at any stage the process of the impenetration of myth by metaphysics and logic—a process without end because the coincidence is never complete. Thus, in the *Gorgias* there is as yet no hint of the idea of Reminiscence, but Socrates' belief in a judgement in the world

---

[1] *Gorgias*, 523 A, 524 A, B.

beyond is very definitely marked; there, however, it is still a purely personal faith, πίστις. But soon the doctrine of Reminiscence prepares the way for a fusion of logic with metaphysics, and from that moment there begins the development which we have described, culminating in the *Republic*. In that Dialogue the objects of faith (πίστις) are the things of sense; it therefore drops to the lower place, and it is reason itself (αὐτὸς ὁ λόγος) which by intuition (νόησις) grasps transcendent objects. It should occasion no surprise that the *Republic* is not a clear instance of the dialogue form, as we have analysed it (although even here Socrates shows proper uncertainty and diffidence when it falls to him in Books VI and VII to expound the main doctrine), for the *Republic* has broken its original mould,[1] which would appear to have been that of a Dialogue on Justice. The very idea of showing Socrates as the founder of an Ideal State meant trespassing beyond the limits of Socratic conversation, both in spirit and in form. Nevertheless, there still remained at the heart of the argument the question as to the nature of the moral life, with which all the properly Socratic Dialogues are concerned. If the *Republic* satisfies this criterion, it is sufficiently in harmony with the Socratic method known to us from the earlier Dialogues. This concern with ethics also accounts for the fact that the *Philebus*, a late Dialogue, once more presents Socrates in the leading part, although his personal characteristics have disappeared; here we must also bear in mind the plausible conjecture of H. Maier (*Sokrates*, p. 587) that the *Philebus* is a final attempt to rally the most important schools of Socratics.

With the *Republic*, at all events, we come to the critical turning-point in Plato's philosophy, as regards the interrelation of form and content—the elements which must be inseparably combined in anything that we name a work of art. When the problems of the Socratic Dialogues are left behind, the artistic beauty begins likewise to vanish, and for this there is an inner reason. Plato's decision cannot have been easy to make, and he may well

---

[1] Δοκεῖ σοι δίκαιον εἶναι περὶ ὧν τις μὴ οἶδεν λέγειν ὡς εἰδότα; (505 A, 506 c foll.) διι-σχυρίζεσθαι (517 B, 533 A foll.).

have felt that with this change in the problems, he had lost his innermost motive for artistic representation (μίμησις). There must have been important material reasons behind his decision; for the moment, it perhaps seemed to him that he was entirely giving up his literary production and would mainly devote himself in future to practical tasks, especially to his work as a teacher in the Academy. If this is the fact, it might be used to prove that we have so far been right in assuming a close relation between his literary work and the personality of Socrates. And even in thus planning to abandon authorship in favour of oral instruction, Plato could feel himself in an intimate accord with his master. Only this can have led him to take the radical view of his decision which appears in the *Phaedrus*: for no doubt it is obvious that in my last words I have been alluding to this Dialogue. In the *Phaedrus* we have an original document stating Plato's principles of authorship; and we must now resume our whole argument, and submit it to this test. Once more the close connexion of form and content appears, for it is impossible to do this without considering the *meaning* of the *Phaedrus*.

So far it might appear that we meant to surrender the great victories achieved by the genetic study of Plato, and in its place to revive the attitude of Schleiermacher.[1] This revival has been openly defended in recent times by H. von Arnim. But in contrast to him, I also think that the *Parmenides*, *Sophist*, and *Statesman* show a fundamental change in Plato's doctrine. Now it is just in these Dialogues that Socrates is replaced in the leading part by other speakers, although, as far as I know, no one has yet considered the fact in this connexion. That the *Phaedrus* stands near to these Dialogues in doctrine is at least the prevalent view to-day; and even the most zealous defender of its early composition, O. Immisch, has recently concluded that there was a second edition. It is therefore not unlikely that we may be able to connect it, in the way already illustrated, with the formal revolution implied by the abandonment of the Socratic Dia-

---

[1] [Schleiermacher, who translated Plato in 1804, took up the position that Plato was from the first in possession of a system, and presented it to his readers in an order suited to their understanding. He placed the *Phaedrus* first of all, because it contained a mythical *Ahnung des Ganzen* (presentiment of the whole).]

logue. And it does indeed give us the key to the reasons which make Socrates henceforward an unsuitable leader of the discussion.

We have seen the form of the Socratic Dialogue arising from certain contrary forces at work in the growth of Plato's philosophy, and the *Phaedrus* is a fine example of this form. In its personal charm, its power of working immediately on our feelings, it is unrivalled by any other Dialogue. From beginning to end, the earnest tone which the theme seems to demand is relieved by a serene irony. If a reader tried to understand the *Phaedrus* without external aid, he would be at a loss to discover how much is seriously meant; and his bewilderment would rise in proportion as he tried to observe the author's own hints, and not merely to surrender himself to the impression of its content. And if this reader came ready armed with some general view about μῦθος and λόγος, he would perhaps decide that Plato's serious intention was no more to be found in Socrates' great recantation than in the two first speeches. Nevertheless, on closer inquiry he would find that this 'hymn' of Socrates contains the proof of Immortality founded on κίνησις, which is propounded, undoubtedly in earnest, by the Athenian in the *Laws*, and which has a large part to play in the *Metaphysics* of Aristotle. In the treatment of Reminiscence, moreover, he would come upon the plainest statement of the method of abstraction from particulars that can be found anywhere in Plato; and he would now notice that Plato's Socrates seems to point this out himself (265 B) : ἴσως μὲν ἀληθοῦς τινος ἐφαπτόμενοι, τάχα δὲ ἂν καὶ ἄλλοσε παραφερόμενοι, κεράσαντες οὐ παντάπασιν ἀπίθανον λόγον, μυθικόν τινα ὕμνον προσεπαίσαμεν ... τὸν ... Ἔρωτα. Most bewildering of all, he would find that the critical inquiry into the nature of λόγοι at the end of the Dialogue is described as a 'jest' (this plainly being the sense of παίζειν here).[1] It is easy, then, to see why professional scholars also have surpassed themselves here in coming to various and contradictory conclusions. They say that the visibly conciliatory attitude to Rhetoric, the art of 'persuasion', an attitude so far removed from that of the *Gorgias*, cannot be meant

---

[1] Οὐκοῦν ἤδη πεπαίσθω μετρίως ἡμῖν τὰ περὶ λόγων (278 B).

seriously at all—it is a camouflaged encomium on philosophy—whereas the praise of Isocrates at the end is an oblique and disguised condemnation. In the *Phaedrus*, all the ambiguities of tone which we found in our earlier analysis of the Socratic Dialogue are accumulated. This is not unconnected with the mood in which Socrates himself appears. His irony is here, from the first, diluted with a drop of effervescent humour. Phaedrus has lured him against his wont into the shade of the plane-trees, into the magic circle of the shrine sacred to the nymphs, and of the cicadas, sacred to the Muses. He is thus prepared to undergo the effects of θεία μανία, madness sent from the gods, without which no success in poetry is possible (245 A). This madness includes three forms: erotic, poetical, and religious. And in his great speech, Socrates undergoes a unique transfiguration in all three ways; Plato, if he wished to be true to his picture of Socrates, was obliged to turn this into irony. Yet he makes him at a later point specially refer back to the division of madness into a good and a bad kind, as an essential part of the speech (266 A). All this is in flat contradiction to the genuinely Socratic method, as Plato himself had represented it in the *Apology* and *Ion*.[1] Socrates valued the clearest possible rationality, and the power of 'giving an account' (λόγον διδόναι), which in the *Apology* (22 B) is explicitly required even from the poets. In the *Phaedrus*, Plato is becoming fully aware of the character of his philosophy, and of his whole activity in writing and oral teaching. He acknowledges his writing to be mere play, παιδιά, and this remains his dominant view. No wonder; when he abandoned the true Socratic Dialogue, without abandoning the Dialogue itself as an artistic form, he did so with the deliberate intention of carrying on the imitative style; he did not intend to confine himself to the prose of the learned treatise. The excursion of the *Phaedrus* outside the limits of Socratic inquiry is not unconnected with a general movement of interest in the realm of reality, in the widest sense, which runs through Plato's later writings. As long as Ethics (in Plato's sense, i.e. knowledge

---

[1] A dialogue whose authenticity seems to be confirmed by Pohlenz's comparison with Aeschines. See *Aus Platons Werdezeit*, p. 186.

of the Good, and the problems related to it) remained the proper
object of his thinking, so long, but no longer, did Socrates continue to dominate. There follows next a series of intensively dialectical writings—the *Parmenides, Sophist, Statesman*—in which
Plato employs a new procedure of synthesis and division, συμπλοκή
and Διαίρεσις, which also earns an emphatic commendation in
the *Phaedrus*. So strongly is the Dialogue affected by Plato's new
interest in the real world that he now considers Dialectic (the
new procedure just mentioned) to be the source of every influence which men may exert in any way upon their fellows,
whether in writing or by speech. Rhetoric, in quite a new sense,
herewith becomes important. The starting-point of the argument is this: Can the fact that a man is a writer of speeches be
made a ground of reproach against him? In favour of the opposite view, it is alleged that all great statesmen are writers—for
laws too are written speeches—and that they have always desired
eternity for their written works. This idea recurs constantly in
the *Phaedrus*, and is so frequent that Plato's emphasis on it must
be intentional. In the *Statesman* likewise, Rhetoric appears in
an entirely favourable light (304 A); this has some connexion
with Plato's conversion to the idea of enlightened despotism in
politics. (This has been depicted by Wendland, who traces it
to Plato's hopes of success in Sicily.) The prospect, which he
found so infinitely attractive, of his political plans being realized
by the strong hand of a monarch, brought home to him the great
value which Rhetoric might have if it could become a force
actually determining the will of men, a ψυχαγωγία in the literal
sense. The persuasion of men through their emotions thus became important in all its aspects; and it is this change which we
find surprising in the *Phaedrus*. Plato is entirely serious when he
praises Pericles on the ground that his speeches have derived
their 'sublimity and force' from the natural philosophy of Anaxagoras.[1] The same example also shows how the new interest in
φύσις is connected with ψυχαγωγία in the political sense. The
point is one which we find again in the 'preludes' of the *Laws*,
and in the *Statesman*—that, in order to prepare the way for the

[1] 270 A—cf. *Parmenides*, 135 D.

Statesman's work, there must be an education in natural philosophy, culminating in Religion (*Phaedrus*, 276 E; *Statesman*, 304 D). This idea of παιδιά (play) for the sake of παιδεία (education) is a *motif* often repeated in the *Laws*. It explains in turn another fact, namely the conciliatory attitude of Plato to popular religion, a feature both of the *Laws* and of the *Phaedrus* (where Socrates definitely opposes the rationalist interpretation of myths, 229 D). In the *Phaedrus*, then, instead of the theoretical method of Socrates, there is a definite leaning towards practical and political activity. With even greater clearness Plato resolves to turn from the writing of books, and proclaims it an aim not unworthy of the philosopher to communicate instruction by word of mouth. To the ordinary reader this is the most memorable thing in the *Phaedrus*. Two of the reasons alleged by Plato are particularly important for our present subject.

1. More than once he declares that the written word can only serve to 'remind' a man who already knows. We need not emphasize that this decisively contradicts the alleged 'ignorance' of Socrates; but we have seen how he, as leader of the conversation, must necessarily obscure the proper meaning of the views attributed to him by Plato. But this phrase 'to remind the man who knows' (275 D), upon which such strong emphasis is laid by Plato, can undoubtedly confirm the conclusion at which we have arrived, that the Socratic Dialogues have only an indirect value as a source of Platonic doctrine. Whether it was that he now assumed readers who were in the position of 'knowing' his chief doctrines, or whether he had merely learned from experience how sadly the Socratic Dialogue could be misunderstood, we find that Plato henceforward presents his dialectical and metaphysical doctrines with less reserve, and that there are not the same sceptical limitations on the part of the leading speaker as before.

2. A second and very obvious *motif* plainly expressed in the *Phaedrus* is that every man who *knows* needs to be in a position to prove that what he has written is a jest, παιδιά; and even, in certain instances, that it is untrue (278 c). With the proof of this, his serious activity (σπουδάζειν) would begin. Once more a close parallel is to be found in the *Statesman*, so that in both

contexts the 'writings' of legislation are not the least of those to which the statement refers. To be able to take back laws which have been given, and to replace them by better ones, is there proclaimed as the highest duty and achievement of the *Statesman* (295 E, 296 B).

There is not much real difference between such Laws and the sketch of an Ideal State in which (we remember) Plato's whole literary activity hitherto has culminated. In any case, if we consider theory as well as practice, it is quite clear that Plato has now reached a critical point. There are two possible grounds for his criticism of the theory of Ideas in the *Parmenides* and *Sophist* (for it is either a reply to misunderstanding by others, or shows a change on his own part), and these fit into the same picture. It is confirmed from all sides that the *Phaedrus* is connected with the *Sophist* and *Statesman*. The political interest in the *Phaedrus* has in the past been little emphasized, and it still needs to be more carefully shown. It may be some agreement about politics which moves Plato to praise Isocrates; at least there is an obvious similarity in thought and style between two passages—Isocrates, *Ep.* i. 2. 3 (to Dionysius!) and *Phaedrus*, 275 E. The latter shows an example of ψυχαγωγία; it helps us to see what Plato means when he strongly recommends paying attention to the individuality of the person whom one is trying to persuade. I hope that it has at least been made clear that political influence is included when, in the *Phaedrus*, Plato speaks highly of the influence of the living word in human relations. Since the *Phaedrus* in its condemnation of writing reaches a negative result, a result which shows an essential point of contact between himself and Socrates, Plato can allow Socrates to reappear in person, and to express ideas from which every Socratic element has disappeared —veiled, however, in the form of irony. By passing such a judgement on the written word, Plato gives us clearly to understand that his Dialogues are works of art, and therefore, by one of his familiar doctrines, 'imitation' and 'play'.

And it is always in this light that Plato, in later years, sees his own literary work. Content and form continue to be interwoven in manifold ways, the ironical play of the Socratic Dialogue turns to mystical resignation; and we come to a view which stands in curious contrast to that of Socrates. 'The affairs of men', which were his exclusive interest, 'are not worthy of great seriousness, though we must perforce be serious about them'— *Laws*, 803 B. And the study of the kingdom of Nature appears in the *Timaeus* to be in the last resort only a dignified amusement (59 D, cf. 29 C). One thing alone is an object of serious Philosophy—a mystical and spiritualized μετεωρολογία, a religious astronomy, with which Plato surely reaches his farthest distance from Socrates.

My observations here are simply a first attempt to understand, with reference to the structure of Plato's Dialogues, certain questions which have hitherto been answered as though the Dialogues were not works of art. For the same verdict must be passed upon the 'philosophical' interpreters; if they ignore literary form, they cannot fulfil their special task of understanding what Plato's problems in themselves mean. We must define the aim of Platonic scholarship as it was long ago defined by Goethe. 'How necessary it is, in reading such a writer (as Plato), to have a clear and critical view of the circumstances under which he wrote, and the motives which made him write! Every reader will feel this, who in reading Plato does not wish for nebulous edification—which he can obtain from far lesser writers—but wants to be acquainted with a remarkable man in his individuality. It is not the appearance of what others may have been that is instructive, but the knowledge of what they were and are.'

PLATO'S METHOD OF
DIALECTIC

My first aim in the present work is to secure an historically accurate view of the meaning of the doctrine of Ideas, which modern scholarship has only succeeded in rendering more and more doubtful. To this end, it seems absolutely necessary to discover, by a systematic analysis which does not go beyond the horizon of Plato's doctrines, what form of Universal it is, and how constituted, that he names an Idea. The most important result of such an inquiry will be that Plato's discovery of the concept comes at the end rather than at the beginning of his evolution. The view which finds in the theory of Ideas a consistent and comprehensive doctrine of the Concept must be rejected as a survival of the obsolete treatment of Plato as a systematic philosopher in the modern sense of the word—equally whether the concepts are held to have been *substantialized*, or are interpreted as 'rules of method'. There is, no doubt, equally little justification for speaking of a continuous development traceable from one Dialogue to the next. The truth here is best described in a phrase of Goethe's, 'the form impressed by Nature, which develops because it lives'. In Plato's work there is both unity and development—unity, because he has a sharply defined manner of viewing things and securing an intellectual grasp of them, and this manner *is* the Platonic Idea or 'vision'; and development, because there is a change in the kind of objects on which his main interest rests at different times. Being objective, his thought necessarily takes on the shape of its favourite objects. Upon these principles I shall here attempt to define more precisely the change of interest which (so much has never been disputed) led Plato to relinquish Socrates and his primarily ethical problems, and to aspire to a wider knowledge of reality; and I shall also try to trace the influence of this change upon the logical function ascribed to the Idea. That being done, it becomes possible to assign the Dialogues of Plato to two periods, according as his predominant interest is in morals and practice, or in theory and natural philosophy. By analysing the central Idea of the Good, we find that in the earlier period the Ideas have the characteristic transcendent existence of an Aretê, in the specifically Greek sense—each Idea is a cause (αἰτία) in the double sense of explanation and end; whereas in the later period, Ideas are the substantial reality implied by the 'permanence of kinds', the classes defined by natural science; and Διαίρεσις, division, is a method whose purpose it is to determine them in order to bring individual reality within the grasp of science. The evidence of outward form points to the same general division of Plato's work; I may refer to my essay on the literary form and philosophical content of the Dialogues. A significant point here is the retirement of Socrates from the centre of the stage; although Plato treats the historical Socrates with the greatest independence, it remains his artistic purpose to preserve the Socratic type of inquiry, wherein some practical problem of ethics is explained, and the 'maieutic' method, i. e. instruction through hints at the positive truth, is employed. This view of the outward form will assist us in our detailed interpretation of the Theaetetus and Sophist; we shall find that the problems solved in the latter of these Dialogues are stated in the former; the artistic device is one which Plato had freely and consciously chosen; and the Theaetetus is a genuine Socratic Dialogue. We shall offer a similar interpretation of the Phaedrus, in which old and new are so mysteriously blended. Plato was consciously employing a form of presentation which would show the continuity between the two periods. More general considerations will lead us from this to a survey of Plato's relationship to Democritus and Aristotle.

The mere announcement of the purpose of my work in these historical and philological terms shows that it will diverge from the 'philosophical' exposition practised by the Marburg school; my only purpose is to restore Plato's views, if possible, in his own sense and in that of his time. Even where I have argued philosophically, it is with the purpose of interpretation. Hence my frequent disagreement with Natorp's study of the Theory of

Ideas, a work which is indispensable for any inquiry which pretends to go deeply into Plato's thought. For just this reason, however, the author feels that he must strongly endorse a remark often made by his teacher Wendland, that 'at no time are Platonic problems so clear as when one engages in careful study of Natorp'.

I. ARETÊ

EVERY philosophical system of the past has some constituent parts which show a remarkable correspondence with later views, and perhaps with those of our own day; and yet a more intimate inquiry may reveal, in the immediate vicinity, features which give us a lively sense of our distance in time. It will depend on the purpose of the individual scholar whether he lays stress on what is familiar or on what is foreign; and a true historical picture can only be attained when we try to supplement one method by the other, until the strands which at first seem so diverse are woven into a single whole. The doctrine must be viewed in the surroundings to which it belongs; the strange features must be made to appear necessary, but, what is more, those which conform more closely to the modern way of thinking must be understood with their individual *nuances*.

The 'divisions' in Plato's *Sophist* and *Statesman* appear at first sight to be no more than elementary exercises in formal logic, wherein a primitive theory of concepts is made to cover a surprisingly wide field. Plato's successors, however, seem to have followed him in laying great weight on 'exercises' of this kind. In the following work we shall consider this unusual part of the Academic philosophy, and try on the one hand to assign it to its proper place in the order of history, and, on the other, to find what part it played in the systems of the time, especially that of Plato. We shall thus be contributing to the history of Platonic *logic*; hence some brief preliminary remarks may be helpful.

As soon as man begins to employ a language, however simple it may be, he makes use of concepts, judgements and inferences. There is an active mutual relationship between speech and thought, and in a language as highly evolved as Greek in, say, the year 400 B.C., we should obviously expect to find an expression for all possible operations of thought. But it is exactly this inextricable blend of speech with thought, expressed by the Greeks in their ambiguous word λόγος, which keeps men unaware of simple logical laws; being unconsciously followed in every significant statement, such laws for a long time elude the attention of the speaker, because they are observed so long as his meaning is rightly expressed, and departures from them in most cases correct themselves through direct insight into the meaning. No wonder that, when concept and word are thus identified, men at first go directly to language to find the laws of thought. It is well known that Plato occupies a half-way position here; he at least recognizes the grossest errors to which Antisthenes had fallen a victim, and he often contrasts 'division into natural kinds' (κατ' εἴδη Διαιρεῖν) with 'following verbal distinctions' (κατ' ὄνομα Διώκειν).

The *Cratylus* is entirely devoted to this problem. Its conclusion gives us an emphatic contrast between 'verbal correctness' (ὀρθότης ὀνομάτων) and the theory that the Good and Beautiful are concepts existing in their own right. But it would be premature to credit Plato at this early stage with full insight into the nature of the concept. Such mistrust may seem to be insulting to him. But in reply to this, I would quote from a modern logician, H. Rickert, who, in his *Theory of Definition*, writes as follows:

'In its concepts our thought requires absolute unity, but such a requirement is not achievable by the human mind. Concepts, then, may also be termed Ideas in the Kantian sense; they are Ideas of a task which, as soon as we discover the true situation, we feel to be impossible. When we speak of a concept as though it were something single, something permanent, we are in strict truth employing a fiction, although a fiction of great logical value. We behave as if we had solved a problem which can never really be solved. Hence the best description of a concept is that it is a complex of judgments imagined to have attained fixity.'

I know no passage which could show more clearly and distinctly where Plato went wrong. His mistake, if I may so call it in a purely historical discussion, was of an honourable kind. Here there is something parallel to that interrelation of speech and thought which has already been noted. Because all concepts are very closely connected with judgements, they are able in innumerable cases to add the function of the judgement to their own, before the difference between them, and their proper relation, has been made obvious by disciplined reflection. Even defenders of the philosophical interpretation of Plato, who as specialists in these matters know how often Plato's Ideas usurp part of the function of judgements, have to admit that it is the singleness and permanent Being of the Ideas that he principally stresses. How often does he himself contrast the stream of appearances with the motionless εἴδος, the single Being (ἐν ἕκαστον) which 'is' in itself! Plato, it may be said, has given us all that we need in order to perceive as clearly as possible the 'fiction' mentioned by Rickert: on the one hand the unity, being, stability, unchanging permanence of the Idea, on the other the concept which only appears when we descend to the act of judgement.

Two phases in the Doctrine of Ideas

If Plato thus normally conceives the Idea as something permanent and substantial, how should we interpret the version given in the *Phaedo*, which makes it an 'hypothesis'? I sketched an answer to this question in my essay on the form and content of the Dialogues. Moreover I there attempted to show how, in Plato's earlier period, which I assume to culminate in the *Republic*, the Idea of the Good may gradually have secured its place as the central doctrine of Socratic ethics.[1] Since the chronology of separate Dialogues is always a matter of great uncertainty, it seemed to me advisable to be satisfied with a general division into two groups, each with its own main tendency. These were:

1. A 'Socratic' period—Socratic in this sense, that Plato here still thought he could present his own doctrines through the mouth of his master; and

2. A later period in which this method was abandoned. Save for the *Theaetetus*, into which I purposely did not enter there, I was able to bring all the Dialogues into this scheme, the *Philebus* being an apparent exception which confirmed the rule. For the rule was that, so long as Socrates was the principal speaker, the moral interest was always paramount, however plainly

[1] In partial agreement with von Arnim, *Platons Jugenddialoge*, 52 ff.

the discussion led on to a more general theory of knowledge.[1] The view thus outlined gives rise to two questions which it is important for us to answer. These are:

Firstly, assuming that the Idea of the Good is the centre of Plato's entire doctrine of knowledge, what in the earlier period is its special effect on his Logic?

Secondly—and here the answer to the first question must naturally be our basis—what inner reformation of Plato's doctrine drove him to make such a drastic change in his manner of presentation as the dismissal of Socrates from the leading part, and the enrolment of other speakers in his place?

Plato's earlier Logic. The Good as its central object

It is only with many reservations that we can credit the historical Socrates with those discoveries in Logic which historians of Philosophy since Aristotle have been wont to ascribe to him. This point has recently been well established by Maier, although it is impossible to prove his assumption that the relevant passages of the *Metaphysics* depend on other authorities. We do not here intend to ask what germs of logical doctrine existed *potentially* in the method of Socrates, but how much is *actually* apparent in the earlier Dialogues of Plato, which give us our most detailed portrait of Socrates at work; how much there is which can be historically understood, and placed in its context of contemporary speculation. What, then, was the logical doctrine of Plato's Socrates? Its purpose was to prove by Dialectic that the virtues are united under a single comprehensive ἀρετή, namely, the possession (κτῆσις) of the Good-Itself. It arrived at this chief end by identifying various concepts which are already separated in language, and in that ordinary consciousness which language reflects. By 'concepts' no more need here be understood than some form of consciousness of a meaning, some image of 'inner speech' corresponding to a word which we use. The 'just' is the good; the 'beautiful' is the good; the truly 'profitable' or 'advantageous' is the good; indeed, if we understand the *Protagoras* literally, even the truly 'pleasant' is the good. All the virtues,

[1] 'Moral' must naturally be taken in the widest possible sense. See below.

even bravery, come round to 'knowledge of the good'; this knowledge is the living force in the logic of the Platonic Socrates. Formally, we see in the *Protagoras* (349) how it triumphs over the fine-drawn logical refutation which it immediately provokes from the Sophist. Philosophically, we see how it drives Socrates in the *Republic* to a valuation of the various sciences which is no less one-sided to Plato in his later phase than it is to ourselves. It was a logical doctrine founded on the identity of virtue and knowledge, although Plato's stupendous energy obviously carried that identity far beyond the view of the historical Socrates. Thus a purpose had already been chosen, for the attainment of which isolated points of merely formal logic could have scarcely any value. Such thinking is an outstandingly good instance of a general remark which has already been made—that on Socratic principles the only guarantee of formal correctness in thinking was a conviction of the truth of one's belief; for the Idea of the Good was the final and unique belief, which no reflection upon method could ever confirm or ever disprove. Plato soars above methodical hindrances. He is never, indeed, conscious of the intuitive character of his νόησις. Since all his contemporaries conceived thinking to be the intuition of an object, his transformation of ethical postulates into the assertion that the Good was a real and necessary entity appeared at a time and place where its errors were least considerable; they would escape notice, in any case, under the strong glare of 'intuition'.

At first the moral Ideas were the objects of Plato's thinking, or rather there was one central Idea, the Good. So long as this remained true, and every other form of knowledge was viewed simply as a propaideutic for the intuition of the Good, his view of the highest Being could be justified by the End he assumed. To form for ourselves a living and effective notion of the Good is our right, nay, as beings possessed of moral wills, our duty; and, on the other hand, belief in the existence of the Good leads directly to a consciousness of a possible moral action to be done. Plato's view simply did not allow him to think of theory in separation from practice—and he could not conceive that even theoretical knowledge might be traced back to an independent activity of the mind. The Good, which to Socrates had remained a postulate, was to him an object of actual knowledge; it was the duty of the individual to realize the Good in his life. He thought of the Good as given in a vision or intuition, ἰδέα, and he had necessarily to bring 'Socrates' within sight of this vision. What Socrates views as *possible*, Plato postulates as *necessary*. Socrates knows nothing, Plato has a positive metaphysical doctrine. One falls short of the mean, which the other goes beyond.

For our purpose the essential fact is that even where Plato's Socrates is alleged to use logical proofs, they are affected by the ethical character of the doctrine he expounds. Take the thesis that when the Good is present as an object to our minds it must, because it is good, determine action, and so 'no one voluntarily errs'. Socrates founds his whole argument on this, as an indisputable axiom (thus assuming for *practical* purposes that the Good which he regards as a bare possibility really *is*); at *Gorgias*, 468 D, for instance, the proof that the tyrant cannot do as he wishes rests on this genuinely Socratic equation of 'wish' and 'wish for the Good'. Yet this equation depends on the popular view of the Good, which identifies it confusedly with the useful and pleasant.[1] This example, to which every reader of Plato could easily add some more, plainly shows us how far this early Logic was from aspiring to any acute grasp of distinctions, and what a firm foundation there was, in the main logical activities of the time, for the synoptical tendency which Plato confessed to be the whole of his Dialectic in the *Republic*: Μετὰ δὴ τοῦτον τὸν χρόνον . . . τά τε χύδην μαθήματα παισὶν ἐν τῇ παιδείᾳ γενόμενα τούτοις συνακτέον εἰς σύνοψιν οἰκειότητός τε ἀλλήλων τῶν μαθημάτων καὶ τῆς τοῦ ὄντος φύσεως (537 C). It is not surprising that the range and meaning of notions were not always clearly seen, and that propositions were unjustifiably converted. Naturally we must expect that Plato, like any other rational man, will often happen to give expression to a true judgement on particular logical points; at *Republic* 491 D, for

[1] A confusion already present in language, where εὖ πράττειν has a twofold meaning. Compare the concluding words of the *Republic*, εὖ πράττωμεν.

instance, he is led to make the distinction between 'evil' and 'not-good', and so between a contrary judgement and a contradictory. Note, however, that his main interest is in an observation of fact—that a higher nature in the absence of proper care is liable to deeper degeneration. It is this which leads him to express the logical rule, 'evil is, I suppose, more opposite to the good than to the not-good', and not *vice versa*. Such accidental observations are entirely different from the careful analysis of logical opposition which meets us in the *Sophist*; and it would be inadvisable to use them to support inferences about the chronology, as some have tried to do in this instance.

Connexion of all Ideas with the Good through the notion of Aretê

So much is clear, that the innermost tendency in the logic of 'Socrates' is the tendency to combine and unite things by the discovery of common characteristics; to retain all that is self-consistent, and to anchor it to one single object, the Good. How natural it was for any doctrine which assumed a plurality of Ideas, as did the so-called Ideal Theory, to group them around the Good as their centre, the following remarks may show. Plato's doctrine of Ideas lies dormant, one might almost say, in the single word ἀρετή. To the Greek, this meant far more than our 'virtue'; he (and Plato follows him) ascribed an ἀρετή to every living creature and to every object.[1] Further, it is very important to notice that ἀρετή does not so much indicate some sort of abnormal efficiency in a thing (as we speak of the excellence or goodness of a knife or a weapon), as the excellence which fits each conceivable thing to perform its specific function (τὸ ἑκάστου ἔργον); consequently its essential character is included in its ἀρετή. When the notion of excellence has to be expressed, it is not found in some single, separable capacity, but by the elevation of the object as a whole nearer to its ideal type

---

[1] Οὐκοῦν ἀρετὴ καὶ κάλλος καὶ ὀρθότης ἑκάστου σκεύους καὶ ζῴου καὶ πράξεως οὐ πρὸς ἄλλο τι ἢ τὴν χρείαν ἐστίν, πρὸς ἣν ἂν ἕκαστον ᾖ πεποιημένον ἢ πεφυκός; (*Republic*, 601 D). There is an allusion to i. 353 B οὐκοῦν καὶ ἀρετὴ ᾿δοκεῖ σοι εἶναι ἑκάστῳ ᾧπερ καὶ ἔργον τι προστέτακται; von Arnim (l.c. 82 foll.) shows how this is connected with the statements made in *Gorgias*, 504 A, B, and discusses the meaning of οἰκεῖος κόσμος.

or εἶδος. (Gorgias, in such a context,[1] introduces of his own accord the notion of an εἶδος, 503 E.) Thus when the ideal type is determined, the essence of the thing, 'what it is good for',[2] is known. We are on the fringe of an interpretation of all Nature in terms of design or End, and a straight path would lead us to the 'entelechy'[3] of Aristotle. But Plato's thought before and in the *Republic* is strictly subservient to one main task, the highest at which such inquiry can aim—he wishes to comprehend the ἀρετή of Man, as the essential nature of man, of the human soul. He wishes (to express the same thing more precisely, and in terms closer to the Greek) to understand this essence, the highest object of our human consciousness, '*absolutely*' and '*as it is*', i.e. in the truth of its objective nature.

Plato's manner of proving the Immortality of the Soul in the Tenth Book of the *Republic* shows plainly that the notion of ἀρετή is the very core of his thought. The proof depends entirely on the twofold meaning which we have learnt from our analysis of this word; or, to be more precise, on the fact that the idea of ἀρετή presents itself to Plato as a single whole. In Book X he introduces an opposite conception to that of 'proper virtue', for which he had elsewhere prepared the way (e.g. *Gorgias*, 477 B)—that of a thing's proper or natural *evil*, ἡ οἰκεία πονηρία καὶ τὸ οἰκεῖον

---

[1] Cf. von Arnim, l.c. 83.

[2] We may thus explain the kaleidoscopic change of meaning to which ἀρετή seems to be subject in everyday speech: cf. Koch, *Quae fuerit ante Socratem vocabuli* ἀρετή *notio*, Jena, 1900: J. Ludwig, *Quae fuerit vocis* ἀρετή *vis ac natura ante Demosthenis exitum*, Leipzig, 1906. For its substantial meaning varies with the speaker's position and sex, and with the ideals of the time. Where natural things, having no moral significance, are concerned, its meaning can easily be assimilated to 'thriving' with reference to some definite perfection, as we can see from the Aristotelian quotations in the next note. In fact the conception of ἀρετή derives its meaning from the bearer of the ἀρετή; consequently Socrates is hard put to it to unify the various meanings by reference to the Idea of the Good. His interlocutors all start out from the popular interpretation which attributes separate ἀρεταί to man, woman, child, and so on: cf. *Meno*, 71 E.

[3] ἡ μὲν ἀρετὴ τελείωσίς τις (ὅταν γὰρ λάβῃ τὴν ἑαυτοῦ ἀρετήν, τότε λέγεται τέλειον ἕκαστον. τότε γὰρ μάλιστά ἐστι τὸ κατὰ φύσιν, ὥσπερ κύκλος τέλειος, ὅταν μάλιστα γένηται κύκλος βέλτιστος), ἡ δὲ κακία φθορὰ τούτου καὶ ἔκστασις, *Physics*, 246ᵃ 13. καὶ ἡ ἀρετὴ τελείωσίς τις· ἕκαστον γὰρ τότε τέλειον καὶ οὐσία πᾶσα τότε τελεία, ὅταν κατὰ τὸ εἶδος τῆς οἰκείας ἀρετῆς μηδὲν ἐλλείπῃ μόριον τοῦ κατὰ φύσιν μεγέθους, *Metaphysics*, 1021ᵇ 20. τὸ γὰρ ἔργον τέλος, ἡ δ' ἐνέργεια τὸ ἔργον. διὸ καὶ τοὔνομα ἐνέργεια λέγεται κατὰ τὸ ἔργον, καὶ συντείνει πρὸς τὴν ἐντελέχειαν, ibid. 1050ᵃ 21. On Xenocrates' doctrine of οἰκεία ἀρετή, see Heinze, 147 foll.

κακόν 610 E, τὸ σύμφυτον κακόν 609 A). Moral evil—which is opposed to Virtue in our modern sense—is at the same time the denial of the Soul's *being*; if the Soul could be destroyed, it would be destroyed by this. Only if we follow Plato in his notion of ἀρετή does his proof obtain the cogency it requires. Again, let us consider his discussion of self-knowledge in the *Charmides*. Once more the logic of his argument is highly suspicious, and it can only be held together by the assumption that Virtue and essence are the same in meaning. (It shows, incidentally, how little Plato, before and in the *Republic*, has a doctrine of method, a reflective theory of thinking.) The subject of discussion is 'Knowledge of oneself', the Delphic γνῶθι σεαυτόν (164 D); an essential ethical idea, familiar to Greek thought since Heraclitus.[1] But how does Plato proceed in discussing the theory of such knowledge? His mind is so accustomed to *objects* of thought that he obviously cannot conceive that one's own personal consciousness could be a subject of inquiry.[2] At any rate when the more naïve Critias continues to entertain the idea, no doubt quite an indefinite one, that such a self-knowledge in the modern sense may be possible, Socrates dismisses it on the ground that knowledge, according to his notion of it, appears unthinkable without a definite object and a definite use. The same objections are raised against the idea of a 'knowledge which reflects on knowledge' when, with logic which is not faultless, this is substituted for 'a man's knowledge of himself' (166 c). A fuller phrase 'knowledge which deals with other forms of knowledge and with itself' (166 c, E) does indeed suggest that there can be a general theory of knowledge; the remarkable thing is that it is not saved from rejection, even though it obviously echoes a view held by the historical Socrates;[3] Socrates fails to see the benefit of such a knowledge. But he welcomes with relief the notion of the Good (174 c); and so this once more stands revealed as the focus of Plato's thought in its earlier stage. 'Monster! I said; you have

---

[1] Ἐδιζησάμην ἐμεωυτόν, Diels, B 101.

[2] Moreover even in the quotation from Heraclitus the reference is entirely to something concrete and objective which his 'reflection' discovers, as K. Reinhardt (*Parmenides*, p. 220) has rightly emphasized.

[3] τὸ εἰδέναι ἅ τε οἶδεν καὶ ἃ μὴ οἶδεν, 167 A.

been carrying me round in a circle, and all this time hiding from me the fact that the life according to knowledge is not that which makes men act rightly and be happy, not even if knowledge include all the sciences, but one science only, that of good and evil.' It is not self-knowledge, but knowledge of the Good, which assures us of Happiness, εὖ πράττειν in its twofold sense. This is certainly the true climax to the Dialogue; for nearly all the earlier Dialogues agree in maintaining that only a 'right use' of things with insight into the highest of Ends, the Good, can lend them meaning and value.[1] Plato is always in search of the 'royal art', the art which 'provides and creates Happiness' (*Euthydemus*, 291 B), but his first detailed description of it as the Dialectic of the Idea of the Good comes later, in the *Republic*. So the *Charmides* also issues in the customary 'Socratic' train of thought. But in order to exhaust its meaning, we must relate its special problems to the general foundation on which they rest—σωφροσύνη, as defined in the *Charmides*, must be explained with the help of the notions of Goodness and Happiness (εὐδαιμονία); for the attempted definition of it is not rejected by 'Socrates'.[2] Far from it—his 'criticism' has a definitely positive character, and he is bound to hold that while the problems of the Dialogue cannot be solved *without* his doctrine of the Good, when it is given they are solved entirely.

If, then, it is ἀρετή which gives unity to the *Charmides*, this is no negligible proof that we were correct in our analysis of that word. From the standpoint of Plato in his Socratic phase, the order of the argument would be something like this: The Good for the soul, her ἀρετή, is at the same time the essence of the soul, so far as she becomes conscious of her own essential nature. If the soul knows herself, her own essence and ἀρετή, she also knows her 'proper Good', performs her 'own function' (οἰκεῖον, τὰ ἑαυτοῦ)[3] and acts so as to fulfil her innermost being; and Socrates holds that this is also the greatest good fortune, the true 'prosperity' of the soul. That is the true sense of his 'eudaemonism'.

[1] *Meno*, 88 E; *Gorgias*, 480 foll.; *Republic*, x. 601 D foll.
[2] See 169 B, D, 172 B, C.
[3] The close relation of this idea to the points we are discussing is well brought out by von Arnim, l.c. 63 foll. He refers also to the *Lysis* and the *Symposium*.

The Idea as Intuition

We have seen what a wealth of meaning can be found in the mixed notion of ἀρετή and εἶδος, derived from its native soil of moral philosophy; what variegated strands were combined, so long as this was Plato's teaching about the Universal. We, it is true, can easily unravel them, but to Plato they are bound together by the Good. Even the *Charmides* shows many clear signs of a strong impulse carrying the thinker along towards a 'universal' which he has yet to secure; impatiently 'synoptic', he thrusts aside the opposite tendency to analysis. Notice the objection of Critias, which we cannot help feeling to be justified: 'but you are assuming that they are alike,' 165 E, and a very similar phrase at 166 B. When we compare this with passages which will be discussed later in detail, on the subject of 're-semblances' and 'differences',[1] we see that only the 'synoptic' side of the later Dialectic, that is, only one half of it, has yet impressed itself on Plato's consciousness. Now what kind of an *organon*, or method of thinking, was he here employing; and can it be what we should now call a *concept?* According to one view the discovery of the concept is traced right back to Parmenides; but the truth is that its discovery was much impeded by the fact that men directed their thought to unusual and difficult objects, such as Absolute Being, which lie at the fringe of human comprehension, and were bound soon to involve the mind in hopeless self-contradictions. This was why the Eleatic logic issued in scepticism. When, under the influence of Socrates, Philosophy found its own proper objects in men's moral feelings, these, because of their subjective nature, were specially liable to the contentious onset of the Sophists, and similar difficulties soon arose. (The similarity lay in this, that Socrates' thought again chose objects which were exceedingly difficult to grasp, like Virtue and the Good. A logical theory had to start with such objects, and to be first applied to them.) Still later, the same difficulties are admitted to have brought Plato into conflict with Eleaticism, for the Eleatic logic had by then been

---

[1] *Phaedrus*, 262 A; *Statesman*, 285 A.

pressed into the service of a form of Sophistry which was diametrically opposed to the spirit of Socrates, at least as Plato
represents him.

Now there could be no hope of defining Virtue or the Good,
or of forming concepts to describe them. When the mind turned
to these objects, it could only take them for granted, and be
content with the assurance that they were really present. We
call such a mode of thinking 'intuition'. And we can follow
the process by which Plato's 'intuition'[1] gradually takes form
among the indefinable objects bequeathed to him by the thought
of Socrates. The process seems to be inevitable, and not at all
to depend on his free will. It has been customary since Aristotle
to think of the Concept as something intermediate between the
Socratic definition and the Idea of Plato's mature theory. But this
is quite wrong. Socrates had real reasons for declining to clothe
his thought in conceptual form; as though he had a dim consciousness of his special function in moral philosophy, he was
content to see a practical proof of it in moral action; how could
one express the Good in terms of other ideas without destroying
its categorical force? The same deep-lying reasons were bound
to lead Plato to think intuitively: it goes without saying that the
Good is an object to be seen, ἰδέα; it really *exists*, and the soul
has only to be turned to it in order to 'apprehend' it. The ἰδέα
(= seeing) therefore obtains its nature very largely from the
objects which are its special province. That Greek thinking
had many traits which were bound to strengthen this tendency
to intuition, until it seemed to be the form of all thinking without qualification, becomes clear as soon as one begins 'to think
or speak in Greek terms',[2] and can see the full likeness of ἀγαθόν
to καλόν, ἀρετή to εἶδος. However careful we are to dismiss
every thought of the ideal and the ineffable, and to concentrate
on the more sober and straightforward work of reflection which
prevails in the Dialogues alongside the element of mysticism
and intuition, still our picture of Plato's logic is scarcely changed;

---

[1] ἰδεῖν, εἰδέναι, ἰδέα, εἶδος.

[2] Wilamowitz, *Aristoteles und Athen*, ii. 410. In the passage we have quoted from
the *Gorgias*, 503 E, it is taken as evident that εἶδος corresponds to ἀρετή.

its essential operations show the same fondness for an intuitive manner of understanding. This will become clear when we proceed to ask, In these circumstances, what is the relation of the particular to the universal? This was the burning question at a later time, which brought about the revision of the theory of Ideas: that is undoubtedly what we learn from the *Parmenides*, *Sophist*, and *Philebus*, and in some degree from the *Theaetetus* before them.

Mathematical Orientation of the Idea

Intuition, wherever found, is the representation of the universal in a particular case, which somehow already includes in itself the marks of that universal. The present-day logician, when he mentions intuition, refers especially to intuition in Mathematics. Now in all the various accounts which have been given of the formation of the doctrine of Ideas, it has always been seen that the influence of Mathematics was important. From this science, as every student of the *Meno* and *Phaedo* knows, Plato takes his favourite illustrations of the participation by the particular in the universal. It is characteristic of intuition in Mathematics that a particular case represents not only others of the same order as itself, but something altogether different, something 'higher', and indubitably certain. There is no question of obtaining the Universal in Mathematics by abstraction from particulars; and indeed mathematical problems must have served to make it clear, even to the ancient thinkers, that some higher principle must be applied to the particular before it is known for what it is, before the 'seal of existence', as the *Phaedo* says, can be stamped upon it. Early philosophy, then, found that the universal of which we are speaking, that of Mathematics in the widest sense, was hard to include in intellectual conceptions of definitions, but very much more easy to represent in intuition. So this philosophy was ever liable to fall back on what is individual and can be intuited, where the thinker can at a stroke, in a single view or survey, μιᾷ ἰδέᾳ, learn the nature of some universal. This is the

παλίντονος ἁρμονία of the Idea, by which its later development
will be determined.

'Separation' (χωρισμός) in relation to the Idea

In the *Republic* Plato had conducted an extraordinarily profound inquiry into the difference between the intuition of
mathematical Ideas and Ideas proper. The essential thing for
our present purpose is that he showed the two kinds of knowledge to be closely related; and in the *Meno* they are not yet
separated at all. It is indeed true that the objects of ethics,
if understood as our account of ἀρετή suggests, become very
closely similar to those of Mathematics. The Good in Plato's
sense must necessarily exist because it is the object of a desire
in which every man shares (see e.g. *Symposium*, 205 E), and no
man is knowingly satisfied with its mere appearance (*Republic*,
505 D, *Theaetetus*, 177 D). Here then, as in Mathematics, there
is an object immediately certain, which has to be grasped in its
purity and simplicity, but which only manifests itself in particular individuals and actions; these, however, are all mere
stages, ἐπαναβαθμοί, on the way to a 'highest' principle which
they never make fully real. When we proceed from the Good
to the theory of the particular Virtues (of which we have already
given some account), the same relation becomes even clearer:
it is much easier to *represent*, in an εἶδος, what the ἀρετή of a
particular living being or object is, than it would ever be to
express it in a laborious definition; and it is at least questionable whether Plato at first understood the object of Socrates'
inquiry to be definition, in the logical sense. Since the Ideas
were thus linked to particulars—to individual form and shape,
in which the universal could be seen—it naturally became the
ambition of a philosopher to escape from this limitation; to
contemplate the Form, not in the particular, with which it is
now so very deeply interwoven, but *in and by itself*; for it was a
fundamental premiss of Plato's thinking in its Socratic stage
that the ever-changing stream of becoming was utterly incapable of giving rise to a permanent reality such as thought
could comprehend; now in the case of moral objects, the Good

and the Beautiful, the upward impulse was bound to redouble its force, till it became a demand for entire transcendence, a religious metaphysic; while the logic of Mathematics, with its ideal objects lying beyond this world, was accepted as a welcome reassurance and confirmation.

Thus the 'universal' to Plato was a representative intuition (called 'Idea'), to which were added all the associations of the Greek word ἀρετή (see above). Briefly, it was what we now, in a narrower field, call an Ideal. And the very existence of such an Ideal meant that the philosopher's urge for 'separation' (χωρισμός), his desire to find 'pure Form in itself', would come to dominate all other motives. No anxiety would be felt about the connexion of the Idea with the particular; for, after all, there it was immediately given to him in intuition! One may go farther and say that, the more keenly we feel the distance between the one pure Form, μονοειδὲς εἶδος, and its many copies, the stronger becomes our power to bridge the gulf, our longing for ἀρετή, κάλλος, εἶδος. It is not man alone who strives for the εὐδαιμονία in which his essential being is fulfilled. All things wish to be 'perfect', to realize their being.[1]

Such a complex structure as the theory of Ideas must necessarily remain open to various interpretations, since it assuredly contains latent forces of which the philosopher himself will only gain full theoretical consciousness in the course of their development. Any view or interpretation which tries with the help of modern concepts founded on separation and analysis to describe the unconscious syntheses of an earlier time, must feel that it is making a *selection*, dividing that which, in the eyes of the ancient thinker, could not really be separated. Admittedly, before we can hope to understand the nature of the ἰδέα we must first expose all the factors inherent in it; but still these factors were present to Plato's own consciousness in very varying degrees of clarity. To take an illustration: the quality of a sound is determined, not merely by the sum of the component tones, but also by the different relative strength of the upper, lower,

---

[1] *Phaedo*, 75 B: προθυμεῖται μὲν πάντα τοιαῦτ' εἶναι οἷον ἐκεῖνο, ἔστιν δὲ αὐτοῦ φαυλότερα. Also 75 A: πάντα . . . ὀρέγεται.

and combination tones. It is just such a personal quality which must be the aim of historical research. Can it be true that, in regard to the theory of Ideas, we have no other criteria than *either* our 'own insight into the theory of knowledge', *or* a 'subjectively satisfactory impression of the whole'?[1] We must necessarily start with such an impression, but it should be possible in two ways to test its historical truth. (1) The individual who is interpreting Plato must remember that his own horizon is, in some respects, wider; and so must correct his interpretation if necessary. (2) Above all our results must be tested by application to the text—the beginning and the end of all our knowledge, even that of Plato. Now, is the view which we have expounded—that to Plato the essence of things is their ἀρετή, and that the εἶδος is its intuited image—in harmony with the general background of Greek thought? On this point we must be satisfied with what has been said already. We will now take some special problems of interpretation, and judge from them whether the assumption that Plato's doctrine had at first an entirely moral orientation will or will not enable us to understand its later development, and the problems of that development.

To begin with the theory of knowledge in the *Republic*: let us prove that the two opposed interpretations of the doctrine of Ideas, the teleological and the 'critical', can be combined when we look at them from our point of view, that of ἀρετή. In the process we can make a summary of our whole previous argument, which will serve as an ἐπίβασις καὶ ὁρμή from which we may try to understand the decisive change in Plato's central position after the *Republic*; or in other words, to understand the *Theaetetus, Parmenides, Sophist, Philebus*, and see their inward relationship.

The Good as αἰτία *and* ἀνυπόθετον.

The Concept is by its nature *universal*; Plato's Idea, on the other hand, was so constituted that it readily showed a certain

[1] [The first phrase is taken from Cohen, and represents the criterion of philosophical students of Plato. The second is taken from Pohlenz, and represents that of philologists.]

parallelism with the particular, and seemed in real danger of becoming a 'thing'. It was natural and necessary that Plato should strive to find objects which were not burdened with such inner diversity, and were really a 'unity' in the sense that they logically excluded any multiplication whatsoever. It is significant that it was moral speculation which furnished to Plato objects of this kind; by their absolute necessity for thought, they confirmed his faith in the Idea as he had conceived it, and for a long time turned his eyes away from that 'abyss of nonsense' (*Parmenides*, 130 D), into which an unrestricted belief in Ideas threatened to lead him.

If in all their actions men aim at the Good, this Good must be the last, the final cause (οὗ ἕνεκα)—or, to start in Greek fashion from the side of the object rather than the subject, the *first* Cause. In the *Lysis* such a Cause, the πρῶτον φίλον, is demanded as a a necessity for thought.

Socratic-Platonic ethics insists on a highest Good which is categorically necessary; desire for it must depend on no conditions, it must be ἀνυπόθετον. This lesson is in fact taught in all the Dialogues of apparent doubt: Justice, Courage, Piety, Self-restraint, really are, in relation to this highest Idea, mere ὑποθέσεις —provisional assumptions, which only secure their meaning when they are made fast to the Idea of the Good. The same conception of the Good as the highest Cause and Aim also serves to make clear the true meaning of 'the absolutely beautiful' in the *Symposium*, and of Platonic Love. Philosophical Erôs leads not only to the supreme beauty, but to the highest knowledge. So that besides the moral *motif* (Love is the impulse towards the highest morality and εὐδαιμονία), the quest for knowledge is already visible. And this last and most extensive aspect of Plato's Theory of Ideas receives its purest and clearest expression in the *Republic*, where the Good is the heart of all knowledge and the object of the highest spiritual power, νόησις. It is not difficult to see that by adding together these three divisions—the πρῶτον φίλον, πρῶτον καλόν, and πρῶτον ἀληθές—we obtain the full meaning which our analysis discovered in ἀρετή: we have (1) the supreme object of all human desire; (2) the visible form of all perfection, the εἶδος; (3) lastly the 'essence', the organization of a thing (κόσμος), which displays itself in a specific function (ἔργον); its 'rightness' (ὀρθότης) which it is our task to understand, if we would know what the thing *is*, and what purpose it serves. The distinctively *intellectual* character of Plato's ethics, an inheritance from Socrates, infuses itself into the 'teleology' which Plato teaches in the *Republic*, enabling him (1) to explain why all existing things strive after an end; because they have a longing (ἔρως) to maintain themselves in their εἶδος, or, as it is expressed in the *Symposium* 'to participate, after a fashion, in Immortality'; and (2) to show, at the same time, how the phenomenal world is knowable; it is through participation in this single archetype, which the philosopher comprehends by reasoning (ἐν λόγοις); the Good, in fact, is, in the words of the *Republic*, the source both of the knowable in things and of their being.[1] From this Idea, in the end, all 'reasoning about causes' must start. The insertion into the same scheme of the doctrine of principles in the *Phaedo* offers no further difficulty. There the survey of pre-Socratic ἀρχαί ended in the demand for a Final Cause (99 c), and this we can safely assert to be the Idea of the Good; as for the 'hypotheses', they have to be connected, as we saw on the last page, with the ἀνυπόθετον of the *Republic*, and this will not be difficult in view of what has just been said of the parallelism in Plato between teleology and the knowledge of a thing's essence. (Another point of connexion is the ἱκανόν, *Phaedo*, 101 e.) The 'philosophical' interpreters of Plato have attributed so much importance to the version of the Ideas as hypotheses that a more detailed demonstration of the close relation between the *Phaedo* and the *Republic* is really desirable. Here I will be content to refer to my earlier Essay.

---

[1] 509 B: καὶ τοῖς γιγνωσκομένοις τοίνυν μὴ μόνον τὸ γιγνώσκεσθαι φάναι ὑπὸ τοῦ ἀγαθοῦ παρεῖναι, ἀλλὰ καὶ τὸ εἶναί τε καὶ τὴν οὐσίαν ὑπ' ἐκείνου αὐτοῖς προσεῖναι.

II. PROBLEMS LATENT IN THE DOCTRINE
OF ARETÊ

LATENT in the theory of Ideas, as it has here been outlined, were four problems whose full difficulty Plato began to see in the Dialogues after the *Republic* (but not till then) and with all the energy at his command undertook to solve. They are partly interwoven with each other, and so also are the solutions which he found; however, they can be described in the following terms:

(1) The absolute existence of the Idea.
(2) The relation between the single Idea and the manifold objects participating therein.
(3) The meaning of such μέθεξις; in other words the problem of 'separation' (χωρισμός).
(4) True and false judgement (ἀληθής, ψευδὴς Δόξα). Their nature is warmly disputed in the *Theaetetus*, and is at last decided in the *Sophist*.

Under the doctrine of ἀρετή,[1] if I may so describe that earlier phase of the Ideal Theory which I have outlined, not only did these problems not arise in the form in which they were later discussed, but the philosopher would necessarily tend at first to exaggerate and lay stress upon the very points which were destined to create his later problems.

1. Firstly, the absolute existence of the Idea. The separation of the final End, and its elevation to a higher realm, were, in the sphere of ethics, logically necessary; for the enthronement of the supreme Good as high as possible above the kingdom of this world was precisely what was needed in order to awaken our longing (ἔρως) for the highest Truth and Beauty, and to give it force enough to cross the intervening gulf by the φιλόσοφος βίος, the ὁμοίωσις θεῷ (*Republic*, 613 A, B). Although we have no right forthwith to identify the Idea of the Good in the *Republic* with the God of the *Timaeus*, some blend of religious elements with his

---

[1] [Stenzel says the ἀρετή-εῖδος doctrine. I think the English reader will be satisfied with a less precise expression.]

philosophy was essential to Plato in working out the view of the Idea as transcending experience. The need for an alliance with Religion is already seen in the *Meno* in the doctrines of Immortality and Reminiscence. And because of this ethico-religious background Plato was not in a position to see that this isolation of the divine might lead to a sort of reduplication of reality—to the problem of the 'third man', which he later expressed so precisely in the *Parmenides* (132 E foll.). Indeed so long as the doctrine of ἀρετή remained as the foundation of his thought, and was not confronted by sober questions of pure Logic, the thought that this kingdom of essences, so nobly exalted above the whole world of sense, might one day be compared with the things of that world, and indeed placed on a level with them, seemed utterly absurd. And it is now clear that the danger of this comparison arose, and that it became unavoidable, as soon as the doctrine of ἀρετή began to evolve in the direction of a general theory of the concepts of all things, and the philosopher claimed to know these things clearly, and to explain them.

2. Hence the second of our problems is immediately connected with the first: what place was there for Unity in the doctrine of ἀρετή? Evidently the virtues (in the narrower sense, limiting the word to temperance and courage, piety and justice) were a Unity. 'Knowledge of the Good' was their inward bond of union. And this 'highest study', far from comprehending the virtues as subordinate kinds, actually *was* all of them. This logical relationship is peculiar, and only understandable on the basis of Socratic-Platonic ethics; no concept exactly represents it. Consequently when, at a later time, the crisis came in the theory of Ideas, and the theory of knowledge began to take a more definite place by the side of the moral interests, Plato looked upon the classification of concepts as a novel and important discovery. (To us this seems a much simpler relationship than the earlier one.) The principle of the Good could only be understood by grasping its content; and this very indefiniteness of form meant that it was well adapted to unite the ἀρεταί (= εἴδη) of all other objects. On the one hand, all the *purpose* in nature culminated in the Good; on the other hand, Plato had

taken what seemed to him the most certain content of thought (that idea of a supreme End, which his ethics required), and made it the typical content of all rational knowledge whatsoever; it was the guarantee which made secure all other branches of 'pure' knowledge (pure Mathematics, Astronomy, &c.), and these must therefore be kept free from all empiricism (see e.g. *Republic*, 530 B). In the *Republic* this union of all knowledge in the light of the Idea of the Good is still simply defended by an argument from politics and education—that only the philosopher, who in his Dialectic surveys the connexion of all the sciences with the highest rational knowledge (νόησις), is in a position to make 'right use' of all these sciences for the welfare of the State. Its true welfare is seen in the light of the Good, which he alone can comprehend. We mentioned that this was foreshadowed by the βασιλικὴ τέχνη of the *Euthydemus*.

Here, then, the same passion for Unity is manifest—the same distinctive idea, so specially characteristic of Plato, that all branches of knowledge aspire towards a single aim. It leads him, for example, to condemn empirical knowledge, and so to pass a one-sided judgement, which he had afterwards to correct, on the science of nature. There is an unrestrained impulse to secure unity by emphasis on the Good—the Good, which behind its thousand appearances, is One. To the 'synopsis' which is knowledge of the Good (*Republic*, 537 c) no opposite process of division corresponds. Given this quite exceptional Unity, whose meaning was more important than its form, all those questions remain open which afterwards disturbed Plato so profoundly. In the *Republic* we never learn how many Ideas there are—whether they are to be assumed for every entity and concept, or whether there are limitations, and of what kind. Those who would find answers to these questions there, must resort to unconvincing inferences from the examples of Ideas quoted in some special context. The answer may well be that the idea of a teleological Unity of all being is so dominant that the dangerous problem of the One and the Many is still left out of account; the Good stands out among all the other Ideas, and the more fully its connexion with particular Ideas is known, the more conditional their proper value is seen to be; the Good tends to become the sole Value sufficing for all the others—and Plato does not dream that it may be logically comparable to them; freedom from all such relationships is precisely its chief characteristic.

3. When, as the range of Ideas is extended, this contrast in values is gradually mitigated, and the Idea begins to turn into a mere unity embracing a manifold or plurality of objects, it is then that the problem of 'participation' becomes serious for Plato. This will appear later. But for the present the entire question of the One and the Many is forgotten; and for the problem of μέθεξις, which is closely bound up with it, we may refer moreover to our general analysis of the nature of an Idea (p. 37).

Following the direction of the philosopher's thought, things themselves share in an upward movement towards that highest Idea in which all contradictions come to an end. There is no stronger expression of this movement than in the *Phaedo*, where, to the dismay of 'philosophical' Platonists, 'chorismos' is at its widest, the gulf between experience and the Idea deeper than ever. But it is significant that in the same Dialogue, the question, what are μέθεξις and παρουσία? is pronounced to be entirely irrelevant.[1] One cannot blame certain earlier Platonic scholars who placed the *Parmenides* before the *Phaedo* in time. The keenly contested argument of that Dialogue, of which we shall speak presently, gave them, on the current interpretation of the theory of Ideas, a conclusive reason for doing so: for the man who could write that sentence of the *Phaedo*, and add οὐ γὰρ ἔτι τοῦτο δι-ϊσχυρίζομαι must, it seemed, have passed beyond the problems of the *Parmenides*, and likewise the elementary logical questions of the *Sophist*.

4. The last difficulty concerns a notion which the advance of Platonic scholarship has only succeeded in rendering more problematic, that of δόξα. With this I can at present deal briefly,[2] firstly because a vast amount has been written on the subject, and more especially because the study of the *Theaetetus* and

---

[1] ὅτι οὐκ ἄλλο τι ποιεῖ αὐτὸ καλὸν ἢ ἡ ἐκείνου τοῦ καλοῦ εἴτε παρουσία εἴτε κοινωνία εἴτε ὅπῃ δὴ καὶ ὅπως προσγενομένη, 100 D.

[2] Cf. Raeder, *Platons philosophische Entwicklung*, pp. 287 foll., who surveys the literature and the problems.

Sophist will give me occasion to examine the question again in detail(pp. 62 foll.). The idea of Δόξα evolves in a most remarkable way in the Dialogues. Here are the main points; with the overwhelming majority of scholars I date the *Theaetetus* after the *Republic*. At first 'Opinion' is defined in such a way that true and false Opinion present no problem (*Meno: Republic*). Nor again is it difficult to determine the boundary between Opinion and Knowledge proper; Opinion occupies a half-way position between Knowledge and Ignorance (*Symposium*, 202 A, *Republic*, 476 C, 506 C). The criterion of Knowledge as distinct from Opinion, is λόγος, the statement of a rational ground, which is understood in various ways: we have the λογισμὸς αἰτίας in the *Meno*, λόγον Δοῦναι καὶ Δέξασθαι in *Republic*, 531 E, *Symposium*, 202 A, *Phaedo*, 76 B, 78 D. The contrast between Δόξα, sensuous apprehension of an individual in the world of becoming, and ἐπιστήμη, knowledge of the universal, dominates all the Dialogues down to and including the *Republic*. Though in the fourfold division of knowledge in Books VI–VII there is nothing which literally corresponds to this favourite contrast, at VIII. 534 A it is distinctly introduced; for ἐπιστήμη then takes the place of νόησις (the highest of the sections in Book VI), and is joined with Διάνοια to form νόησις περὶ οὐσίαν; and to this is opposed Δόξα περὶ γένεσιν, which, as we are definitely told, is an inclusive term, wider than πίστις or εἰκασία; it is thus preserved in its old meaning. In the Dialogues down to the *Republic* the distinction between Δόξα and ἐπιστήμη is as plain as that between γένεσις and οὐσία. Having no other interest, in his earlier phase, than to bring fully home to our consciousness the superiority of the realm of the eternal and immutable to that of Becoming; purposely emphasizing, as we have shown, the 'separation' in value, in order to encourage us to strive upwards and bridge the gulf; Plato naturally finds no uncertainty in the sense of Δόξα; it is only too well known to human beings, and to rise above it is, to the wise man, the whole moral problem. Nowhere is the nerve of the doctrine of ἀρετή more clearly perceptible than here; and the point shows how great an influence a word, in the wealth of its unanalysed senses, may exert upon the process of theoretical speculation. Subjectively, δόξα is *opinion*; on the side of the object, it is *appearance*—either fallacious reputation, such as even an impostor can attain, or the good appearance which, at least, does no harm.[1] Let us remember the detailed picture drawn by Plato in *Republic*, Book II, and in the *Gorgias*, of the completely unjust man, who, throughout his whole life on earth, has preserved the *appearance* of the just. When the Soul in the *Gorgias* has passed over into the realm of truth, and stands naked before its inexorable judges in the next world, it learns at last the true nature of the Good, as distinct from its *appearance*. If the unjust man had known this before, he would have done what is 'good', or 'fitting' for him—would not have hazarded the 'prosperity' and happiness of his soul. A man may be content with an appearance of the Just, but no one is satisfied with a mere appearance of the Good (see above, p. 39). Knowledge of the Good preserves a man, and that alone; he who in his endeavour to reach this goal has made the eye of his soul strong and keen, is set free from all appearance; for all things unconsciously strive for their proper good. Just as, in the strict sense, there cannot be an *appearance* of the Good, so, in the end, there cannot be *opinion* about it; the true Good can never become an object of δόξα, because it is an unconditional final End; it is only to be grasped in an absolute and final knowledge. But is this attainable? The sciences, which have no need to call in the aid of sensation, and can proceed by a 'pure' method, prove to us that it is. Or rather, these sciences have to be related to the Good (so Plato continues in the *Republic*) in order to become certain of their own presuppositions, which are otherwise assumed without proof. For, in its absolute necessity to thought, this highest End, elevated above all that is 'conditioned' or earthly, is the prototype of all νόησις whatsoever. Its ground lies in itself, and here the ontological proof is justified; a supreme End, if once it is understood, *is* real; because here our consciousness is free, and, in the necessity of thought, becomes aware of its own highest freedom. Knowledge about this end is ἐπιστήμη, in the same sharp contrast with opinion which is clearly expressed by Aristotle (*Meta-*

[1] Cf. Wilamowitz on Euripides, *Heracles*, 292.

physics, 1039ᵇ 33) : knowledge does not change in a moment and become ignorance, 'but such a state is opinion'. As Plato so often repeats, all things save the Good itself are sometimes good and sometimes not good.

So we see once more the peculiar tension which seems to be an essential accompaniment of Plato's conception of Knowledge, and which was destined actually to determine the history of the Platonic εἶδος; it has been indicated here before; the Idea is linked to the particular, but strives to acquire the nobler character of Universal. Just in the same way, it will often seem to the philosopher that there is nothing in the lives of most men but δόξαι, and that in this sense it is the lot of man always to be a 'lover of wisdom', never 'wise'. Yet Plato, even where, as in the *Meno*, he seems to lean to a milder judgement of the virtue 'of the citizen', never doubts that unless reflection leads us to the highest cause, the Good-in-itself, our true opinions cannot be 'bound', and become the property of the Soul. For by an intimate logical necessity this mysterious yet all-pervading power can only be comprehended in knowledge; and conversely the final 'unconditional' knowledge is only conceivable in connexion with it. Socrates had professed ignorance, had made no claim to knowledge; in the last resort he started out from the particular case, confident that, in its examination between man and man, he could most convincingly prove the necessity of standards of conduct; Plato, by the whole trend of his doctrine, was obliged to emphasize that *universal* insight is the presupposition of each particular moral action; and this is another reason why true insight into the particular case did not claim his interest. Consideration of the moral side therefore confirms his tendency to pass over the particular, and strive to obtain a 'synoptic' view of various strands converging towards the Good, around which, as we have now shown, all his problems can be grouped. The thought and action of the philosopher moves in the kingdom which is not of this world. To ascend into that kingdom is the aim of Dialectic; and its descending process, at the end of the Sixth Book of the *Republic*, is definitely limited to Ideas: τελευτᾷ εἰς εἴδη. The κάθοδος can only confirm the relation of Ideas to the supreme Idea of the Good; in so doing it establishes, as has been noticed before, the conditional principles of the other sciences, and shows that they too, by being connected with the unconditioned Idea, can be elevated into the realm of νόησις: *Republic*, 511 c '(arts) which proceed from hypotheses only; these also are contemplated by the understanding, and not by the senses: yet, because they start from hypotheses and do not ascend to a principle, those who contemplate them appear to you not to exercise the higher reason upon them, although when a first principle is added to them they are cognizable by the higher reason.' Only in the world of Ideas is knowledge possible; and this scheme of Dialectic definitely bars any further descent to the realities of empirical observation. Such things cannot be known.

III. THE EMERGENCE OF THE FOUR PROBLEMS

WE must now ask what problems await this theory of knowledge, what crises and changes it must face, when the time comes to defend the view that 'only the universal can be known' (Aristotle, *Metaphysics*, $1086^b 5$) and maintain it in relation to empirical reality. Hitherto this view has been boldly assumed. What will happen when knowledge of individual realities is no longer simply dismissed as δόξα, but viewed as a fact to be explained? In the discussion of this question, an important part falls to the *Theaetetus*. Here the very foundations on which Plato's earlier thought rested are subjected to an incisive and, moreover, an entirely positive criticism. This can be shown quite clearly with reference to the problem of δόξα.

Even the assumptions which seemed most certain are found to be doubtful; coming to the essential thesis of the Sophists that there is no such thing as a false opinion, Plato questions the possibility of any distinction between true and false δόξα, after an analysis which is both impartial and remarkable for attention to detail, and no road to a solution is revealed. Nor is this all. On the assumptions which he now makes, Plato has to reject not only the remaining attempts to decide the essence of knowledge, but also its definition as ἀληθὴς δόξα μετὰ λόγου, which is undoubtedly in harmony with his view in the first period (see above, p. 48). However, the first part of the *Theaetetus* in all respects continues that main contrast which we found in the earlier period, the contrast between knowledge of Ideas and knowledge through the senses; and the ethical orientation clearly remains.[1] There is only a gentle hint that the theory requires completion. Hence some scholars would actually make the *Theaetetus* precede the *Republic*, as representing the same doctrine of knowledge at an earlier stage. They must then, of course, abandon any attempt to explain the 'dogmatic' second part. (Natorp, pp. 112 foll.) But the *Sophist* is there to show us that we ought to pay full respect to what is said of δόξα in the latter half of the *Theaetetus*. Plato

---

[1] Cf. for example, 157 D, 169 D, 172 A, B, 176 C.

gives in the *Sophist* a definition of true and false opinion which has never, indeed, been made completely clear; but it is stated with full assurance; it is proved that false opinion exists, since 'Not-Being', to which it is related, exists. This is in direct conflict with *Republic*, 478 B, and *Theaetetus*, 189 A, B, where Not-Being was declared to be not only unknowable, but inconceivable, because nothingness cannot be conceived. Thus this problem of Δόξα brings us to the same result as before: precisely those propositions which seemed to Plato to offer no problem on his earlier assumptions and amid his earlier intellectual interests, because he still held the doctrine of ἀρετή with its moral orientation, appear to him at a later stage to be burdened with a special difficulty, which he energetically undertakes to resolve.

This clearly prescribes the plan of our inquiry. We must show how the four problems which have been mentioned were bound to emerge in the process of extending the doctrine of ἀρετή into a genuine 'theory of Ideas'; we must show how they presented themselves to Plato, and how he tried to solve them.

There is a remarkable situation in modern scholarship as regards this 'genuine' theory of Ideas. If asked to name four extreme interpretations of the theory, one might mention (*a*) the view of Zeller that the Ideas are concepts of all things 'hypostasized', or made into substances; (*b*) in contrast to this, the view which emanates from 'modern philosophy' that the Ideas are 'methods', i.e. their function is to enable the manifold given to the senses to be comprehended as a single object of thought. Then, in another dimension, we have more opposites: (*c*) For some the theory is the foundation of Plato's 'system', suffering no essential change, and in some way, more or less clearly and distinctly, assumed in all the Dialogues. But (*d*) others allege a complete break in Plato's development; the theory, they say, was modified in a manner which can practically be described as a surrender. There must be some real ground for all these views, since they can continually be defended by arguments which may or may not be novel; and we must look for a standpoint from which none of them need be simply thrust aside, but a kernel of truth can be discovered in all.

1. *The Ideas in the 'Parmenides': abandonment of the standpoint of value*

What is the main distinction between the doctrine of ἀρετή outlined by us above, and these mutually contradictory 'theories of Ideas'? According to them, Plato very soon postulated Ideas of all things; here we have proved that this extension to 'all being' was indeed in harmony with the earlier doctrine, but that its real interest lay in morals, and in objects which lent themselves to moral and teleological treatment, those, in brief, which could have an ἀρετή. That such was the origin of the whole doctrine, and likewise that Socrates was all-important in the earlier period, is clearly shown by Plato's own account of the genesis of the theory of Ideas in the Dialogue with which the 'destructive' criticism of it begins: *Parmenides*, 130 B (tr. Jowett):

'Was this your own distinction between ideas in themselves and the things which partake of them? and do you think that there is an idea of likeness apart from the likeness which we possess, and of the one and many, and of the other things which Zeno mentioned?

I think that there are such ideas, said Socrates.

Parmenides proceeded: *And would you also make absolute ideas of the just and the beautiful and the good, and of all that class?*

Yes, he said, I should.

And would you make an idea of man apart from us and from all other human creatures, or of fire and water?

I am often undecided, Parmenides, as to whether I ought to include them or not.

And would you feel equally undecided, Socrates, about things of which the mention may provoke a smile?—I mean such things as hair, mud, dirt, or anything else which is vile and paltry; would you suppose that each of these has an idea distinct from the actual objects with which we come into contact, or not?

Certainly not, said Socrates; visible things like these are such as they appear to us, and I am afraid that there would be an absurdity in assuming any idea of them, although I sometimes get disturbed, and begin to think that there is nothing without an idea; but then again, when I have taken up this position, I run away, because I am afraid that I may fall into a bottomless pit of nonsense, and perish; *and so I return to the ideas of which I was just now speaking, and occupy myself with them.'*

Socrates' perplexity would have no meaning if the εἶδος in question were already the concept. Why should there not be concepts of mud and hair? If a 'separate' and substantial Idea of Good is necessary to give us the concept of goodness, then an Idea of mud is no less necessary to enable us to form a concept of mud. It is obvious what was the hindrance which Plato found— it was the distinction in value; but value is quite irrelevant to the existence of concepts. We have, then, the clearest possible sign that the εἶδος is laden with moral and aesthetic qualities; Plato declines to speak of an ἀρετή of mud, or of an εἶδος which would have to be mud of a purer and clearer quality than mud on earth. And yet (so he now believes) there is no doubt that εἴδη of all things must be assumed. With this their nature is assuredly modified, and in a way which makes them more like concepts. We must try to understand how this step came to be so difficult for Plato. He does not have to fight his way to the Ideal—that comes naturally to his spirit—but to something which seems to the modern mind vastly simpler, although in the case of those humbler things which are mentioned here, it may not be as simple as it seems—to the concept. When the theory thus spread beyond its original horizon, the interest in knowledge necessarily gained in importance relatively to other interests. A theory of knowledge had been implied in the view that all things have 'essences'. But it is bound to become much stronger when Plato has to decide how we grasp the essence of things which cannot be known *a priori*; and which, on the contrary, make a contest between theory and observation inevitable.

Plato's theory was made to gravitate in this direction by its own law of development. But the scientific interest of the age as a whole must have reinforced this tendency, once it had begun. The strands which had been interwoven were sorted out. When it became Plato's ambition to know everything without distinction of value,[1] the first change was the disappearance of that teleology which had been implied in the notion of ἀρετή. It has to be purified and remodelled before it can reappear, clearer and more conscious, as a genuine teleology—I mean in the *Timaeus*. Plato's entire later speculation about the World-Soul and the

---

[1] In the *Sophist* and *Statesman* he distinctly denies any intention of respecting value. *Sophist*, 227 B, *Statesman*, 266 D, and similarly *Philebus*, 58 C.

Creation is, it may be said, nothing but a remodelling of elements which had been contained from the first in the doctrine
of ἀρετή; but only when a theory of knowledge had been worked
out in the Eleatic Dialogues could these elements be disentangled
from the original skein and show their proper nature. In the
later philosophy the threads are sorted out, and run parallel,
though it is true that each continues to be very necessary to the
others; this is why a theory of knowledge *alone* still seems to be
unobtainable without simplification, and such a theory is far
from exhausting the true meaning of the *Parmenides*. But it is
precisely because Plato now faces the question of knowledge in
its whole extent, including even empirical knowledge, and because this is a novelty to him, that he formulates the problem
in its bare and elementary simplicity. And this has made scholars
repeatedly propose to place the Dialogues concerned (even the
Theaetetus, until our own day) before the *Republic* in order of time;
for it has always been dimly perceived that the Dialectic of the *Republic* is the culmination and ending of a stage of development.

Two moments have so far been emphasized: Plato has (*a*) extended the Ideas to everything that exists, and (*b*) in connexion
with this, he has raised in a simple form the question, What is a
thing's essence? (τί ἐστιν;). The *Parmenides* shows what were the
first effects of this: Plato begins intentionally to neglect the contrast between higher and lower value, which he had previously
so often stressed, and which gave colour to the separation of the
Ideas, and made it justifiable on the original ground. The
Phaedo is no exception. True, Plato seemed there to be giving
clear expression to a 'critical' view of Knowledge, when he spoke
of the Idea as a 'seal' placed by reason on the data of experience.
Nevertheless it was in that Dialogue also that he had most vigor-
ously stated the defective character (ἐνΔεεστέρως ἔχειν) of things
of the sensible world, in contrast to the realm of essential Being
towards which they aspire (ὀρέγεσθαι); there was never any idea
in the *Phaedo* that the philosopher should aim at knowledge of
these μετέχοντα, and they were mere steps in his ascent to the
highest forms of knowledge.[1] And how Natorp is obliged to

---

[1] ἐπαναβαθμοί, *Symposium*, 211 c—but the term itself does not recur in the *Phaedo*.

struggle against the 'separation' which is so plainly acknow-ledged in the *Phaedo*! But in the later phase it is just these μετέχοντα which have to be known—no longer the *a priori* and mathe-matical aspects of empirical reality, but real things themselves. And this is just where a distinction in value can serve no useful purpose. In the *Parmenides*, therefore, Plato, knowing that he has a solution ready, prefers to expose without reserve the full difficulty of such a distinction; he says that such knowledge of a higher Being could never serve to give us knowledge of this world, nor could even God come to know *our* objects by it alone; hence the cause of change must lie in the nature of Ideas, and not in things; and they must themselves undergo change, if they are to help in our study of observed reality.

The 'absolute' existence (τὸ ἄμεικτον) of the Ideas has thus become a most serious problem, because the comparison in point of value, which had been the chief motive for 'separation', has been entirely abandoned. Does this mean that the Idea is now a concept, instead of the older ἀρετή or εἶδος or intuition? Is it a mere predicate of judgement, uniting the manifold of sensation? If so, the absolute existence of Ideas would be abandoned, and at the same time their 'separateness'. But Plato is bent on pre-serving 'separation'; for in the introductory part of the *Par-menides* he twice plainly rejects the view which would make the Idea a predicative concept: 'when many things appear to you to be great, perhaps you seem to see one form (ἰδέα) in them all, and hence you think that greatness is one' (132 A). The reason why he rejects this theory is the peculiar τρίτος ἄνθρωπος argu-ment which cannot be considered until later, when we come to the problem of Δόξα; and here it is enough to mention Plato's repeated remark. The Ideas, then, remain ὄντα; they do not tend to become 'conceptions' of the soul (νοήματα). The reason given is very typical of ancient philosophy: 'in that case every-thing would consist of thoughts, everything *would think*' (132 c). 'Separation', therefore, remains, and is in no way abandoned, even though its logical difficulty is now nakedly exposed in the absence of the all-pervading desire for the Good. The view, however, that 'these Ideas are established as patterns in Nature',

132 D, which would recall the teleological relationship once more, *is* decidedly rejected, and for logical reasons, which correspond to the 'Third Man' argument.

Thus as soon as the 'Ideal Theory' had to be adapted to serve as a general theory of Knowledge, two of the difficulties which we have mentioned sprang up in its path. Both the absolute existence and the 'separation' of the Idea become problematic, and it is in consequence clarified and remodelled. It may thus be said that there was never any 'general theory of Ideas'—that name is a relic of the one-sided 'systematic' interpretation of Plato. When the original theory had to be *made* general, it at once changed its nature.

2. The 'Parmenides' and the problem of the One and the Many

Nowhere in the argument of the *Parmenides* do there seem to be such obstinate logical difficulties as in the contrast between the One and the Many; and this contrast does in fact now become fundamentally important for the Ideas. Previously the εἶδος, unique and uniform, had been fixed as a 'pattern' in the world of Being, where it drew things to itself by its beauty. Since it moved them 'like an object of love and desire', it must naturally be *single*. (The Aristotelian phrase may serve to remind us how great an importance all these views were to acquire later in the philosophy of the Academy.) But now this active relationship ceases. In place of the living Idea infusing its own moral force into all earthly things, there is now a simple logical 'participation'; and again the questionable point is just that for which the earlier Plato had contended—unity. If the εἶδος is one, how can it at the same time be 'in' the many μετέχοντα? It was not necessary for the earlier theory to be concerned about this question. We observe once more that the earlier εἶδος cannot have been a general concept. Had it been so, and had other reasons in the meantime led Plato to make the remarkable 'substantialization' of concepts, he could always have found his way back to the view of the universal as an abstraction, and so solved this problem at a stroke.

But here we must remember once more the relationship

between Plato's Idea, an act of intuition, and the particular: it is indeed a close relationship, but so long as the εἶδος is really an Ideal Form, this guarantees it against any unwelcome parallelism with the particulars known by sense. But the more closely the εἶδος comes to resemble a concept, the nearer does it draw to the sensible particular. How, indeed, can a concept have other and higher properties than the objects which it includes? An existent, ὄν, it remains—for how, asks the *Parmenides* (132 B), can there be a thought (νόημα) of nothing? Upon this the Idea suddenly turns into an unnecessary duplicate side by side with the sensible particular; in order to comprehend in one group the Idea and the particulars which 'share' in it, a new universal of the same kind would be required; and this, too, must be one of the specifically Platonic, hence really existent universals; an infinite regress begins; and the One, i.e. the universal, is indefinitely multiplied. This is the so-called 'Third Man' argument, resting on the assumption that the Idea and its particulars are comparable. And this assumption is a necessary consequence of Plato's intuitive manner of thinking, as soon as that thinking has lost its idealizing aspect; i.e. as soon as the particulars which should be subordinated to the Idea become important on their own account; are no longer instruments of, and points of departure for, a higher knowledge, but objects of knowledge.

3. *The 'Parmenides' and* μέθεξις

But the problem of the 'One and the Many' has, in another way, an even greater importance.

The question of μέθεξις has been altered. The 'participating' things and the 'form' in which they participate stand on one plane; each 'participant' *is* that 'in which it participates', and *vice versa*. Again the difficulty appears that an Idea is at the same time one and many (*Parmenides*, 131 A foll.). This adds point to Plato's whole statement of his problems in the *Parmenides*. The standpoint of Socrates coincided exactly with Plato's own at *Phaedo*, 102 D, *Republic*, 523 B and elsewhere, and undeniably this was in some way parallel to the Eleatic doctrine.[1]

[1] Reinhardt, *Parmenides*, pp. 202 foll.

The world of sense is the subject of contradictory predicates. Knowledge, therefore, must relate to a Being which exists beyond the range of sensation. It is just the contradictions of the senses which induce the soul to look upwards to the higher realm. In that realm no contradiction is found; and it is significant that Plato (in *Republic*, 525 D, E) thought he could thus simply dispose of the problem of the One and the Many which later aroused his lively concern, by referring us to a pure Unity beyond experience which is absolutely One and nothing besides, and which has no parts. Not so in the *Parmenides*: Socrates finds that Zeno has set himself too easy a problem, and all depends on the question whether the One-in-itself can also be Many. 'But if any one can show that the essential One (ὃ ἔστιν ἕν) is many, and again that these many are One, I shall indeed be surprised' (129 B). Parmenides laughs, and appears not to enter into this question. Instead, he examines the theory of the young Socrates, by which he had hoped to set a new problem to the Eleatics. But suddenly it turns against its author. He had believed, like Plato in the *Phaedo* and *Republic*, that the proof which he demanded was impossible. Now it is shown that the theory of Ideas stands or falls with this impossible fact. If the One-in-itself *cannot* be many, all the objections raised against participation are justified. But this 'impossibility' is in fact quite possible; both the young Socrates of the Dialogue and the earlier Plato, in his Ideal Theory in the *Phaedo* and *Republic*, had unwittingly assumed an important principle, although they had not really recognized it, and had not found a solution.

4. *The 'Parmenides' and Opinion*

We have already anticipated what should come later; for we have still to consider in this connexion our fourth problem, that of 'opinion'. It has been shown how Plato had come to realize in the *Parmenides* that the problem of 'participation' was the vital point in the doctrine of Ideas, and how this eventually brought him to the old Eleatic contrast between One and Many. Consequently he had to reconsider a problem also raised by Eleaticism, that of the nature of 'appearance' (δόξα) and truth. This contrast likewise becomes clear if we approach it from our former angle, i.e. from the connexion between universal and particular. In the Idea, deprived of its former ideal significance, the universal and the particular were clearly combined in three different ways, or, to use the Eleatic terminology, in the concept of 'the One', three different meanings were dormant: (1) the indefinite article (*a* man); (2) unity or singleness; (3) the number one. All these meanings are operative in the Idea, and the exceedingly difficult task of separating them is not yet attempted. So the problem of Individuality—which was, in fact, to play a decisive part in Academic philosophy in its later developments—begins to raise its head. In our own day it is still one of the hardest problems in the theory of Knowledge, Knowledge being by nature universal.

We have seen, then, how Plato's special view of the connexion between universal and particular, which was the consequence of his intuitive and objective way of thinking, came, on account of the problem of the 'third man', to influence and alter the nature of the Idea. But there are two sides to any such influence or alteration. Either extreme may come to resemble the other. If it is legitimate to say that the Ideas 'were turned into sensible things', it may be said with no less emphasis that particular things were 'conceptualized', and it was this factor in the mutual process of assimilation which had the greater historical influence. So long as the theory of Ideas took its bearings from mathematical objects which could be constructed *a priori*, it might seem to be capable of extension to objects which really can never be grasped save in experience; one might hope to secure an immediate, intuitive knowledge of their essence or virtue. Such knowledge of the purpose of particular things was only intended to make wider and more complete the empire of the Idea of the Good; and the true meaning of the Good lay in its practical effect in morals and education.

But when the extension of Ideas to all things, with the express purpose of obtaining actual knowledge of their essences, was seriously undertaken, it became clear that a particular thing's definite nature, which we try to reproduce in words, was in no way an object of immediate certainty. And if, on the other hand, Plato was really to maintain, in face of the new empirical objects, that view of the εἶδος as intuition which before he had boldly assumed, and which gave to the word εἶδος its proper sense, the result was that Ideas were brought perilously near to αἴσθησις, and to the 'judgement (Δόξα) which arises from αἴσθησις' (*Theaetetus*, 179 c). And the once despised 'opinion' about particular cases was now precisely what was needed. Previously, intuition had often been compared to a vision—a vision of that which no mortal eye can see; such was the comparison between the Sun and the Good. This metaphor, once harmless, must now lead to the gravest difficulties where empirical objects were concerned —indeed it must endanger the very foundations of Socratic-Platonic philosophy, which was of an *a priori* type, and limited itself in principle to 'reasoning' (λόγοι). If, however, the intuitive side of the Ideas were sacrificed to their logical function, nothing was left of them but definitions; mere definition was adequate to reproduce the full content of the new universal.

The 'Theaetetus': a Socratic Dialogue devoted to Δόξα

The *Theaetetus* states in their natural order the problems of αἴσθησις, Δόξα, and definition, but only hints from afar at their solution. The unsolved problems in the interpretation of this Dialogue have already been mentioned. They may be summarized in this way: Firstly, should it be given a place before the *Republic*, or with the *Sophist* and *Statesman*, to which it has, at least, a close *external* relationship? Natorp decides in the former sense. He makes the main weight fall on the earlier part, where the view that 'sensation' is identical with 'knowledge' is criticized. He finds that the whole Dialogue more or less culminates in the sentences 184 D, 186 c; here the view that knowledge cannot be secured by the senses, but only ἐν λόγοις, is brought home to us, especially on the negative side. Since knowledge of the Ideas assumes a more positive shape in the *Phaedo* and *Republic*, Natorp takes this for a sign of progress. He finds the whole second part of the Dialogue to be of no philosophical importance, and his ground for this is very instructive; here, as in the *Sophist*, it is Ἀόξα which offers stubborn resistance to the remorseless logic of his interpretation.

He thinks that any genuine union between the two parts of the *Theaetetus* is impossible. 'It is only too clear that Ἀόξα, which in the earlier part meant judgement, has now come to mean opinion' (p. 113).

Natorp's interpretation can give us one useful point which is worth retaining: that, judging from a general impression, the earlier part of the *Theaetetus* might very well have been written before the *Republic*. In terms of our own earlier argument, we may say that the doctrine upon which the conclusions of this part of the Dialogue are founded still has a moral orientation. It will, however, soon appear that the first and second parts harmonize very well with each other; that in reality the second part displays by far the more important features, and that these give a direct hint of the *Sophist*; and above all that the first part too acquires a much clearer meaning if we give it the later date which external criteria in any case recommend.[1]

A point which at once strikes the reader is that the proof that sensation can furnish no knowledge is far more thorough, and makes contradiction far more difficult, than its counterpart in the *Meno*, *Phaedo*, and *Republic*. Nevertheless, there is not a syllable here about the doctrine which, in the *Meno* and *Phaedo*, was the presupposition of all knowledge that transcends sense-experience, namely Reminiscence. Natorp might perhaps suppose that the *Theaetetus* was here giving expression to the genuine significance of the Ideas as 'rules of method'—that they were less encumbered than elsewhere with the ballast of mysticism; but, assuming his view of the sequence of the Dialogues, Plato would then actually progress towards mysticism, only to retrace his steps later. This, then, can scarcely be the main reason why the metaphysical doctrine of Reminiscence is never mentioned in the *Theaetetus*, *Parmenides*, *Sophist*, *Statesman*, and *Philebus*. The truth is rather that Plato's thought, being especially objective in nature, bore the impress of the objects which came to interest him as he advanced. His philosophical method had not yet taken

[1] Cf. Eva Sachs, *De Theaeteto Atheniensi*, Berlin, 1914.

on the rigid form of a system; much more readily than has hitherto been supposed, it was apt to follow the problems as they arose,
without losing its own inner structure in the process. Whilst
Plato's first interest was the moral one, he was primarily concerned with objects which could be understood *a priori*; later,
when he came to deal with empirical objects, he had to recon-
struct his method. Reminiscence can now obviously give him no
help, for it is sensation which now appears as the principal source
of knowledge, and Plato does not underestimate the difficulty
of deposing it from that rank. His manner of arguing the case
in detail need not be repeated here; and I will merely mention
a few signs from which we may infer that, although the result
seems the same, the positive doctrine of the *Phaedo* and *Republic*
has really undergone a complete change. There is a striking
passage devoted to the praise of movement, the more remarkable
as it occurs within the criticism of the theory which reduces
sensation to a flux (153 B). 'Learning is a κίνησις': this is said in
clear anticipation of the *Sophist*, where some 'movement' of the
Ideas, hitherto supposed to remain fixed in Eleatic rigidity, is
made a presupposition of their becoming accessible to knowledge. According to Socrates, the chief point in this connexion
is the eternal movement of the Cosmos.[1] This idea, as I have
shown elsewhere, is foreign to Plato's earlier works. Above all, it
is to be observed in this passage that although Plato gives a proof
that the Heraclitean standpoint puts an end to all knowledge,
and indeed to all understanding, yet he postpones, on grounds
of mere form, his refutation of the contrary attitude of rigid
Eleaticism. But he marks it very definitely as a task for the
future (184 A), and, as we know, it forms the main theme of the
Sophist. On this important subject, the criticism of sensation and
movement, the *Theaetetus* is therefore remarkably ambiguous.
Plato proposes to prove that the view which he is attacking is
false; but the contrary view, to which we should naturally turn,
is equally far from being true. These are all signs that he has in
preparation a higher synthesis of the earlier contrasts.

Very similar is our impression when we look more closely at the

---

[1] ἐπὶ τούτοις τὸν κολοφῶνα, 153 C.

arguments to which Plato appeals in refuting the flux theory. As once before in a very similar context at the end of the *Cratylus*[1] so here, certainty and true being are found in the sphere of ethics: 'Tell me, then, again if you agree that nothing *is* good and beautiful, or has those qualities that we now enumerated—there is no being, only becoming' (157 D). If Protagoras will but admit the distinction between better and worse, Socrates is confident that he can refute him. In the context he had actually renewed the defence of Protagoras in order to give a profounder statement of the relativistic view; the meaning of all Rhetoric was found to lie in the power which it gives to the better man to impose his better opinions upon another, i.e. to communicate 'right opinion'. Thereupon the style rises to the most exalted *ethos* of the *Phaedo* and *Republic* (176 foll.); once again Plato with great clarity elaborates the contrast between the orator who is clever in the affairs of this world, and the philosopher who soars above the earth, and finds true wisdom and virtue in an 'assimilation to God'.[2] 'True opinion' in the political sense, as the observance of what is just 'by law', and as the opinions acquired by persuasion, fails to make good its claim to be knowledge,[3] despite a brilliant defence of mere probability (εἰκός) assigned to Protagoras. 'Opinion' (Δόξα) in the moral sphere is found to coincide with 'the probable', by means of the proposition to which we have referred as the very centre of Plato's moral speculation, that there is no 'appearance' (Δόξα) of the Good; any one who said so would be merely playing with words, 177 D. As might have been foreseen, Plato in the *Theaetetus* is no more in the mood than elsewhere to make concessions to Δόξα in morals.

In literary style the Dialogue attains its supreme height in the sketch of the character of the true philosopher, which brings it into line with the *Phaedo* and *Republic*. But as regards the special problem of the Dialogue, it is a digression (πάρεργον);[4] the

---

[1] εἰ Δὲ ἔστι μὲν ἀεὶ τὸ γιγνῶσκον, ἔστι Δὲ τὸ γιγνωσκόμενον, ἔστι Δὲ τὸ καλόν, ἔστι Δὲ τὸ ἀγαθόν, ἔστι Δὲ ἐν ἕκαστον τῶν ὄντων, . . . ῥοῇ οὐΔὲν οὐΔὲ φορᾷ (440 B).

[2] σοφία καὶ ἀρετὴ ἀληθινή, 176 C; ὁμοίωσις θεῷ, 176 B.

[3] τὸ κοινῇ Δόξαν, 172 B, clearly alludes to the ἔΔοξεν used in official decrees.

[4] περὶ μὲν οὖν τούτων, ἐπειΔὴ καὶ πάρεργα τυγχάνει λεγόμενα, ἀποστῶμεν—εἰ Δὲ μή,

Theaetetus studies the nature of ἐπιστήμη in quite a different sense
from the philosophical knowledge extolled in this digression—
knowledge of objects which were not *a priori*, and did *not* seem to
be immediately explained by the appeal to a higher world. Its
question is: In what sense can there be ἐπιστήμη of the objects
of becoming? In the *Republic* they had been abandoned to
'sensation' and 'opinion'; now it is shown, in the earlier part of
the argument, that sensation in itself cannot be a source of knowledge, and it is typical enough of the new attitude to knowledge
that this seems to deserve such a detailed proof; 'opinion' still
remains, and naturally its relation to knowledge will henceforward be the main question. So the second part of the *Theaetetus*
is as important as the first; if it be taken as the statement of a
problem, it is actually more important; we can agree that it comes
no nearer to a *solution* than the first part. The whole course of
our argument will have made it clear that the treatment of δόξα
in the *Theaetetus* will be very differently viewed if we place this
Dialogue before the *Phaedo* and *Republic*, and bring it into their
train of thought. Natorp considers that the second part gives
a superfluous, merely polemical criticism of δόξα as 'naïve, dogmatic representation' of the particular. Though in our judgement of the situation we must firmly disagree with Natorp, his
view gives a valuable indication that Plato, for quite definite
reasons, had become interested in the particular. It will be
found that here, as usual, Natorp's penetrating analysis leads
to some quite essential difficulties, which urgently require
explanation.

We saw that Plato rests his criticism of 'sensation' in the first
part upon the same grounds as in the *Republic*, except that his
attitude to the problems there was one of much greater assurance—i.e. upon the ideas of ethics, and upon those *a priori* or
'pure' elements in the sciences which he connected with ethics in
a characteristic way. When he wrote the *Theaetetus* he had, it
will soon appear, already obtained a clear grasp of the conception of knowledge which we find in the *Parmenides* and *Sophist*, in

πλείω ἀεὶ ἐπιρρέοντα καταχώσει ἡμῶν τὸν ἐξ ἀρχῆς λόγον—ἐπὶ Ἀὲ τὰ ἔμπροσθεν ἴωμεν, εἰ
καὶ σοὶ Ἀοκεῖ, 177 B, C.

its essential outlines. That is to say, Dialectic had been completely freed from dependence on the Idea of the Good, which
had been its essence in the *Republic*, and had become a logic
which, if not purely formal, was at least free from a specifically
moral content. In the *Theaetetus*, using to the full his liberty as an
artist, Plato gives us a genuine Socratic Dialogue treating of the
very problems which will afterwards be presented to us as solved,
when Socrates has handed over the leading part to the Eleatic
Stranger. Plato there is no longer a man who 'knows nothing',
but one who has full consciousness of his knowledge. The
Theaetetus is intended to show once more that he depends upon
Socrates' teaching, yet has an independent doctrine of his own,
concealed behind the 'maieutic' method of Socrates. Hence the
theme of Socrates as a midwife is important, and he dwells upon
it at unaccustomed length (150 B foll.). Hence also the moving
protest against erring disciples of Socrates, which is an attack by
Plato upon his contemporaries. In the digression, with its moral
and religious tone, Plato had re-entered the sphere in which
Socrates could serve as the representative of his own philosophy.
Socrates must, indeed, search rather than find—he could not discover a positive theory of knowledge, definitely going beyond the
region of will and action. But Plato intended here, just where the
Socratic influence seemed to be losing its hold, to show in unmis-
takable terms the unwavering conviction to which he had come
within those narrower Socratic limits: that knowledge requires
to be established by a thought which is more than empirical.
At 186 c, therefore, Socrates summarizes his earlier criticism of
αἴσθησις: all 'reasoning concerning the being or the usefulness
of things' refers to something more than the affections, παθήματα,
of the senses. In the first chapter we saw that these two, being
and usefulness, were intimately connected aspects of the Good,
which together made up its importance in the theory of knowledge. Socrates' remark is entirely natural in a Dialogue composed later than the *Republic*. But it obtains a deeper meaning in
view of what happens in the second part of the argument.
Reference to the Good (i.e. the ὠφέλεια or 'usefulness' above) is
now discarded, and with great caution the possibility of *mere*

being—simple οὐσία divorced from any connexion with an End
—is raised. And a memorable passage of the *Sophist* tells us that
the notion of mere being, as hitherto understood, is no more
intelligible than the μὴ ὄν, which is the favourite weapon of
scepticism. (I recall once more the fact that in *Theaetetus*, 184 A,
there is a clear allusion to the coming criticism of the notion of
'being' in the *Sophist*.)

A very surprising fact is the absence not only of 'Reminiscence'
and the Idea of the Good, but also of the theory of Ideas as a
whole; surely this theory, once established in the *Phaedo* and
Republic, must be the strongest refutation of a view which takes
αἴσθησις to be knowledge? Instead, we have an argument,
which on comparison with Plato's earlier position can only be
called scanty, to prove that certain reasonings (συλλογισμοί)
about the affections of our senses cannot be due to the agency of
sense,[1] but must be traced to a common source, 'whether we call
this the Soul, or give it some other name'. As examples of such
reasoning Socrates suggests the ideas of Being, Not-Being, Likeness, Unlikeness, the Same, the Other. (All these are explained
afterwards in the *Sophist*.) Theaetetus, responding readily to
further questions, adds of his own accord a few mathematical
examples—the even, the odd, 185 c, D. Special emphasis is
again laid upon Being, 186 A. Then the main ethical Ideas,
the beautiful, the good, and their contraries, are added. The
passage concludes with references to Being (yet again), and to
our power of conceiving opposite properties, and the nature of
opposition itself. Finally, this region in which the Soul 'by itself',[2]
without help from the senses, studies the nature of Being, is
described in two phrases which have been quoted, 'reasonings
concerning the being and usefulness of things', and 'inference
about our affections' (συλλογισμὸς περὶ τῶν παθημάτων: to
the Soul's activity, the disputed word Δοξάζειν is definitely
applied).

Natorp mistakes the drift of this passage. Knowledge, he says,
is clearly traced back to the concept, i.e. to 'the universal func-

---

[1] εἰς μίαν Ἰδέαν, 184 D. But Ἰδέα can scarcely be used in its technical sense.
[2] 185 E, 186 B.

tion of synthetical unity'. Concepts are traced back to 'basic concepts, fundamental types of synthesis, or in other terms, basic functions of judgement'. A further advance is made, he thinks, in the *Phaedo* and the *Republic*, because their logical inquiries concern the basis of knowledge as a *system* of judgements, and 'they presuppose throughout the decisive result reached here'.

Natorp has here applied the maxim for understanding Plato stated by Cohen (see p. 41).[1] It can only be some 'subjective theoretical insight' of his own which reveals to him, either in the form or the meaning of Plato's phrase at 184 D, anything akin to the modern view of a synthetical unity in knowledge. His own 'insight' is to him a sufficient criterion 'of what is genuine, mature, essential, and one might almost say seriously meant, in Plato'. And in the *Theaetetus* he considers only the earlier half to be seriously meant; the latter part is condemned outright as 'dogmatic'. But Plato's very first sentence when he passes to the discussion of 'true opinion' shows us that this interpretation is unsatisfactory. Plato states at 187 A that knowledge has not yet been found; so far, we know only that it is not identical with sensation. Then he passes immediately from the term Δοξάζειν to ἀληθής and ψευδὴς Δόξα. Here, if Natorp were right, Plato must have obscured his own argument by changing the meaning of Δόξα within two consecutive sentences. Moreover, what Natorp himself regards as the most definite instance of Δοξάζειν in the sense of 'judge' (not 'believe') occurs far on in the 'dogmatic' part, which according to him is planned as a *reductio ad absurdum* of the other meaning, 'belief'. In this passage (190 A), Δόξα is identified with a proposition (λόγος) 'spoken, not aloud to another, but silently to oneself'.

This recurs almost word for word in the *Sophist* (263 E) as a simple assertion, no longer with any pretence of Socratic ignorance: 'Thought (Διάνοια), then, and speech are the same. But the inner dialogue of the soul with itself, which takes place without vocal utterance, is called by this very name of Διάνοια.' Since Δόξα is defined as Διανοίας ἀποτελεύτησις (264 B), there

[1] i.e. the maxim that we can judge Plato's meaning from our own theory of knowledge. Cf. p. 27, note (1).

is full agreement between the passages. The precise correspondence in terminology should be noticed. Λόγος is the equivalent of Δόξα or of Διάνοια (cf. also *Theaetetus*, 206 D); the latter is in both contexts a general term for 'thought'. Of the finer distinctions made in the *Republic* no more is heard; they were plainly designed for quite another purpose, viz. to show the relation of knowledge to the Good. The new Dialectic does not yet require them. The mathematical objects assigned to the special care of Διάνοια in the *Republic* occur side by side with objects of a more concrete nature (195 E); so likewise do the objects attributed in the first half of the Dialogue to the 'reasoning about our impressions', such as τὸ ἕτερον; indeed, in the passage devoted to the explanation of false opinion, 'difference' is mentioned most significantly in connexion with Not-Being. Here the two Dialogues, *Theaetetus* and *Sophist*, are complementary to each other—the *Sophist* arrives at the explanation of τὸ μὴ ὂν δοξάζειν as τὸ ἕτερον δοξάζειν; in the *Theaetetus* all attempts to give a definition of ἑτεροδοξία or ἀλλοδοξία fail, just because this implies having a representation of 'not-being', and this is still held to be impossible in conformity with what had been said in the *Republic* (478 B).

In these ways the close connexion between δόξα, in the second half, and αἴσθησις, in the first, becomes very clear.[1] The psychological meaning of δόξα is also plain. Notice how the inferences follow in strict sequence:

'But if a man sees some one thing, he sees something which *is*. Or do you think that oneness can exist among things which *are not*? —No—He, then, who sees one thing, sees an existing thing—It seems so—Likewise he who hears, hears one thing, and so a real thing?— Yes—And he who touches something, touches what is one, and if it is one, it is real?—This also follows—Does not he who thinks think one thing?—Certainly—And does not he who thinks one thing think an existent thing?—Granted—He, then, who thinks what is not existent, does not think' (188 E).

If we take μὴ ὂν in the sense of absolute non-existence, and attempt to think of it, i.e. intuit it as an object; and if each object

[1] Cf. αἱ αἰσθήσεις καὶ αἱ κατὰ ταύτας δόξαι, 179 C, and the whole argument at 163 D.

of thought is derived from sense-perception, Plato thinks that a contradiction results. The person who in this sense has opinion must naturally have opinion *of something*. The use of the word εἰδέναι in this context (which we quoted above for a purpose of our own) shows how strongly Plato felt its etymological connexion with ἰδεῖν, at least as long as his thought was concerned with the moral objects which interested him. Εἰδέναι therefore confirms the assertion which we have often made that ἰδέα is intuition rather than abstract thinking. But did Plato believe that the problem of false opinion was serious and real? The fact that he resumes the discussion at the same point in the *Sophist*, and goes on to give a new sense to 'not-being', shows satisfactorily that he did. (The *Sophist* gives no new sense to δοξάζειν.)

We turn next to the attempts in the *Theaetetus* to prove that 'true opinion' is knowledge. These also point clearly to the *Sophist*; for their undertaking is without hope of success from the start, when the attempt to define 'false opinion' has proved a failure. (Socrates is right in his observation (200 c) that, before trying to define false opinion, we should have defined knowledge.)

The first view expressed makes a reference to Justice, and shows a characteristic alteration of its earlier practical sense. As evidence that true opinion is distinct from knowledge, Socrates quotes the fact—which he takes to be certain—that judges pronounce their judgements in accordance with right opinions. The reason why, at the very best, they can only have right opinion is not that they have no knowledge of the Just in itself (which, at an earlier time, would have been the reason given), but that they were not eyewitnesses of the crime.[1] So that even in ethics the same entire change in Plato's view of knowledge is noticeable.

It occurs to Theaetetus that, if right opinion is accompanied by a rational explanation (μετὰ λόγου), it may be knowledge—if not, they are distinct. Such a view of the nature of knowledge, as we briefly explained on p. 43, coincides with Plato's own at an earlier time. And he preserves it in a modified form; so much

---

[1] *Theaetetus*, 201 B: Οὐκοῦν ὅταν δικαίως πεισθῶσιν δικασταὶ περὶ ὧν ἰδόντι μόνον ἔστιν εἰδέναι, ἄλλως δὲ μή, ταῦτα τότε ἐξ ἀκοῆς κρίνοντες, ἀληθῆ δόξαν λαβόντες, ἄνευ ἐπιστήμης ἔκριναν, ὀρθὰ πεισθέντες.

may be said in anticipation. We saw how the λογισμὸς αἰτίας in his earlier system would lead ultimately to the Idea of the Good. This is now confirmed. But Plato's attitude has changed; he is interested in mere knowledge and definition; and he has turned to objects which it would, on the face of it, be meaningless and unnecessary to bring into a teleological connexion with the Good —even the Good in its function as the corner-stone of rational knowledge. When the Good falls into the background, the λογισμὸς αἰτίας goes with it. The definition (λόγος) of right opinion is sought in three directions. Failure is the result in every case, but all three views recover their meaning after the *Sophist* has solved the problem of definition, to which they all lead.

It appears that Plato is, as a matter of fact, clearly referring here to certain doctrines of Antisthenes. But I propose to ignore this, and to concentrate on the philosophical connexion between the *Theaetetus* and *Sophist*. This is, I believe, what Plato intends: 'We are not concerned with these persons—our aim is to discover the truth' (*Sophist*, 246 D).

He takes as his basis a doctrine which is clearly described at *Theaetetus*, 201 E. The elements (στοιχεῖα) of all things are unknowable—they can only be *perceived*. But things compounded of these elements can be defined by a formula which combines the names of the constituents (συμπλοκὴ ὀνομάτων). Any one whose attention has been called to the relationship between the two Dialogues will think of the συμπλοκὴ εἰδῶν which serves for the determination of concepts in the *Sophist*. Now to come to the three forms which λόγος may take: they are enumerated (208 C), and the first named is 'the image of thought in speech'. An unfriendly description of it is given (206 D): 'In the first place, the meaning may be: manifesting one's thought by the voice with verbs and nouns, imaging an opinion in the stream which flows from the lips, as in a mirror or water. Does not such an act appear to you to be λόγος?' (tr. Jowett). This account of λόγος is dismissed when Plato, anticipating the *Sophist*, shows that it makes no difference whether thought finds expression in words or not.

The second form of λόγος Plato calls 'the approach to the whole through its elements', διὰ στοιχείου ὁδὸς ἐπὶ τὸ ὅλον. The manner of its refutation shows still more clearly that the *Theaetetus* forecasts the main problems of the *Sophist* and *Parmenides*. The example of letters—an important illustration in the *Sophist* and *Philebus* also—is taken: we see from this example that if the 'syllables' are to be known, knowledge of the elements must be presupposed; for a whole composed of unknowable parts could not be knowable. But perhaps it is incorrect to consider the 'syllable' as the sum of its elements, and it must rather be regarded as a new entity,[1] 'a single kind having a single form of its own, and different from the elements' (203 E). Here is the most interesting point in the argument. Plato has employed the word ἰδέα in the sense which he had assumed in his earlier Dialogues, and then subjected to criticism in the *Parmenides*. Theaetetus is brought to the admission that πάντα, πᾶν, and ὅλον in such a case must all mean the same; for if this whole, the 'syllable', were *not* constituted by its elements, it would be an indivisible Idea (μία τις ἰδέα ἀμέριστος, 205 c); but this would make it an un-compounded thing like the element, and equally unknowable. As though it were not sufficiently obvious that this alludes to qualities ascribed to the earlier Idea, Socrates repeats the reason why it is unknowable. 'Can some other cause than this be found for its being uniform and indivisible (μονοειδὲς καὶ ἀμέριστον)? For my part I cannot see one.'[2] Ἀμέριστον and μονοειδές are two of the honourable titles of the Idea in earlier days—and here they are expressly mentioned as features which make it unknow-able! This precisely coincides with the point at which the first part of the *Parmenides* left the earlier theory of Ideas; and the *Parmenides* had hinted that there must be a revision which would begin with the relation between Whole and Part, One and Many. And this task also is fully performed in the *Sophist*: it is shown how One and Many can, without contradiction, be united.

To the problem of definition, again, we are directly led by the last of the three forms of λόγος, according to Socrates a very well-known one: ὅπερ ἂν οἱ πολλοὶ εἴποιεν, 208 c. By this view,

---

[1] ἕν τι γεγονὸς εἶδος, ἰδέαν μίαν αὐτὸ αὑτοῦ ἔχον, ἕτερον δὲ τῶν στοιχείων.

[2] *Phaedo*, 78 D, 83 E: μονοειδεῖ καὶ ἀδιαλύτῳ, 80 B: *Symposium*, 211 A, E.

λόγος consists in the statement of some distinguishing mark whereby the object in question differs from all others. The *Theaetetus* takes us, therefore, as far as the 'specific difference'. But it has nothing at all to say of the *genus proximum*. (Mention is, however, made of common properties—κοινά—without which no definition in terms of *concepts* is possible, 208 D.) Since the argument does not advance beyond opinion about an individual case (this is clearly shown by the example chosen—the 'snub-nosedness', σιμότης, which is a property of the individual Theaetetus), all attempts to change 'true opinion' into knowledge by this criterion must move in a circle. For he who has a right opinion must necessarily have opinion about the individual characteristic, if such an opinion is possible at all.

Socrates adds that the problem would indeed be solved if a *rational explanation* of such a 'difference' could be obtained (209 E). 'If, my young friend, when we are bidden to obtain λόγος we are bidden to *know*, and not merely have an opinion of the difference, this most promising of all the definitions of knowledge would have come to a pretty end. For to know is surely to acquire knowledge.' But on such conditions this last and best λόγος would already contain ἐπιστήμη, i.e. the definition would involve that which is to be defined. The Dialogue thus seems to close with no hint of a positive result. The fact is that the various lines of argument which here seem unfruitful are all made to bear fruit in the *Sophist*. On the other side, fresh light is thrown on the problems of the *Sophist* by its close relation to the *Theaetetus*. There is a unity, philosophical and artistic, between the two Dialogues; Plato has dealt with the same questions in two distinct artistic forms—in the maieutic Socratic Dialogue, which states a problem, and in the scientific Dialogue, which finds its solution.

IV. A NEW FORM OF DIALOGUE AND A NEW METHOD

The 'Sophist'

IN the Essay already mentioned I began to work out, in broad outline, an answer to the question: What importance has the literary form of the Socratic Dialogue for the philosophical understanding of Plato? The results of this Essay might be neglected for the purpose of our present discussion, which relies mainly on a comparative philosophical study of two works, were it not that in his later Dialogues Plato still writes as an artist; if one does not realize this, one cannot begin to understand them; there is never a time when form and content can be separated. Hence it will be well here also to take it for granted that our problem is somehow bound up with the perplexing question of Plato's artistic form, and to mark as clearly as possible the stylistic distinction between the *Theaetetus* and the *Sophist*. We may here leave aside the undoubtedly important questions of dramatic setting and of the narrated dialogue; the substantial teaching of a Platonic Dialogue is not really touched by these modifications. But it will be useful to compare the judgement pronounced by Theaetetus, at the end of the dialogue called by his name, upon his own part in the discussion, with the part assigned to him (no doubt with some apology) in the *Sophist* by the Eleatic Stranger. (1) In the former case, Socrates has remarked very pointedly on their failure to attain any definite result, *Theaetetus*, 210 B: 'And are you still in labour and travail, my dear friend, or have you brought all that you have to say about knowledge to the birth?' and Theaetetus answers: 'I am sure, Socrates, that you have elicited from me a good deal more than ever was in me.' Plato has again carried out his usual principle; he evidently supposes that it is the primary purpose of Socrates' method to be 'maieutic'. It is the function of Theaetetus to produce, that of Socrates to examine and contradict. (2) In the *Sophist*, the stranger from Elea is introduced by Theodorus as a philosopher; and the remark made in commendation of him leads Socrates to ask a

faintly ironical question: what is meant by 'philosopher'? Are
the sophist, the statesman, and the philosopher one, two, or three
classes? This question, in which the theme of the Dialogue is
stated, shows from the beginning how far we are from the ideas
of the *Republic*. There, the identity of the philosopher and the
true statesman (Philosophy is the 'kingly art') was no less self-
evident than the distinction between the philosopher and the
sophist, which in turn was as clear as that between knowledge
and appearance, ἐπιστήμη and λόξα. Here, however, the philosopher is discovered, later on in the course of the Dialogue, as
though by accident during the search for the sophist. Whether
it is possible to distinguish them depends in the last resort on the
question whether there is a true and a false opinion. Thus the
problems of the *Sophist*, and not less those of the *Statesman*, are
formulated in a way which shows that Plato's philosophical
interest has entirely changed its direction. And we have already
shown that it had. Theory and practice were still intimately
connected in the *Republic*; now they fall apart, leaving separate
provinces for the philosopher and the statesman; and 'opinion'
becomes the object of dispute, over whose true nature the philosopher contends with the sophist. The doctrine of the *Republic*
could still be represented as coming within the purview of
Socrates, for whom knowledge was virtue, and virtue a form
of knowledge. But the new picture requires another frame.
Socrates begins to ask questions; and one who knew nothing of
the work which follows might perhaps guess that the wise man,
introduced with such lavish compliments, would be put to confusion by him, just as Protagoras and Gorgias had been in days
gone by. One need only recall to mind the dispute between
Socrates and Protagoras about long and short speeches, and
about question and answer, and it will be clear how the dialogue
form has been *deliberately* given a new shape, answering closely
to a new type of philosophy. Socrates offers to the Stranger the
choice between two methods of stating his case: a lengthy speech,
or a series of questions. He illustrates the second method by the
mention of his own conversation with Parmenides, as though he
wished to put out of our heads any thought of a genuinely

Socratic Dialogue of the 'maieutic' kind. The Stranger, also, immediately decides that for him no other mode of conversation is possible, 217 D: 'I prefer to talk with another when he responds pleasantly, and is light in hand; if not, I would rather have my own say.' The respondent is thus entirely debarred from taking any active part in the production; the dialogue is a mere external form—it simply seems more convenient than a continuous speech; the Stranger has therefore to apologize to his listeners because, on his first appearance among them, he makes a long connected speech instead of engaging in true conversation; this gives us another indication that the difference between monologue and dialogue is unimportant, 217 D: 'I feel ashamed, Socrates, being a newcomer into your society, instead of talking a little and hearing others talk, to be spinning out a long soliloquy or address, as though I were giving an exhibition.' In apologizing for his procedure he claims that the problem now set demands the lengthy continuous speech: 'For the true answer will certainly be a very long one, a great deal longer than might be expected from such a short and simple question.' Socrates had already recommended Theaetetus to him as a suitable partner in the dialogue, and some may be inclined to infer from this that Socrates had already got to know Theaetetus as a docile answerer, in the dialogue to which he gives his name; whence it follows that the difference in his part in the two dialogues cannot be so important in practice; for the very generous characterization of Theaetetus is certainly carried on into the *Sophist*. But it must be admitted that it is often Plato who here speaks through the mouth of the Stranger (265 D); the latter has only made the acquaintance of Theaetetus on the way thither (218 A). But then, the direct pronouncement on the question at the opening of the *Sophist* has all the more importance, for it shows that Plato regarded the distinction as essential. The function of Socrates in the *Theaetetus* is to ask and to examine; the Stranger, on the other hand, may fairly be called dogmatic; he states the solutions obtained by Plato's new method. The dialogue form has acquired an entirely new purpose, more in accordance with the work of a professional teacher; it helps to make sure at every moment that the answerer, representing the public in the widest sense, understands the argument. By means of the Dialogue, even a philosopher who professes knowledge and expounds his doctrine, may partly avoid those disadvantages of the 'silent' book which were deplored with such deep feeling in the *Phaedrus*.

But what is Plato's new method? It was not yet mentioned in the *Theaetetus*, but all the problems of this Dialogue converged towards it, and Plato did not fail to give a clear indication of his future course. He raised a significant question: what is the *essential formula*, which can raise right opinion to the plane of knowledge? Now it is the science of definition which gives such a formula. Definitions are the subject of the *Sophist* and *Statesman*; and the 'philosophical' scholars are quite right in saying that method, and again method, is the content of both Dialogues. From the first word of his argument in the *Sophist* to the last word of the *Statesman*, Plato leaves us in no doubt what *is* his method (*Sophist*, 218 C, D; *Statesman*, 286 D, 287 A): it is that analysis of class-concepts, Διαίρεσις, which leads in every case to a definition. The train of thought seems so clear, that there must be some profound and remarkable reason why scholars have constantly tried to wrest another meaning from these Dialogues, something 'more valuable' which they can fancy to be Plato's real philosophical lesson. This reason lies in the aim and the method of the procedure of 'Division'. (1) Firstly, it seems incredible that Definition can have been Plato's last word on method, since Socrates, his predecessor, is credited with its discovery. (2) Next, it is said that Διαίρεσις, if by this is meant the pedantic analysis of simple concepts practised in the *Sophist* and *Statesman*, cannot have been regarded as a valuable method by Plato. The resulting knowledge of the inclusion of lower classes within higher ones—briefly, of the κοινωνία τῶν γενῶν in this purely formal sense—must have been self-evident to Plato when he displayed to view the complex structure of his dialectic in the *Republic*. As regards the former point, we have already (p. 37) mentioned H. Maier's treatment of the question how far Socrates' inquiry aimed at definitions; and we need not at present argue against the opinion which has so long prevailed.

Even for Plato, the Universal at first had none of those characteristics which would equip it to serve as a distinct concept, displayed in definition. Indeed the truth is that it was not yet a
concept, but an Idea, an intuition. This we have tried to prove
at length. The Good, the Beautiful, and the objects of Mathematics required no definitions in the sense in which the *Sophist*
and *Statesman* could provide them, and there was thus no need
to employ them in elaborating a method whose simplest elements come unasked to human thought; and to whose further
refinement the theory of Ideas, and the kind of thought which
this theory encouraged, was bound to offer a special obstacle.

'*Division*' in the '*Republic*'

'But', some one will long have been wanting to say, 'these
general considerations are refuted by the fact that both the
division into classes (κατ' εἴδη διαιρεῖσθαι), and the κοινωνία τῶν
γενῶν which is implied in it, are distinctly mentioned in the
Republic, and 'already' in the *Phaedrus*. We may, I hope, leave
the *Phaedrus* out of account in a question of this kind. But the
two passages from the *Republic* are constantly quoted as proving
that there is nothing at all new in the doctrine of Ideas as presented in the *Sophist*. Probably it is Apelt who has carried furthest
this harmonizing tendency; but the two passages have hindered
others as well from obtaining a proper view of the growth of
Dialectic down to the *Sophist*. Naturally to the 'philosophical'
school also it is of the highest importance to be able to show that
the place of honour in the Eleatic dialogues belongs, not to the
offending 'trivialities of formal logic', but to some quite different
'methodical' principles of Plato's. Here both Natorp (p. 286)
and, following him, Hartmann (*Platons Logik des Seins*, p. 124),
who take the *Phaedrus* to be early, are involved in some perplexity
by the two entirely consonant definitions of Dialectic at *Phaedrus*,
266 B, &c., and *Sophist*, 253 D. They are only able to extricate
themselves by what we shall later find to be a very unnatural
interpretation of the passage from the *Sophist*.

But let us come now to the two passages in the *Republic* which
bear witness to the 'division into species' and the 'participation

of kinds'. The first passage certainly gives us one such phrase: 'Many a man falls into this practice against his will. When he thinks that he is reasoning he is really disputing, just because he cannot define and divide (κατ᾿ εἴδη Διαιρούμενοι), and so know that of which he is speaking; and he will pursue a merely verbal opposition (κατ᾿ αὐτὸ τὸ ὄνομα Διώκειν) in the spirit of contention, and not of fair discussion' (454 A). But a glance at the context shows that there is not the most distant allusion to Dialectic in the later sense. Plato here simply wishes to contrast his method with the eristic fashion of playing with words, of which he had already made fun in the Euthydemus; Διαιρεῖσθαι is simply the power of making distinctions, and so of grasping the εἴδος under discussion in its real relations. The point is that Socrates appears to have become involved in a contradiction. Earlier, he declared it to be just and right to require from every one only the function (ἔργον) adapted to his proper nature (τὸ τὰ ἑαυτοῦ πράττειν). But now, men and women are to be trained for the same functions in the State. Socrates meets the contradiction in this way: instead of fastening upon the word 'nature', we ought to consider from what point of view we formerly visualized the notion of φύσις (454 B): 'We valiantly and contentiously insist upon the verbal truth (πάνυ ἀνΔρείως τε καὶ ἐριστικῶς κατὰ τὸ ὄνομα Διώκομεν) that different natures ought to have different pursuits, but we never considered at all what was the meaning of sameness or difference of nature, or why we distinguished them when we assigned different pursuits to different natures and the same to the same natures.' Thus Διαιρεῖσθαι merely means to distinguish, like ὁρίζεσθαι 'limit'. Socrates had not offered to 'define' nature. And so the technical meaning of the word—the procedure of analysing a 'whole class' into its parts, and then obtaining a definition by a συμπλοκὴ εἰΔῶν—does not arise here. It is another instance of our view that the thinker, borne along by the unconscious effect of language, and by the demands of truth in a concrete case, may use some of the laws of Formal Logic. This was shown once before (p. 32) in regard to the Contraries. In the words Διαιρεῖν and Διαιρεῖσθαι, language has given expression to the fact that all knowledge rests on a separation or distinction. In his earlier Dialogues Plato of course had often divided things into parts. Lukas, who has devoted a careful monograph to the 'Method of Division in Plato' (Halle, 1888), is able to quote examples from nearly all the Dialogues. Thus the words Διαιρεῖν and Διαιρεῖσθαι also were often used of division into parts. But it must have been quite different considerations which led Plato to the explicit theory of division he gives in the *Sophist* and *Statesman*.

The second passage from the *Republic* is still more instructive. All commentators, from Stallbaum onwards, adduce as a 'parallel' to it the 'participation of kinds' in the *Sophist*. It is as follows: 'And of just and unjust, good and evil, and of every other class, the same remark holds: each in itself is one, but they appear everywhere in manifold combination with actions and bodies and with one another, and each one seems to be many' (476 A).

If this were an allusion to the method of Διαίρεσις, there would have been a clean sweep of all the problems of the *Parmenides* and *Sophist*, and of the doctrine of Methexis in the *Phaedo* (see above, pp. 47 and 56). We should have to credit Plato with a perfectly clear answer to the question how far the 'one' Idea can likewise be many, how far the Ideas can participate in one another. But we are, indeed, 'valiantly and contentiously insisting upon a verbal truth'! What does the 'participation' of the Ideas achieve in the *Sophist*? It makes them objects of knowledge, enables them to enter into judgements—an exalted function. Here, on the contrary, the 'participation' appears in a most unfavourable light. The Ideas 'seem to be' many; the 'appearance' is actually expressed twice over. He who knows them only in their many instances is the φιλοθεάμων; the possessor of *knowledge* tries to isolate 'pure being', he does not confuse the Beautiful itself with the things which participate in it, or *vice versa* (476 D): 'He who, on the contrary, recognizes the existence of absolute Beauty and is able to distinguish the Idea from the objects which participate in it, neither putting the objects in its place nor it in theirs—what of him? Is he a dreamer also, or is he awake?' (476 D). Firstly, then, the passage confirms what is also seen from the *Phaedo*, that Plato is here completely indifferent to the genuine problem of 'participation'; and secondly, it reveals clearly the situation in regard to the problem of 'separation'; a pure view of the Ideas in themselves, transcending experience, absorbs all the philosopher's attention; in so far as the Ideas admit of 'participation', they belong to the realm of becoming, and fall under opinion, which, in the sense previously examined (p. 48 fol.), is the exact opposite of knowledge. But the most valuable result of this passage is that it gives us help in explaining the 'descent' (κάθοδος), mentioned at the end of the Sixth Book, and there contrasted with an ascending process. Among those who hope to find at least a uniform doctrine of Ideas in Plato's works, no one has failed to bring this dialectical movement into relation with the later 'division', even if he otherwise follows the genetic method of study and abandons the question of Plato's 'system' as an unreal one. If the participation among Ideas (κοινωνία) is here on the same plane as that of Ideas in 'actions and bodies'[1] which is admitted to be prejudicial to the true being and purity of the Idea, then there can be no relation at all between the κοινωνία and that 'descent' of which we are expressly told that it 'ends in Ideas' (511 c). Hence this κοινωνία cannot be connected, however obscurely, either with the doctrine of the *Sophist* or with this 'descent'.

Another κοινωνία, which *is* connected with the 'descent', is in fact mentioned in the *Republic*, but again this has no connexion with any form of Division. We have often mentioned the 'synopsis' of the dialectician, his concentration upon the Idea of the Good and its unity: now at 531 B Socrates describes the 'experiments' of the Pythagoreans in the spirit of disdain everywhere shown in the *Republic* for empiricism which does not mount upwards to the true 'problems', i.e. to laws of an *a priori*, mathematical character. The true aim of experiment is then described, 531 c: 'But it is useful, I replied, if sought after with a view to the beautiful and the good; but if pursued in any other spirit, useless.' Plato goes on to use the term κοινωνία in a sense highly characteristic of the *Republic*: Οἶμαι δέ γε, ἦν δ' ἐγώ, καὶ ἡ

---

[1] As a sign of the moral orientation, note that actions come first; and for the idea see above, p. 50.

τούτων πάντων ὧν διεληλύθαμεν μέθοδος ἐὰν μὲν ἐπὶ τὴν ἀλλήλων κοινωνίαν ἀφίκηται καὶ συγγένειαν, καὶ συλλογισθῇ ταῦτα
ᾗ ἐστὶν ἀλλήλοις οἰκεῖα, φέρειν τι αὐτῶν εἰς ἃ βουλόμεθα τὴν
πραγματείαν καὶ οὐκ ἀνόνητα πονεῖσθαι, εἰ δὲ μή, ἀνόνητα.

More light is thrown on these passages, and some earlier
observations of our own are confirmed, by a summary of the
whole work of education later in the *Republic*. It immediately
precedes his familiar statement that the work of Dialectic is a
'synopsis'. He says (537 c): τὰ . . . χύδην μαθήματα παισὶν ἐν
τῇ παιδείᾳ γενόμενα τούτοις συνακτέον εἰς σύνοψιν οἰκειότητός
τε ἀλλήλων τῶν μαθημάτων καὶ τῆς τοῦ ὄντος φύσεως. Thus the
'synopsis', which is a feature of Dialectic, is a view not of the
κοινωνία τῶν εἰδῶν, but of the affinity of all the sciences. These
are members of one family in so far as each contains *a priori*
features leading to immediate rational certainty. To bring out
this family likeness, to discover the relation between the unconditioned Idea of the Good and the lower forms of knowledge, whose
hypotheses depend on it, is the task of Dialectic. The purpose of
the 'descent', κάθοδος, is simply to confirm this 'synopsis' on the
side of the special sciences.

Κατ' εἴδη διαιρεῖν *in the 'Sophist'*

After our survey of the passages in the *Republic*, which are
perfectly clear when their purpose is understood, we may perhaps
be more disposed to take Plato at his word in the unambiguous
explanation of his new method which he gives in the *Sophist*. We
must here examine with greater care some passages to which a
brief allusion has already been made. First, let the ending of
the *Theaetetus* be remembered. After the failure of all attempts
to determine the nature of 'true opinion', Plato concluded:
'This most promising of all the definitions of knowledge would
have come to a pretty end if we were merely bidden secure
knowledge, as contrasted with mere opinion, of a thing's distinctive nature.' And the discussion of the essential nature of the
Sophist in the Dialogue of that name is opened by the Eleatic
Stranger as follows: 'You must join me in my inquiry, and I think
we should begin with the Sophist: you must inquire what he is,

and make it plain in discussion (λόγῳ). For at present we are only agreed about the name; but of the thing to which we both apply the name, possibly you have one notion and I another; whereas, in any inquiry, we ought to come to an understanding about the object itself by means of definition (διὰ λόγων) rather than about a mere name without a definition.' The Stranger recommends that, before proceeding with the task, we should 'take an easier example which will give us previous exercise in our method';[1] and so a definition is first found for the art of angling. (Here the procedure of the *Republic* is reversed. Justice, as it appears in the larger outline of life in the State, had then been used to decipher the smaller writing in the individual soul.)

A passage in the *Statesman*, exactly parallel to this, explains even more clearly the universal importance of the procedure of 'division'. There also we find definitions of this familiar type, and the art of weaving is defined in order to facilitate the main task, the definition of Statesmanship. Plato says that the procedure of classification, which we may practise at first on objects perceptible to the senses, can render a still higher service. He is speaking of the definition of the Statesman, which is, in appearance, the main task of the Dialogue (tr. Jowett):[2]

Str. And is our inquiry about the Statesman intended only to improve our knowledge of politics, or our power of reasoning generally?

T. Soc. Clearly, as in the former example, the purpose is general.

Str. Still less would any rational man seek to analyse the notion (λόγον) of weaving for its own sake. But people seem to forget that some things have sensible images, which are readily known, and can be easily pointed out when any one desires to answer an inquirer without any trouble or argument (λόγον αἰτοῦντι, χωρὶς λόγου); whereas the greatest and highest truths have no outward image of themselves visible to man, which he who wishes to satisfy the soul of the inquirer can adapt to the eye of sense, and therefore we ought

---

[1] ἐν ἄλλῳ ῥᾴονι τὴν μέθοδον προμελετᾶν, 218 D.

[2] The context is as follows: Plato has given (285 A) great prominence to the art of τὸ κατ' εἴδη διαιρεῖσθαι and to the discovery of common factors, κοινωνία, and of distinctions—διαφοραί, ὁπόσαιπερ ἐν εἴδεσι κεῖνται. The reason why a definition was not reached in the *Theaetetus* was because κοινά were neglected.

to train ourselves to give and accept a rational account (λόγον) of them; for immaterial things, which are the noblest and greatest, are shown only in thought and idea (λόγῳ), and in no other way, and all that we are now saying is said for the sake of them. Moreover, there is always less difficulty in fixing the mind on small matters than on great.

The meaning of this passage will be examined in Chapter VII. It should be observed that, from the *Theaetetus* onwards, great prominence is given to λόγος. In this passage the phrase λόγον 2οῦναι καὶ 2έξασθαι has obtained the definite meaning which was sought in vain in the *Theaetetus*: 'to give the proper logical definition of something'.

The same idea is differently expressed by a later passage in the *Statesman*; it shows how deeply attached Plato is to his method, and the attempt to make it clear. He says that Division (τὸ κατ' εἴδη 2υνατὸν εἶναι 2ιαιρεῖν, 286 D) aims at performing a great service, which must outweigh any complaints of excessive length: it can make those who engage in dialogue 'more dialectical, and better able to make plain the nature of reality by reason'. He himself, in fact, regarded his method as new—for why else should it be expounded with such care?—and well adapted to the solution of serious intellectual problems. Even *after* the *Republic*, he certainly thought himself entitled to regard it in this light. So much for the formal side of the method; we must deal next with its material effect.

V. THE 'ATOMIC FORM'

IT will be found that all four of the problems which provided the framework of our argument in Chapters II and III can in Plato's opinion be resolved by the process of διαίρεσις. Firstly, the character of absoluteness in the εἶδος is essentially altered; and the Idea, once an intuited universal, comes more and more to resemble a concept.

Secondly, an immediate result of the method of Division is to show that the εἶδος is not 'indivisible', as hitherto assumed, but divisible.

Thirdly, the *Philebus* will show that Plato relies on the same method to overcome the 'separation' of Ideas, and to show how it is that particulars 'share' in them. But in this work we will begin with the fourth problem, that of δόξα; for the method of Division is specially designed for its solution, and by it any interpretation of the *Theaetetus* and *Sophist* must be tested.

It is probably admitted by all—certainly it has been a basic premiss in our own argument—that as Plato's distance from Socrates became greater, he in some way became more and more deeply interested in contemporary science. The keynote of science, in the fourth century, was the knowledge of the given realities of nature, in the widest sense. Scholars were led to consider this historically probable by reflection on the important achievements in the field of natural science which proceeded from the Academy; surely this knowledge was founded upon the organization of scientific work in the school. An advance of the highest importance was made by Usener and Wilamowitz when they took this opinion a stage further, and showed that even in Plato's writings we can find traces of extensive empirical knowledge, sufficient alone to explain his pupils' success in science. The inquiry came to an end, however, with the study of the copious scientific material displayed in such Dialogues as the *Timaeus*; and even here many problems still await solution. Our judgement of Plato's philosophy, in the narrow sense, has remained almost unaffected by the discovery of this new relationship. One is surprised to find that it is the 'philosophical' interpreters who have seen the problem with the greatest clarity, and given an answer, on their own lines, to the question: how did Plato adapt his method to allow for a form of knowledge based on experience, yet truly scientific? The result has been that the gulf between Plato and Aristotle in scientific method appears to us to-day wider than ever, whilst, on the other hand, in particular branches of science it has been possible to show the continuity of the research begun in the Academy with that carried on in the Lyceum.

In a previous discussion of the problem of δόξα we arrived at this point: Plato, to apply to him an earlier phrase of his own, became a φιλοθεάμων; the world of becoming, with its changing forms, now seemed to him to deserve the most serious exploration. As the *Parmenides* shows, this was bound to lead him into a difficulty, for which his earlier view of the structure of knowledge was responsible. The things which 'participated', and the Idea in which they participated, suddenly seemed to be on one level. In the *Republic* Plato could still warn us with complete confidence against such a confusion (476 D, quoted above). In our earlier discussion of the problem of δόξα we showed how the universal and the particular underwent a process of mutual assimilation; the universal was in danger of being 'reified' (but above all the particular acquired some *traits* of universality). One side of this change has been discussed in connexion with the τρίτος ἄνθρωπος criticism; the other side is our present concern.

Because his conception of knowledge had been framed with reference to that which is known *a priori*, the problem of δόξα brought Plato into difficulties of a simply insuperable kind; he was not the man to spare himself a single one of them; what other thinker would have stated the objections to all the merely *possible* consequences of his own doctrine as keenly as Plato did in the *Parmenides* and *Sophist*? He had inherited from Socrates, and never lost, a conviction that only by thinking (ἐν λόγοις) can objects of any kind whatsoever be known. His consistency on this point makes Plato the founder of science in the strict sense. Now it was in the hope of maintaining this belief that he faced the objections. Obviously he tried to attain his end in a way of his own; but that in no way diminishes his service in having stated the problem in this form at all. It was necessary—and this is what has so often been misunderstood—for him to try to extend his knowledge to objects which are commonly accounted empirical—i.e. to take up arms against sense-perception—before he could see the full extent of the problem. Where sensation is of no account as a source of knowledge—where the moral interest prevails—it was relatively much easier for him to push home his principle; only those things were admitted as ὄντα (realities) from his earlier standpoint, wherein he could find some genuine Being; when he spoke of 'everything that *is*' the illusory things of our earth were simply excluded. From this the peculiarities of his philosophy result. In the *Republic* he has an elaborate doctrine of knowledge, complete in itself—a map of the various spiritual activities. If we insist on finding his later problems in the *Republic*, we are bound to be surprised at his falling back into simple questions, and into solutions which, at first sight, seem surprisingly primitive. But, given the terminology of the *Republic*, the new task was bound to appear to Plato in this light: Can there be any alliance between knowledge, which is of the universal, and 'opinion', which is of the particular? Can opinion be conveyed to the mind through reason, λόγος—the specific instrument of knowledge—and so be proved *true*? Even in its 'descending process', the Dialectic of the *Republic* possessed no instrument for solving this problem. In the *Republic*, δόξα and the εἶδος had belonged to quite separate worlds, and both now required to be radically remodelled. That they were bound to approach nearer to each other as soon as the Ideal Theory became general, we have already shown.

In the *Sophist*, λόγος, δόξα, and αἴσθησις are eventually placed side by side; Plato clearly indicates how they differ, and what they have in common. Undoubtedly that is his final word in the Dialogues; but just here, as all the interpreters agree, there lies an essential obscurity which seems to upset its entire foundation.[1]

---

[1] [Stenzel gives quotations from Apelt and Natorp in which they complain

The problem arose for Plato owing to the peculiar status of the Idea, half-way between universal and particular. It was neither general concept nor 'presentation' of a particular, but a representation of the universal *in* the particular; a concept, in our sense, it was not. Plato confirms this by his attitude in the *Sophist*, where, when he sees the concept functioning in a way which seems to us perfectly natural, he is overcome by surprise and philosophical wonder. The Idea is by its very nature totality, wholeness; it is not merely a wider universal, including what 'falls under it'—it simply extinguishes other things and makes them invisible. The light which streams from the Good is so blinding that all else is left in darkness; in the logical sense also there is an essential difference between the Good, the unconditioned, and the 'assumptions' which are conditional. Such is the character attributed to the Idea in the *Symposium*, where also its indivisibility is most plainly expressed.

Διαίρεσις *aims at the 'atomic form'*

What, then, could Plato make of a method which clearly confirmed this property of the Ideas (indivisibility), and yet endowed them with all the functions of the concept? Every logical Διαίρεσις, if continued long enough, brings us to an 'indivisible' (ἀΔιαίρετον, ἄτμητον, ἄτομον). Otherwise reality will be parcelled up indefinitely, and hopeless scepticism will be the result (κατὰ σμικρὰ Διαθραύοντες, *Sophist*, 246 B). And Plato had now to face a new formal and stylistic problem: how far could certain technical terms, which had become customary in his school, be used in his works of imitative art, whose entire reference was to the intellectual life of earlier periods? It would certainly be a serious error for us to infer, from the fact that some term is absent from a Dialogue, or is often avoided by paraphrase, that it had 'not yet' been coined. Once more only a careful attention to the literary form of the Dialogue can save us from two contrary errors, the reading of later ideas into a Dialogue, and the abandonment of any attempt to interpret Plato's hints of a system

that Plato's explanation of false judgement in the *Sophist* is vitiated by a confusion about the meaning of μὴ ὄν.]

with constant terminology; which would amount to a refusal to consider the Dialogues as *philosophy*.

To apply this to the present instance: Plato says (*Sophist*, 229 D): 'But we have yet to consider another point, whether it is now indivisible (ἄτομον) as a whole, or admits of some further division worth mentioning.'[1] The division of concepts is the road to the new εἶδος, and this is an 'atomic form', whether this is the precise term used or not. Διαίρεσις cannot call a halt until it arrives at an object which is indivisible, or, as it is expressed in a half-figurative way, has 'embraced' this object (περιλαμβάνειν, συλλαμβάνειν). But both this indivisibility and the newly found unity are relative. Just as it was necessary to split up one unity after another by division in order to arrive at wider and wider differentiation, so also even the final 'atomic form' may be both one and many; that possibility can no longer be excluded. The example of the higher unities shows this, since, although divided, they too are wholes (ὅλα). Thus the εἴδη, beginning with the higher and more abstract ones, come to possess, after much effort and still within strict limits, the character of concepts; lower εἴδη 'fall under them'. And Plato, as we shall see, holds that the problem of 'separation' is thereby practically solved.

The 'atomic form' is reached by Deduction

If we entirely leave out of account the direction in which Plato's thought changes: if we attend solely to its results, and ask how we should nowadays describe the method which could have produced them, we shall reply that Plato's method here has some distant resemblance to abstraction or induction. But Plato regarded it as the purest *deduction*—he believed that the *content* of the 'atomic form' could be derived by division from the most general concept. By mere analysis he thought that he could 'constitute' the object. The ontological character of Plato's thinking is nowhere plainer than in this expectation that he could make an inference from mere concepts to a reality with a definite content. The 'philosophical' scholars are wont to

[1] Cf. *Phaedrus*, 277 B: Πρὶν ἄν τις τό τε ἀληθὲς ἑκάστων εἰδῇ πέρι ὧν λέγει ἢ γράφει, κατ' αὐτό τε πᾶν ὁρίζεσθαι δυνατὸς γένηται, ὁρισάμενός τε πάλιν κατ' εἴδη μέχρι τοῦ ἀτμήτου τέμνειν ἐπιστηθῇ.

derive from this a mere general assurance that 'Plato finds reality in thinking'. This, they say, is a timeless truth—*ergo*, this is Plato's serious meaning. But Plato's method of Division is intended to explain the actual particular in its determined being; i.e. Division is intended not merely to establish a general form for the judgement, but to prove the truth of particular judgements, having a definite content. This interpretation of Plato comes to grief, therefore, over the question of Δόξα.

Aristotle, whose polemic aims at showing that Διαίρεσις is not a valid form of proof, must have understood it in this way. His arguments also enable us to see precisely where Plato supposed the factor of logical necessity to lie in his method of 'constituting' a definite object (*Anal. Priora*, 1. 31. 46ᵃ 31). Aristotle does not deny that the proposition that all beings are either mortal or immortal is certain; but Διαίρεσις, he says, leaves the most essential question open—namely, under which of these two concepts should we include the thing whose nature we want to know? Expressed in terms of formal logic, his objection is that the middle term in a valid syllogism must always have such-and-such a character, and in this sense it hits the mark,[1] though it may be said that the syllogism is no better able to solve the problem proposed by Plato, and that Aristotle is throughout his logic building on Plato's results. But his remark shows the point on which Plato obviously laid greatest weight: one need only divide a higher εῖδος at some point which nature has determined, some 'joint' (Διαφυή, *Statesman*, 259 D), or to take another metaphor, one need only divide it 'organically', as the skilled man dissects the limbs of a sacrificial victim (*Statesman*, 287 c; *Phaedrus*, 265 E) (or 'specifically', κατ' εῖδος. Cf. Διαφοραί, ὁπόσαιπερ ἐν εῖδεσι κεῖνται, *Statesman*, 285 B), in order to find determinations which logically exclude each other, under which by a simple process the next εῖδος is fitted. For in most cases we do in fact accurately know whether the creature to be defined is e.g. mortal or immortal; the only thing is to make sure that no other possibilities are left besides those which have been discovered by the natural 'dissection'. The dissection, therefore, is always the

---

[1] Cf. Maier, *Syllogistik des Aristoteles*, ii b. 70 foll.

crucial thing. The case of dichotomy is easiest; here we have to answer a simple question, Is it *X* or *Y*? e.g. is the sophist a layman or a specialist? Now it is true that this question can generally be answered as soon as it is rightly put. Hence it seems that the process has only to be continued in order to give us, by pure method, the grasp of a definite object; Διαίρεσις seems to be a 'manifestation through reason of the things that are', Δήλωσις λόγῳ τῶν ὄντων. The demonstrative force which Plato finds in Διαίρεσις undoubtedly depends on there being a contradictory relation between the two species discovered in the next stage of Division. It is therefore easy to understand why he devotes a special discussion to this point at *Statesman*, 262 B foll. The 'pedantry' of the entire method, which has aroused so much antipathy to it, is simply a consequence of the resolution not to omit, for the sake of brevity, any single step in Division, and not to establish prematurely any single obvious classification, but to advance by means of exclusive contraries which will conduct us by necessary stages to the concept which we want. The subdivisions ought, if rightly found, to stand in the relation of 'being' and 'not-being'. (Plato's new discovery, which he considers so essential, is that 'not-being' may be understood in the sense of 'difference'.) He must have found the demonstrative force of Division precisely at the point where Aristotle complained of its absence. To take the classic instance of dichotomous division: we ask, In which of the two parts must the form we seek be placed—this or 'the other'? Not *that*, therefore *this*. The divider knows what the desired form *is not*, and knowing also that the alternatives are exclusive, he can recognize what it *is*. Many scholars think that it was the main purpose of the *Sophist* to show how not-being and being are related, viz. that they correspond to 'this' and 'not this'; now the value of Διαίρεσις is that it is a never-ending attempt to show the intricate relation of being and not-being. Plato himself tells us that μὴ ὄν and Διαίρεσις are connected: Μία μέν ἐστί που καὶ ἐκείνη (sc. ἡ θατέρου φύσις), τὸ δ' ἐπὶ τῳ γιγνόμενον μέρος αὐτῆς ἕκαστον ἀφορισθὲν ἐπωνυμίαν ἴσχει τινὰ ἑαυτῆς ἰδίαν. Διὸ πολλαὶ τέχναι τ' εἰσὶ λεγόμεναι καὶ ἐπιστῆμαι (257 c). Every stage in Division shows a being and a not-being side by side. To take an instance from the *Sophist*: According to the end we have in view, we may designate the art of acquisition as 'being' and that of production as 'not-being' (it excludes the former, i.e. it is not it, i.e. it is other); or if we are interested in one of the productive arts, we shall designate these as 'being'. And just as the two divisions of art are connected by their participation in the ὅλον εἶδος of τέχνη, so, in the next stage of division, the form which has at present been described as 'being' will be split open, and a new bifurcation of being and not-being discovered. The art of acquisition is a unity including two lower arts—acquisition by trapping or stealth, and (exclusive to it) acquisition by violent appropriation. The process goes on and on, until the method has served its purpose and an 'indivisible' is reached, whether it be the angler or the sophist, the art of weaving or the art of statesmanship.

The συμπλοκή εἰδῶν *in the 'atomic form'*

Here a new surprise appears, at least for philosophers who, as we all know, had not yet successfully overcome the problem of predication. The process of division ends in one of union and connexion. This point has received only a minimum of recognition, owing to misunderstanding of the essence of the whole method, yet Plato, both in theory and in practice, placed it in the foreground. When any concept has been finally determined, all the various higher concepts on the side of 'being' are 'brought together',[1] and the 'proper' definition of the concept results. This is a συμπλοκή εἰδῶν, corresponding exactly to the συμπλοκή ὀνομάτων in the *Theaetetus*, though from that it proved impossible to derive a definition. A precise explanation of this συμπλοκή is given at *Sophist*, 221 A: 'you and I, therefore, have now not merely agreed upon the name of the angler's art, but also upon the definition which describes its functions.' The Indivisible, the 'atomic form', possesses all the predicates which are woven together in its definition. Here we should turn back to a problem stated in the *Parmenides*, viz. where the subject is a concrete real thing, it

---

[1] συνάγειν, *Sophist*, 224 C; συμπλέκειν, συνδεῖν, 268 C.

is easy to show that it may without contradiction combine in itself various predicates, but can this be shown of the εἶδος as well?[1] Socrates wished that it could, and his wish has been realized. The εἶδος is one, an indivisible result of Division. At the same time it is many, inasmuch as the concept of its essence, its λόγος, is a combination of all the higher concepts. But this combination separates it from all other things, and preserves it from any chance of confusion with what resembles it. Plato often described in the clearest terms this very important κοινωνία, cf., for instance, Sophist, 264 D, E: 'Let us, then, renew the attempt, and in dividing any class, always take the part to the right, holding fast to that set of qualities in which the Sophist partakes, until we have stripped him of all his common properties, and reached his peculiar nature—cf. Statesman, 285 B: πρὶν ἂν σύμπαντα τὰ οἰκεῖα ἐντὸς μιᾶς ὁμοιότητος ἔρξας γένους τινὸς οὐσίᾳ περιβάληται —so that we may exhibit him in his true nature, first and foremost to ourselves, and secondly to kindred dialectical spirits.' This is again reminiscent of the phrase οἰκεῖος λόγος in the Theaetetus. Plato there argued that the οἰκεῖος λόγος proposed by Antisthenes was not properly a λόγος at all, but only a 'name'. It included no common factor, no genus proximum (208 A). By the true method of definition described in the Sophist, it is just by 'preserving the common features' (ἐχόμενοι τῆς . . . κοινωνίας) that we are able to draw a line between κοινά and the 'essence', proper to the desired form, which survives when they are taken away, and so to discover its οἰκεία φύσις. The term περιελεῖν, 'to remove from the circumference', is chosen by Plato to show that in this process all other εἴδη are 'separated off'. The word recurs at Statesman, 281 c: 'Well, then, suppose that we define weaving, or rather that part of it which has been selected by us, to be the greatest and noblest of arts which are concerned with woollen garments—shall we be right? Is not the definition, although true, wanting in clearness and completeness; for do not all those others arts require to be first cleared away?' (πάσας περιέλωμεν);

---

[1] Πολὺ μεντᾶν ᾧδε μᾶλλον, ὡς λέγω, ἀγασθείην εἴ τις ἔχοι τὴν αὐτὴν ταύτην ἀπορίαν ἐν αὐτοῖς τοῖς εἴδεσι παντοδαπῶς πλεκομένην, ὥσπερ ἐν τοῖς ὁρωμένοις διήλθετε, οὕτως καὶ ἐν τοῖς λογισμῷ λαμβανομένοις ἐπιδεῖξαι, Parmenides, 129 E.

cf. also 268 c. And in this last quotation there is also a clear allusion to *Theaetetus*, 208 c, d. Plato mentions a wrongly assigned *differentia*: . . . 'the popular notion of telling the mark or sign of difference which distinguishes the thing in question from all others. . . . As, for example, in the case of the sun, I think that you would be contented with the statement that the sun is the brightest of the heavenly bodies which revolve about the earth.' (Here language has left its trace. Διαφέρειν means either 'to distinguish oneself' or 'to be distinct', i.e. different.) Finally, at *Statesman*, 258 c, we have the two processes placed side by side: the 'separation' of the remaining μὴ ὄντα, which 'are not' the form desired, and the process of collection which gives the desired unity: 'Where shall we discover the path of the Statesman? We must find and separate off (χωρὶς ἀφελόντας), and set our seal upon this, and we will set the mark of another class upon all diverging paths.' Compare 268 c: the Statesman is not precisely determined until 'we have disengaged and separated him from those who hang about him, and claim to share in his prerogatives'—and 279 A: 'We must put all these aside, until the Statesman is left alone.'

Τὸ κατὰ γένη Διαιρεῖσθαι καὶ μήτε ταὐτὸν εἶδος ἕτερον ἡγήσασθαι μήτε ἕτερον ὂν ταὐτὸν μῶν οὐ τῆς Διαλεκτικῆς φήσομεν ἐπιστήμης εἶναι;

Οὐκοῦν ὅ γε τοῦτο Δυνατὸς Δρᾶν μίαν Ἰδέαν Διὰ πολλῶν, ἑνὸς ἑκάστου κειμένου χωρίς, πάντη Διατεταμένην ἱκανῶς Διαισθάνεται, καὶ πολλὰς ἑτέρας ἀλλήλων ὑπὸ μιᾶς ἔξωθεν περιεχομένας, καὶ μίαν αὖ Δι' ὅλων πολλῶν ἐν ἑνὶ συνημμένην, καὶ πολλὰς χωρὶς πάντη Διωρισμένας· τοῦτο Δ' ἔστιν, ᾗ τε κοινωνεῖν ἕκαστα Δύναται καὶ ὅπη μή, Διακρίνειν κατὰ γένος ἐπίστασθαι.

W E have seen that when the common predicates are combined 'vertically' (so to speak) a definition is the result. It would be most remarkable if just this process were missing from Plato's explicit definition of the dialectician, wherein definition is made the whole purpose of dialectical method, at *Sophist*, 253 D. And it is in fact included in the third section of the formula, which has given rise to so much conflicting discussion.

This passage gives a general account of the meaning of the new Dialectic, and sets some new problems. There are two summaries of what it has to say, one at the beginning and one at the end. Both times two parallel activities are ascribed to the Dialectician. Τὸ κατὰ γένη Διαιρεῖσθαι καὶ μήτε ταὐτὸν εἶδος ἕτερον ἡγήσασθαι μήτε ἕτερον ὂν ταὐτὸν μῶν οὐ τῆς Διαλεκτικῆς φήσομεν ἐπιστήμης εἶναι; is the first summary. Then follows the disputed passage; and this is again summarized in the final definition, which again has two parts, τοῦτο Δ' ἔστιν, ᾗ τε κοινωνεῖν ἕκαστα Δύναται καὶ ὅπη μή, Διακρίνειν κατὰ γένος ἐπίστασθαι.[1] Between

---

[1] The following passages from the *Phaedrus* (265 c foll.) should be noticed: they show a very close resemblance with the Dialectic of the *Sophist* and *Statesman*. Ἐμοὶ μὲν φαίνεται τὰ μὲν ἄλλα τῷ ὄντι παιδιᾷ πεπαῖσθαι· τούτων Δέ τινων ἐκ τύχης ῥηθέντων Δυοῖν εἰδοῖν, εἰ αὐτοῖν τὴν Δύναμιν τέχνῃ λαβεῖν Δύναιτό τις, οὐκ ἄχαρι (note the *two* kinds). Εἰς μίαν τε Ἰδέαν συνορῶντα ἄγειν τὰ πολλαχῇ Διεσπαρμένα, ἵνα ἕκαστον ὁριζόμενος Δῆλον ποιῇ περὶ οὗ ἂν ἀεὶ Διδάσκειν ἐθέλῃ (note that definition is the aim). ΦΑΙ. Τὸ Δ' ἕτερον Δὴ εἶδος τί λέγεις, ὦ Σώκρατες; ΣΩ. Τὸ πάλιν κατ' εἴδη Δύνασθαι Διατέμνειν κατ' ἄρθρα ᾗ πέφυκεν, καὶ μὴ ἐπιχειρεῖν καταγνύναι μέρος μηδέν, κακοῦ μαγείρου τρόπῳ χρώμενον (cf. *Statesman*, 287 c, κατὰ μέλη . . . οἷον ἱερεῖον Διαιρώμεθα). Then comes the summary: Τούτων Δὴ ἔγωγε αὐτός τε ἐραστής, ὦ Φαῖδρε, τῶν Διαιρέσεων καὶ συναγωγῶν, ἵνα οἷός τε ὦ λέγειν τε καὶ φρονεῖν· ἐάν τέ τιν' ἄλλον ἡγήσωμαι Δυνατὸν εἰς ἓν καὶ ἐπὶ πολλὰ πεφυκόθ' ὁρᾶν, τοῦτον Διώκω "κατόπισθε μετ' ἴχνιον ὥστε θεοῖο". καὶ μέντοι καὶ τοὺς Δυναμένους αὐτὸ Δρᾶν εἰ μὲν ὀρθῶς ἢ μὴ προσαγορεύω, θεὸς οἶΔε, καλῶ Δὲ οὖν μέχρι τοῦΔε Διαλεκτικούς. With the Homeric quotation compare the playful description of the

these two bipartite phrases there comes the disputed passage, which is in four parts: Οὐκοῦν ὅ γε τοῦτο Δυνατὸς Δρᾶν | μίαν ἰΔέαν Διὰ πολλῶν, ἑνὸς ἑκάστου κειμένου χωρίς, πάντῃ Διατεταμένην ἱκανῶς Διαισθάνεται, | καὶ πολλὰς ἑτέρας ἀλλήλων ὑπὸ μιᾶς ἔξωθεν περιεχομένας, | καὶ μίαν αὖ Δι' ὅλων πολλῶν ἐν ἑνὶ συνημμένην, | καὶ πολλὰς χωρὶς πάντῃ Διωρισμένας. Some external signs render it likely that even here we are not to think of *four* co-ordinate things,[1] or again of a climax in three stages followed by a relatively unimportant afterthought, as Natorp would suppose; but rather that there are two pairs of related terms. These external signs are: first, the αὖ at the beginning of section 3; secondly, the fact that μίαν ἰΔέαν is parallel in 1 and 3, and πολλάς (*sc.* ἰΔέας) in 2 and 4; lastly, the occurrence of the term ἕν (unity) in 1 and 3. Ritter has searched the *Sophist* and other Dialogues for examples of each of the processes mentioned here, with the intention of deciding the meaning of these words by inference from the examples which illustrate them. Now it is doubtful whether Plato's view of a logical relationship would be the same as a modern one, and, apart from this, Ritter's test has failed, as he admits, to bring to light a uniform terminology on the part of Plato. Obviously, if we pay no attention to his language, and hope that considerations of meaning may, by good luck, enable us to impress some sense upon the stubborn, half-figurative sentences, our result will inevitably be an arbitrary one. No certain explanation even of segments (2) and (4) has been given, although it is normally supposed that in (2) Plato is describing the inclusion of subordinate classes within a higher one, and in (4) contrary classes, mutually exclusive to each other, such as Rest and Motion. But Maier rightly draws attention to the point that (2) and (4) partly coincide: 'sheer disparity between them', he says, 'is unthinkable.' He is entirely in the right. At 255 E Plato has certainly declared Rest and Motion to be 'altogether different', but he believes that combination is possible even between 'being' and 'not-being' (the proof of this is indeed the principal aim of the Dialogue), hence Motion and Rest also

Eleatic Stranger as a God: *Sophist*, 216 B. On the *Phaedrus* as a whole, see Chapter IX.   [1] It is not clear how this passage is related to 254 B, C.

cannot exclude each other as it is inferred from this sentence that they do; both participate in 'being' which 'comprehends' them (250 B, a reference also quoted by Maier). It must, after all, be possible, says Plato, to bring them into relation with each other (256 B). And, above all, if this is not so, what purpose is served by 'concepts which, passing through all the kinds (γένη), hold *them* together, so that they may be combined?' (253 c: the sense is the same whether we take the traditional text, or Wagner's conjecture.) Or again by the concepts which 'may without obstacle pass through all and be combined with all' (254 B)? Plato also definitely declines to discuss the ἐναντίον (258 E); his sole concern in this Dialogue is with the newly discovered notion of difference, ἕτερον in its new identity with μὴ ὄν. And it is *a priori* probable that the doubtful fourth segment has something to do with this kind of contrariety. Moreover this assumption may also make it possible to throw light on the obscurity which, in the opinion of all scholars, surrounds the doctrine of contraries in the *Sophist*.

The conflict of interpretations in regard to the first section is most instructive. Natorp, wishing to obtain a climax, keeps this section down, and finds in it only the simplest application of the unity of a concept, its application to a manifold of objects given separately and individually to the senses. It would then correspond to the union of individuals in a universal which, in the earlier phase, Socrates had so often been made to demand. His expressions occasionally had the same ring as in the present passage, e.g. at *Meno*, 77 A: 'Αλλ' ἴθι Δή, πειρῶ καὶ σὺ ἐμοὶ τὴν ὑπόσχεσιν ἀποδοῦναι, κατὰ ὅλου εἰπὼν ἀρετῆς πέρι ὅτι ἐστίν, καὶ παῦσαι πολλὰ ποιῶν ἐκ τοῦ ἑνός, ὅπερ φασὶ τοὺς συντρίβοντάς τι ἑκάστοτε οἱ σκώπτοντες, ἀλλ' ἐάσας ὅλην καὶ ὑγιῆ εἰπὲ τί ἐστιν ἀρετή.[1] In substance, therefore, this view at first seems perfectly possible; but some serious objections arise. Apelt and most other scholars with him assume that here the allusion throughout is to Ideas only, and not to sensible things 'quae in mundo mutationis fluctibus obnoxio posita et a dialectica aliena sunt'. And indeed the constant concern of the whole Dialogue

---

[1] But the meaning here is entirely different, see below.

is with the κοινωνία τῶν γενῶν or εἰδῶν. Moreover it would be striking if the πολλά of the sensible world were termed ἕκαστον ἓν χωρίς, as units already separate and distinct. This question must for the time being remain open. We need only remember that the whole process of development here described has been one of *rapprochement* between individual and εἶδος, each coming to resemble the other. The conflicting interpretations here give us an external sign of the fact.

The third section is explained in the most various ways, and even the traditional text has been questioned: Apelt reads ἓν ἑνί for ἓν ἑνί.

Segment (3): the συμπλοκή *εἰδῶν in the 'atomic form'*

It is the third segment which makes this disputed passage relevant to our argument. Now in the light of our quotation from 264 E (see above, p. 94), we can see that the third and fourth segments belong closely together. Plato has in mind a completed classification. An Idea passing through several 'wholes', ὅλα, is combined to form a 'unity'. This unity is the form whose definition is sought. Words for 'bind together', 'combine' recur in the passages quoted on p. 93 (συνδεῖν, συμπλέκειν). Now both the text of these passages and their sense informs us that, by the same process, many other forms are *utterly separated* from the desired one. The final segment, therefore, is not intended to describe some reciprocal relationship between classes—this would have needed a definite mention, as in (2); its purpose must be to show how the remaining concepts are dissociated from the unity achieved in (3). Thus the argument does not concern definite concepts like Rest and Motion, but only the relationships between concepts of which every διαίρεσις and definition provides fresh instances. Upon this view, we can explain something which causes the interpreters to puzzle their brains, viz., why Plato is so strangely inconsistent about the relation between concepts; the only contrariety which he here recognizes in so many words is that of difference, τὸ ἕτερον.

A special word must be said of the phrase δι' ὅλων πολλῶν. The reading of Proclus, ἄλλων πολλῶν, disposes of any linguistic difficulty, but gives a colourless sense. The use of ὅλων for πάντων is unlikely as early as Plato, though Apelt and Natorp unhesitatingly take it in this sense. (The former translates 'quae cum quavis alia notione copulari possint', which ignores πολλων; the latter 'through all the many'.) Natorp quotes as a parallel 253 A, 253 C, but all that this really shows is that Διὰ πάντων is Plato's phrase for 'throughout all', and moreover, he could scarcely have used Δι' ὅλων in the same sense two lines further on (253 D). The parallel is nevertheless of some assistance. The term ὅλον, in a logical context, always indicates unity. Now the division of unities is the special service performed by Διαίρεσις, and Plato's mention of the ἀμέριστος ἰδέα (Theaetetus, 205 C) shows clearly that he has Διαίρεσις in mind. Not long before, Plato has actually examined the notion of the ὅλον, but, on the assumption that it must be indivisible (204 E), which is carefully retained in the Theaetetus, he is faced with the contradiction that ὅλον cannot be distinguished from πᾶν. The Parmenides is likewise careful to keep in the background the solutions which are to be offered in the Sophist. Now here the quality of ὅλον[1] is attributed three times to the εἶδος[2] in a few lines, to emphasize that it would be a contradiction for the 'many' to participate in it. (So also καθόλου is connected along this road with the meaning of ὅλον. Later it becomes a rigid technical term, and Plato had prepared the way.)

But the Sophist rests on entirely different assumptions, and on new knowledge. Plato naturally reminds us of the old contradiction which has now been solved. The whole εἶδος, he has found, is divisible into lesser εἴδη, and yet it need not lose its character as a whole, a unity. And at 253 c he openly says: καὶ πάλιν ἐν ταῖς Διαιρέσεσιν, εἰ Δι' ὅλων ἕτερα τῆς Διαιρέσεως αἴτια. But could he possibly have used Δι' ὅλων here in the sense of Διόλου (throughout) without bothering to distinguish them? The fact is that his terms differ according as the reference is to Division or Collection. (1) Where he is concerned with the Division of wholes or unities, he says Δι' ὅλων. From the point of view of

[1] Parmenides, 137 C.
[2] Cf. the phrase ἑκάστου ὅλου in Theaetetus, 174 A, explained in B.

sense, the important thing is not that Division extends through 'all', but that it passes through wholes or unities. (2) Conversely, where the process of Collection is described, as it was in the preceding phrase, the essential thing is to include *all* the kinds (γένη) under certain higher ones; hence we there had 2ιὰ πάντων. And this 2ιὰ πάντων makes it obvious that the 2ιὰ in 2ι' ὅλων has not the force of *dis*section. Διά may merely denote that which 'passes through', and affects more subjects than one; although, owing to the proximity of 2ι-αιρεῖν, the literal sense of the word seems occasionally to come to life.

On our view, then, ὅλα takes the place of the plural of ἕν. In the *Philebus* ἑνάδες and μονάδες occur in this sense, and in other respects Plato does not hesitate to borrow largely from Pythagorean terminology. However, when he comes there to speak of Division, he seems to have boldly used ἕν as its own plural in τῶν ἓν ἐκείνων.[1] Μονάς in *Phaedo*, 101 c, 105 c, has quite a different meaning—the Idea of Unity, participation in which renders a thing one, precisely as it obtains any other predicate by sharing in the Idea. This is a very clear indication of the distance between his earlier view, and the new notion that every εἶδος is a unity and a 'whole'. In the *Sophist*, for reasons which we have seen, ὅλον seems to him a more significant term than ἕν. Perhaps he chooses it just because he is at the same time emphasizing that the Idea is divisible. If so, his choice of a term is governed by deliberate intention; '*many* wholes, or unities' may be a somewhat violent combination, but in sense at least the expression is clear and understandable.

We have so far reached the following result: segments (3) and (4) are closely related, and describe the process of obtaining the definition, λόγος, of a single form, μία ἰδέα. We break up the many higher unities, and connect together the predicates so obtained. This blend of predicates constitutes the new unity (ἕν) which we require, and at the same time sharply separates off all other Ideas from the required one. Upon the same basis we must try to understand the first half of the definition, i.e. segments (1) and (2), and it will be natural to expect that these

[1] Cf. Bury's note on the passage in his edition (Cambridge, 1897).

also are closely connected. There are significant points of resemblance between (1) and (3) and between (2) and (4). Hence
we may not only expect that (1) and (2) will be connected after
the pattern of (3) and (4), but also, since each of the four segments has its complement, that (1) can be explained from (3),
and (2) from (4); from the way in which the whole passage is
constructed, there must be two pairs of related opposites, which
together frame our definition of the activity of Dialectic.

Now in segments (1) and (3) we find the term ἕν, and in
(1) it is used in the plural, in (3) in the singular. But we also
notice in (3) the expression ὅλων. It has just been discovered
that ὅλα is the plural of ἕν, and that the ἕν mentioned in the
latter half of the definition is the 'atomic form'. The 'atomic
form' is the conclusion to a Διαίρεσις; it is something which
results when the μία Ἰδέα, mentioned in segment (3), has been
dealt with by the method of (3) and (4). A clear-cut distinction
has been found between it and the many other Ideas (χωρὶς
Διωρισμένας). Now the unity in segment (1) had been provided
from the start, ἑνὸς ἑκάστου κειμένου χωρίς. The use of κεῖσθαι
deserves special notice, since it must apply to something attained
by logical *activity* (τιθέναι). Plato does not, however, bring to
the front·this implication of activity, as he does in segment (4),
where it is required by the sense (Διωρισμένας contrasted with
Διορίζειν). If, then, the operations of (3) and (4) aim at separation, those of (1) and (2) will aim at uniting terms given to us as
separate. This meaning is in fact expressed with great clarity
in (2): 'many different forms comprehended from without by a
single form'. There could scarcely be any doubt that this expresses the subordination of a lower Idea to a higher one, if this
sense had not already been provided by segment (1). No doubt
many scholars are deterred from taking this obvious view of the
phrase 'comprehended from without' by the fact that it had
earlier been applied to the inclusion of Motion and Rest within
Being (250 B, where συλλαβεῖν is added in expansion of περιέχε-
σθαι). It is difficult to think of Being as a *higher* class, which includes the other two. But surely it may well be the case that
Plato, seeing in the method of Διαίρεσις the source of all his logical

knowledge, judges that its classifications are the fundamental type of all communion (κοινωνία) between forms, and applies it to cases where, to the modern mind, some different logical relationship is involved.[1] Since it can scarcely be doubted that segment (2) refers to the subordination of lower classes to higher ones, if only an appropriate sense can be found for segment (1)— the device used by Natorp has been mentioned—let us here take this meaning for granted. What, then, is left for segment (1)? (1) is related to (2) as (3) to (4). In (3) and its counterpart (1) we have the preconditions of the result successfully achieved in (4) and its counterpart (2). The unity in (3) is formed by a con- nexion, based upon Διαίρεσις, of the higher unities; the appro- priate predicates, which are called ὄντα because they 'are' the object defined, are collected to form a definition. When that is done, the work of segment (4) can take place: the desired class can be finally separated from the many other classes. And we have shown by immediate parallels from the *Sophist* and *States- man* that this explanation is correct. In segment (1), accordingly, we are shown the precondition of the real and decisive *synopsis* of forms under a higher unity which takes place in segment (2): the objects which are to be united must first be known in their separation; it is necessary to grasp the *principle* of the separation, which extends through all the instances, and explains why we are confronted, as we are, by many discrete unities. Or, to allow Plato to explain this in his own words (255 D, E):

ΞΕ. Πέμπτον Δὴ τὴν θατέρου φύσιν λεκτέον ἐν τοῖς εἴδεσιν οὖσαν, ἐν οἷς προαιρούμεθα.

ΘΕΑΙ. Ναί.

ΞΕ. Καὶ Διὰ πάντων γε αὐτὴν αὐτῶν φήσομεν εἶναι Διεληλυθυῖαν· ἐν ἕκαστον γὰρ ἕτερον εἶναι τῶν ἄλλων οὐ Διὰ τὴν αὐτοῦ φύσιν, ἀλλὰ Διὰ τὸ μετέχειν τῆς Ἰδέας τῆς θατέρου.

This passage has, on the surface, such a striking family likeness to the first part of the definition that it has often been quoted for elucidation. But at the same time it also teaches us how closely the first and second segments belong together; for we cannot know how and why any 'unity' is 'other (ἕτερον) than the

[1] See what is said below in Chapter VII, on Being as the highest general concept.

definiendum until we understand, and treat as an independent ἰδέα, the principle upon which its 'otherness' depends—until, in fact, we discover the μὴ ὄν to be no less real than the ὄν. Thus once again Διαίρεσις is found to be Plato's guiding idea. He describes it (235 C) as a method of inquiry which 'investigates particular instances, and includes them all' (τῶν οὕτω δυναμένων μετιέναι καθ' ἕκαστά τε καὶ ἐπὶ πάντα). Here is a new description of the method of Dialectic, additional to the various two-fold divisions which occur as illustrations of its working. And it is completely in harmony with our passage (253 D). In segments (1) and (2) the inquirer starts out from the particulars (ἕκαστα), searches for a comprehensive form, and strives to 'include all' (ἐπὶ πάντα); this is the process of connecting the separate units. In segments (3) and (4), on the other hand, he carries out the actual separation, coming down from a higher εἶδος until the final goal of Διαίρεσις is reached. The result is a unity sharply distinguished and marked off from many others; and this was just what Plato had in view when he said in the preceding sentence: 'Shall we not say that it is the work of the science of Dialectic to divide things into their kinds, not considering classes to be different when they are the same, or the same when they are different?' (i.e. we must avoid both wrong divisions and wrong connexions). At the same time the plan of a Διαίρεσις, according to Plato, displays all the various possibilities of κοινωνία, and this he expresses in the summary at the end: τοῦτο δ' ἐστίν, ᾗ τε κοινωνεῖν ἕκαστα δύναται καὶ ὅπῃ μή, διακρίνειν κατὰ γένος ἐπίστασθαι. If we think of higher and lower concepts arranged in the form of a pyramid, it is easy to understand Plato's meaning when he says (254 B): 'We have agreed that some of the species are willing to communicate with each other, and some are not; and that some combine to a slight extent, others more often, and there is no reason why a few should not combine in all cases with all.' The higher the concept, the more numerous its subordinate species. And it is perfectly true that the method of Division shows in the clearest possible way how certain concepts are exclusive to each other, i.e. cannot be combined; this follows from our discovery that there is μὴ ὄν in each stage of Division

(p. 92). This is Plato's solution of the contradictions in which scholars claim that he is involved in his treatment of Motion and Rest.[1]

After the interpretation which has been given, it will be easier to solve some of the problems of our passage. On our view the unusual combination of terms ὅλων πολλῶν will be parallel to Διὰ πολλῶν in segment (1). Why is ὅλων added in one place if it could be dispensed with in the other? In the first case, the meaning of πολλῶν was elucidated by the addition of ἑνὸς ἑκάστου κειμένου χωρίς, but in segment (3) there was no such support, and the higher unities, the 'many', were mentioned in a different grammatical case from the desired new unity, designated as ἕν. Plato could not thus rely on the former clause to explain the latter, and so he added the synonym of ἕν, ὅλον, putting it, as was necessary here, in the plural.

But this last remark may give rise to another and more serious objection. The detail in segments (1) and (2) is fuller than in the other pair, and the necessary acts of thought are made clearer. To explain how the mind understands the separateness of the rejected forms, a special act of synthesis is introduced, whereby the 'other' or 'not-being' is itself found to be based on a uniform principle (μία ἰδέα). Only then is it possible to apply, as we do in segment (2), a higher and more comprehensive unity. Hence in the latter half—in segments (3) and (4)—one stage must be wanting. Which is it? Segment (3) describes to us the combination of the properties of higher classes in order to form the definition. Now this necessarily presupposes the cleavage of these higher classes into their species, and this is the missing stage. It must be remembered that only *one* of the classes which result from each new Division can be chosen, and become a component part of the definition (cf. 264 E, πορεύεσθαι κατὰ τοὐπὶ Δεξιὰ ἀεὶ μέρος τοῦ τμηθέντος and ἐχόμενοι τῆς τοῦ σοφιστοῦ κοινωνίας). In our discussion we have quoted a parallel passage, 264 D, E— from which the phrases just quoted are taken—and it gives a

---

[1] We must return later to this point; for we are far from having exhausted the difficulties of this definition, although it occupies but a few lines. See below, Chapter IX. The concrete individual is only real for Plato, in so far as it represents a general type.

description of the same operation as that in (3) and (4), namely τὸ συνᾶῆσαι, συμπλέκειν, συνάγειν. And here once more the division of the higher kinds receives special mention. Why, then, was it omitted at 253 D? Perhaps because it had already been so strongly emphasized in segment (1) that any union of classes under a higher Idea presupposed a Division. Hence when Plato came to the second half of the process of Dialectic, the Division proper, it could be taken for granted that before any synoptic act could be performed, Division was necessary. He had just mentioned that the most basic necessity for *all* Dialectic was the 'art of division into kinds'; and it is emphasized again immediately afterwards, Διακρίνειν κατὰ γένος, 253 E. Διαίρεσις, in fact, is the fundamental idea in our passage. We must now show in detail that it is equally essential to the doctrines of the *Sophist* as a whole.

We have already, in our discussion of 'not-being', embarked on the proof of this fact; and in analysing the meaning of segment (4) we have shown how Διαίρεσις explains the unusual theory of contraries in the *Sophist*. We shall soon find an opportunity to put together and amplify what has been said.

VII. ΔΟΞΑ AND ΔΙΑΙΡΕΣΙΣ

WE have thus obtained an idea of Dialectic in the *Sophist*, and we must forthwith try to use this idea to throw light on the last and most difficult problem of this Dialogue, its attitude to Δόξα. Philosophically, the main impression left by the passage into which we have just completed a careful inquiry is likely to be that 'separation' and 'combination' are two logical operations in indissoluble union; each method depends on the assistance of the other. Plainly this is what is meant by the correlation of the four segments into two pairs. This systematic interdependence of the two methods is indeed much emphasized by Plato. But that in no way prevents us from asking, even if the reasons which lie behind Plato's preference are merely historical and psychological, which of them, separation or combination, is presented to us in this passage as the really novel, and therefore the more important one. Now as regards our passage, the answer comes of itself: it is Division (separation) which is the pillar of Dialectic; at the close of our discussion, where we dealt with an apparent fault in the symmetry of the definition, we found a proof of this; we also found it implied beyond doubt in the recurrence of such phrases as τὸ κατὰ γένη Διαιρεῖσθαι (253 D), Διακρίνειν κατὰ γένος (253 E). If we once more attempt to compare the Dialectic of the *Republic* with that of the *Sophist* (it must be remembered that the former does not contain the slightest allusion to the division of concepts—it mentions an ascending and a descending process, but these, as we have often stressed, are related quite differently from the later Διαίρεσις and συναγωγή), the result of the comparison is to show how completely different was the aim of Plato's earlier method; the *Republic* (537 C) identified the dialectician with the συνοπτικός. It may be said that in both places we have an upward and a downward process in necessary logical connexion with each other, and that the obvious difference of emphasis is an 'accident'. However, the main theory which we have presented enables us to discover motives of doctrine in this 'accident'. We found that the upward look, the strong emphasis on 'separate' Ideas, was fundamental to the view of the *Republic*; it required, even in its logical doctrine, a movement towards what was absolute and unconditioned. Now, in the *Sophist* and its kindred Dialogues, any such relation to the unconditioned Idea of the Good has utterly disappeared, at least for Dialectic proper; about this it is too late for us to hesitate. In the Dialectic of the *Sophist*, even the reference to a supreme unity, by which all Being is comprehended, is relegated to the background. (It occupies Plato once more in his latest speculation, but we have not yet come to this.) The most important form of κοινωνία between classes, expressed in the words συμπλέκειν, συνΔεῖν, συνάγειν, was the blend formed of the concepts of widest range in order to define the narrowest; this we were able to place beyond doubt. Διαίρεσις, then, is the proper object of the whole dialectical procedure, towards which even συναγωγή is directed; 'division' being undertaken not on account of the highest unit, but of the lowest. The new Dialectic, therefore, aims at discovering an εἶΔος which cannot be further divided; and this is found at the bottom of the scale.

Λόγος *as the criterion of truth in 'sensation' and 'judgement'*

We saw above that the Idea was essentially an intuition by which the universal is represented in a particular, and we followed its development to the point at which it seemed about to lead Plato on to the problem of individuality.

Our study of the *Theaetetus* and *Sophist* has now carried us to the same point. The question which now arises is one which we foresaw as inevitable in our first outline of the theory of Ideas, What does sense-perception (αἴσθησις) contribute to the knowledge of particulars?

Here again the *Sophist* responds to the *Theaetetus*, like the image in a mirror. Just as the latter rejected, patiently but firmly, the claim of sensation to be the sole source of knowledge—denied that αἴσθησις could be equivalent to ἐπιστήμη, and showed that opinion, whilst it was unaccompanied by λόγος, could not derive from within any knowledge of its own truth or falsity, so in the second half of the *Sophist* it is conceded that both sensation and λόγος help to frame the object which we know. Many would say that this is too readily granted. This correspondence between the Dialogues must be the basis of our present study; only if it be observed shall we learn what are the 'objects' or 'judgements' of which Plato is primarily thinking.

In a brief and mysterious sentence, Δόξα and αἴσθησις appear side by side with λόγος (264 A). They may participate in 'being' or 'not-being', and so become true or false; this is an instance of the 'connexion' or 'communion', used in the *Sophist*—with such a bewildering variety of meanings—to solve all difficulties. As for the 'theory of the judgement', this too is solved in virtue of κοινωνία: a proposition must be composed of substantives and verbs, and cannot consist of substantives alone or verbs alone. (The remark is indeed commonplace, and Natorp remarks that 'it pays too much respect to grammatical form', p. 293.) Then once more the question, how do propositions secure true or false meaning? is simply put aside with an allusion to their sharing in 'being' or 'not-being'. Are we to suppose that all these questions occurred to Plato in such a form? Did he really intend to propound a theory of the judgement? It may appear so, but it tells in favour of the contrary view that, if these are the questions of the Dialogue, it gives the scantiest of answers to them. Plato obviously regarded them as minor questions, mere phases of a more essential problem; and if it is found that, within the framework of this problem, the questions can be more satisfactorily answered, our guiding interpretation will have received further support. For us, it is very easy to explain the special affinity which exists between sensation and judgement (αἴσθησις and Δόξα) and λόγος, as its nature appears in the *Sophist* and *Statesman*.

'Not-Being' not a mere formal principle

The Διαίρεσις of Plato is designed as an instrument which may bring experienced fact within his conception of knowledge. He sees in it a means of descending, by stages of pure thought

independent of experience, or so he believes, to the objects somehow presented by our sensation and the δόξα founded upon it.
But before the object so presented, or reproduced in idea, can be
judged true or false, another factor—λόγος or definition—must
be added. Such a λόγος forms a unity (ἕν), as we found in our
long examination of *Sophist*, 253 D; but it does far more than
merely establish the unity of the object—it also informs us,
through definition, of the *content* of the object. That 'not-being'
has a definite sense—a sense which may change, but is never
merely formal—is often emphasized by Plato. The clearest
statement of this comes at 257 c,[1] where we are distinctly told
that 'not-being' 'when it is added to something—and so not surveyed as a whole—always has a special name'; thus it is quite
logically made responsible for the variety of arts and sciences
with their different names: Plato definitely has the analysis of
concepts in his mind. 'Not-being', for him, never has the meaning of a bare formal principle, of somewhat the same kind as the
law of contradiction. He always thinks of it as having meaning
and substance. When a form is analysed by Division, the various
elements are 'scattered', but they continue to influence each
other. So Division can account for truth and falsehood in a
material sense, even in the sphere of observed fact.

A glance at the plan of a διαίρεσις will show how Plato
supposes that a λόγος, by being blended with 'not-being',
becomes false (260 c). (The primary meaning of λόγος is
definition; of this, more will be said presently.) The definition
is true if one keeps to the proper side of the διαίρεσις (cf. ἐχόμενος
τῆς τοῦ σοφιστοῦ κοινωνίας), and combines the ὄντα, which will
vary with the object he has in view. It is just because μὴ ὄν has
a precise and easily understandable meaning, that a false step
into ψεῦδος is so easy to imagine. E.g. in the Division which is
intended to discover the Sophist, 'being' is τὸ εἰδωλοποιητικόν,
'not-being' τὸ αὐτοποιητικόν. Hence Plato regards it as unnecessary to give special warnings against this danger; and surely
even here his thought is less abstract than it appears at first sight.
One single slip from the right side, i.e. one interchange of 'being'

---

[1] We have quoted this passage in an earlier examination of μὴ ὄν.

with 'not-being', makes the λόγος false, applies false predicates
to the required notion, and attributes to it some 'other' which
it really 'is not'.

That Plato hopes to discover through Division a Being whose
content is thoroughly definite, comes fully to light in connexion
with Δόξα and αἴσθησις. Indeed one has only to recall what
Plato's ultimate purpose was, in his great digression about μὴ
ὄν, in order to understand numerous passages in the Sophist
—like 257 c which was recently quoted. The basis which comes
to light in these passages is that on which the whole Dialogue,
even the seemingly general theory of objects, rests. The purpose
of the Dialogue is to explain error and truth, appearance and
reality; and the whole design of the latter part is such that the
reader or listener expects a solution to drop easily into his hands.
If Plato's thought in the decisive passage appears to involve some
sudden leaps, no doubt we ourselves are to blame for this by our
manner of interpretation. The vital passage is 263 D foll., where
λόγος, Διάνοια, Δόξα, and φαντασία are distinguished. 'Judgement' (λόγος) is defined, in the way we already know, as a 'combination of names with words of time'. As to false λόγος, its
'real and true' origin is that the speaker asserts 'the different
as the same', 'the unreal as real'. By this statement the
Stranger holds that the question as to Δόξα and φαντασία is
already solved: Τί Δὲ Δή; Διάνοιά τε καὶ Δόξα καὶ φαντασία, μῶν
οὐκ ἤδη Δῆλον ὅτι ταῦτά γε ψευΔῆ τε καὶ ἀληθῆ πάνθ' ἡμῶν ἐν
ταῖς ψυχαῖς ἐγγίγνεται; but it proves to be necessary to distinguish between these three things. In the first place Διάνοια
is identified with λόγος, where possibly there is some play on
the etymological similarity of Διάλογος and Διάνοια. The only
distinction between them, the only special mark of λόγος in
contrast to Διάνοια, is outward physical expression. And since
by the whole structure of the Dialogue, it follows that the full
meaning of λόγος is what we call, in grammar, a sentence,
and, in logic, a judgement, the same meaning must apply
equally to Διάνοια. Whether this view of λόγος is right or
wrong, we need not here ask. One may see from this how remote the question, whether we can think without an inner

form of words, still is from Plato's mind. The connexion between thinking and inner speech seemed to him so natural that
he could scarcely even have put this question. But what meaning
is to be attributed to 'thinking' in such a case? This must be
decided, if we are to obtain clarity about these problems and
their solutions.

Φάσις *and* ἀπόφασις

But this, like everything that follows, depends on the way in
which assertion and denial (φάσις, ἀπόφασις, 263 E) are understood.[1] Plato says that they are an 'experience' (πάθος) which
occurs as soon as judgements are made (ἐν λόγοις). If the experience is confined to 'thinking within the soul', it is called δόξα;
if it arises not by the soul's own agency, but in response to sense-
perception (δι' αἰσθήσεως), it is then called φαντασία. It
is to be observed that *when assertion and denial occur* in the soul
(παρῇ) through sensation, φαντασία arises. Throughout the
argument the main stress is laid on this act of saying yes or no;
when Plato refers to the completion or ending of thought
(ἀποτελεύτησις)—a description of δόξα given presently in the
general summary, 264 B—it is this act which is meant. And the
reason is plain: Plato is using the connexion of things with μὴ ὄν
or ὄν to solve all his difficulties. Δόξα and αἴσθησις are capable
of this connexion in virtue of their affinity with λόγος. Thus
they can become true or false. To Theaetetus this is instantly
clear (πῶς δ' οὔ;), and the Stranger observes with satisfaction
that an answer has been found 'unexpectedly soon' to the problem which had seemed insuperable.[2] And the attempt to define
the Sophist by classification is promptly continued from the
point where it was abandoned before the great digression, namely
the distinction between true and false copies. The existence of
the latter has been proved, since it has been shown that deception
truly *is* deception, and exists (266 E); and on this the definition
of the Sophist depended.

[1] Cf. *Theaetetus*, 189 E (ἡ ψυχὴ) αὐτὴ ἑαυτὴν ἐρωτῶσα καὶ ἀποκρινομένη, καὶ φάσκουσα
καὶ οὐ φάσκουσα.
[2] Κατανοεῖς οὖν ὅτι πρότερον ηὑρέθη ψευδὴς δόξα καὶ λόγος ἢ κατὰ τὴν προσδοκίαν ἦν
ἐφοβήθημεν ἄρτι . . . ;

Does the old artistic purpose at all survive in the *Sophist*? If so, the difference between true and false Δόξα must follow as clearly from the premisses of the Dialogue as Plato assures us that it does. If it is not a work of art, it is open to us to call it a 'pedantic school-book for the youngest members of the Academy', but in that case Plato was less justified than ever in enveloping in the cloak of entire self-evidence all the obscurities which are detected by Apelt and Natorp. On their view, the author of the *Sophist* would himself be an arch-sophist—one who 'does not know', yet asserts his knowledge and is confident of victory. Now if a commentary on this passage had survived from the contemporary Academy, obviously every interpreter of the *Sophist* would feel bound to employ it for the discovery of Plato's fundamental view of λόγος, δόξα, and αἴσθησις. But we are actually in a much more favourable position. Plato examines in the *Philebus* the entire set of problems which are involved, and shows us quite definitely how he supposes that δόξα and αἴσθησις are connected with 'assertion' and 'denial'.

'Philebus' (38 foll.) as a commentary on δόξα *and* αἴσθησις *in the 'Sophist'*

By a train of thought which is itself interesting, Plato is led to diverge from the special problem of the *Philebus*, and to con- sider true and false opinion. Here (38 A foll.), as throughout the *Philebus*, Plato has in mind the pair of contraries which he had discussed in the *Sophist*—'being' and 'not-being' in their more precise sense as 'true' and 'false'; his task is to employ these for the analysis, and hence the more precise knowledge, of Pleasures. 'Can we find no difference at all between the Pleasure which arises in us accompanied by right opinion and by knowledge, and that which is accompanied by error (ψεῦλος) and ignorance (ἀνοίας MSS., perhaps ἀγνοίας)?' Now follow some vitally important remarks on δόξα (38B): Οὐκοῦν ἐκ μνήμης τε καὶ αἰ- σθήσεως δόξα ἡμῖν καὶ τὸ διαδοξάζειν ἐγχειρεῖν γίγνεθ' ἑκάστοτε; The text at the end is again very uncertain; ἐγχωρεῖν may be the right reading. Διαδοξάζειν is a carefully chosen word, which must obviously be retained just because of the connexion, which it recalls, between Διαιρεῖσθαι, Διάνοια, and Δόξα.[1] Like many other compounds of Διά—for example, Διαισθάνεσθαι—it is designed to express the work of 'distinction' between different things; hence the similarity between Δοξάζειν and 'judge'.

In spite of this we are told, and in no uncertain terms, that Δόξα is the result of memory and sense-perception; i.e. in close proximity to the word Διαδοξάζειν, Δόξα occurs as a term of psychology, meaning 'presentation'. This is strikingly parallel to the last part of the *Theaetetus*. That Plato's notion of knowledge has, with the change in the objects known, become deeply imbued with psychology, appears at the very beginning of the *Philebus* in the list of mental activities, all intended to be instrumental in knowledge, which are opposed to Pleasure; memory occurs side by side with thinking, right opinions and right inferences. And the same impression becomes even stronger when we read the description of 'inner and outer speech'.[2] Here Plato might literally be giving a commentary on *Sophist*, 263 E and *Theaetetus*, 189 E.

Theaetetus, 189 E: 'For it seems to me that thought is simply a conversation in which the soul asks questions of herself and makes answer, and says yes or no.' The following words are important: 'But when, attaining the goal either more slowly or more rapidly, she now makes one answer and is no longer in doubt, we call this her opinion (Δόξα).' We have not yet appealed to this for help in understanding the *Sophist*, but it is important, and the *Philebus* will presently give it new meaning.

Philebus, 38 C: 'Imagine that a man, looking from afar, sees some object not quite clearly—would you thus describe his state of mind, that he wishes to judge what is the thing he sees?—Yes, indeed.—Would he not now begin to ask certain questions of himself?—In what form?—'What can be the thing which appears to be standing beneath a tree beside the rock?' If such were the thing he saw, might he not ask this of himself?—Yes.— Might he not after this make the appropriate answer to himself,

---

[1] For the meaning, compare Διαγιγνώσκειν, ΔιειΔέναι, ΔιιΔεῖν, *Phaedrus*, 262 A, 277 B.

[2] 11 B: τὸ φρονεῖν καὶ τὸ νοεῖν καὶ μεμνῆσθαι καὶ τὰ τούτων αὖ συγγενῆ, Δόξαν τε ὀρθὴν καὶ ἀληθεῖς λογισμούς . . .

namely that it was a man?—Certainly.—Or again, he might go astray, and describe what he saw as an image made by some shepherds.' The examination of λόγος which follows is important for this reason, that it shows λόγος as dependent on Δόξα, the meaning of which has already been made clear, whereas in both the *Sophist* and *Theaetetus* this relationship is reversed. Since it is extremely difficult to make sure what the author means by such a word as λόγος, which one simply cannot follow through all its changes of meaning, it is a great advantage that λόγος appears here as a function of Δόξα, and not the reverse: (38 E) 'And if some one is with him, he gives expression by the voice to the words which he has spoken to himself; and thus what we formerly called judgement (Δόξα) becomes λόγος.—Just so.— But if he is alone, and considers this same thought within himself, often he goes on his way preserving the thought within him for a longer time.—Certainly.' These statements are now illustrated by the comparison of the soul to a book. Every reader is reminded of the waxen tablet in the *Theaetetus*; but there is a considerable difference between the two cases. In the *Theaetetus* no union between Δόξα and λόγος was yet possible, and this was why the attempt to determine true opinion proved a failure; but towards the end we were referred, in terms of optimism, to a form of λόγος which would solve all the difficulties. It is significant that the waxen tablet, a receptacle for mere 'impressions', has now, in the *Philebus*, become a book, in which λόγοι are written. Who writes these 'speeches'? 'Memory, coinciding with the impressions of the senses—and the experiences which this awakens.'[1] These παθήματα become in the next sentence a single 'experience', of which it is said that, if it writes truly, true opinion and true speech (λόγος) are formed.[2]

---

[1] 39 A: Ἡ μνήμη ταῖς αἰσθήσεσι συμπίπτουσα εἰς ταὐτὸν κἀκεῖνα ἃ περὶ ταῦτ' ἐστὶ τὰ παθήματα φαίνονταί μοι σχεδὸν οἷον γράφειν ἡμῶν ἐν ταῖς ψυχαῖς τότε λόγους.

[2] καὶ ὅταν μὲν ἀληθῆ γράφῃ [τοῦτο τὸ πάθημα], Δόξα τε ἀληθὴς καὶ λόγοι ἀπ' αὐτοῦ συμβαίνουσιν ἀληθεῖς ἐν ἡμῖν γιγνόμενοι· ψευδῆ Δ' ὅταν ὁ τοιοῦτος παρ' ἡμῖν γραμματεὺς γράφῃ, τἀναντία τοῖς ἀληθέσιν ἀπέβη. For the difficulties of the text, see Bury's commentary. That the πάθημα writes *actively* is necessarily implied in the context, in which αἴσθησις and μνήμη are now given an active part; moreover it is important to remember, especially in textual criticism, what difficulties a writer incurs when obliged to invent technical terms in his own language—and when perhaps, if his

Two results of this passage may be mentioned. On the one hand it is clear that, while Plato seems to give a psychological treatment of knowledge, he still makes as absolute a distinction between true and false opinion and λόγος as in the *Sophist* (Natorp, p. 322, thinks otherwise). On the other hand δόξα and λόγος are shown here as two aspects in a complex psychological experience (πάθημα), in which Plato singles out memory and sense-perception for special mention. In fact we are again confronted with the trio of related πάθη which were such a remarkable feature of the *Sophist* (λόγος, δόξα, and φαντασία, or αἴσθησις). The only difference is that perhaps in the *Philebus* a still more important part in constituting the object of knowledge (the sole concern of this passage) is assigned to αἴσθησις and μνήμη.[1]

Thereafter λόγος seems to diverge still further from our modern 'judgement'. It will be remembered that the notion of an image or copy (εἰκών) was of essential importance in the *Sophist*. It was the starting-point of the whole digression there; and upon it rested Plato's answer to the special problem of the Dialogue, the definition of the Sophist. In the *Philebus*, Plato wishes to show how λόγοι and copies are related. There is at work in the soul, besides the writer of λόγοι, a painter who produces 'images'. Images arise when we somehow visualize within our minds something which has formerly been an object of simple δόξα or λόγος; they can also be formed through the agency of other senses than sight (for ὁρᾶν in the Greek is used by zeugma to denote a general faculty of forming images).[2] The pictures of true opinions and 'sayings' are true, those of false ones are false: οὐκοῦν αἱ μὲν τῶν ἀληθῶν δοξῶν καὶ λόγων εἰκόνες ἀληθεῖς, αἱ δὲ τῶν ψευδῶν ψευδεῖς; Since the 'deceptive picture' plays such an essential part in the character given to the Sophist, this discussion in the *Philebus* is of vital importance.

---

artistic form demands it, he wishes to forget the terminology which is at his disposal for scholastic purposes. This may well explain the sometimes forced style of the late Dialogues; cf. what has been said above on ὅλων πολλῶν, *Sophist*, 253 D.

[1] Cf. ἡ μετὰ δόξης τε ὀρθῆς καὶ ἐπιστήμης ἡδονή, 38 A.

[2] *Philebus*, 39 B: Ὅταν ἀπ' ὄψεως ἤ τινος ἄλλης αἰσθήσεως τὰ τότε δοξαζόμενα καὶ λεγόμενα ἀπαγαγών τις τὰς τῶν δοξασθέντων καὶ λεχθέντων εἰκόνας ἐν αὐτῷ ὁρᾷ πως.

Clearly when he made such a surprising transition from the digression on μὴ ὄν to the Sophist's art, and when he examined the relation between αἴσθησις and φαντασία,[1] he had at the back of his mind the same views which are expounded at greater length in the *Philebus*. We here learn something which is indeed remarkable, viz. that there are εἰκόνες of λόγοι. On the assumption that λόγος meant judgement, it would be difficult to attach meaning to this idea. The 'pictures' are of an intuitive character—they are presented to the imagination. Δόξα, on the other hand, which by the account in the second part of the *Theaetetus* was still intuitive in nature, has now become quite separate from mental pictures or imagery. Does this mean that it is now equivalent to 'judgement'? If so, it can no more be represented in an imaginative picture than λόγος can, for such images, Plato has distinctly told us, are 'derived from, drawn away from (ἀπάγειν), sight or some other of the senses'. At all events Δόξα and λόγος stand here in the same close connexion as in the *Sophist*; once more the thought which they contain is distinctly said to be the same (τοῦτο ταὐτὸν πρὸς αὑτὸν Διανοούμενος), and there is only a very external trait to distinguish between them, viz. that, in λόγος, the inner speech is conveyed by the voice to another (*Philebus*, 38 E). In the *Philebus*, then, the meaning of Δόξα is no less 'logical' than in the *Sophist*, but it has come to include the λόγος within the soul, and nothing now remains over for the *specific* meaning of λόγος but audible speech.

The changing relation of Δόξα to λόγος.

Let us consider, with reference to this point, the various phases of Δόξα in the *Theaetetus*, *Sophist*, and *Philebus*. In the *Theaetetus* Δόξα does not yet include λόγος, and this is just the reason why every attempt to find the test of its truth or falsehood collapses; it is a 'subjective' imagination of what is simply particular; as such it eludes every objective criterion. In the *Sophist*, there is a fundamental emphasis on λόγος right from the beginning of the Dialogue proper. To the λόγος is opposed the mere name. The problem of definition, upon which the *Theaetetus* had come

[1] This was where our discussion of the *Sophist* came to an end.

to grief, is now solved; λόγος, in the sense of definition by the method of the division of concepts, is firmly established. Then, with a surprisingly matter-of-fact air, the problem of true and false Δόξα is declared to be solved, and consequently that of the truth and falsity of sense-impressions. Plato passes forthwith to the question of true and false *copies* of impressions, and with this the task of the Dialogue is concluded. The *Philebus* arranges the required terms in our proportion as follows: Δόξα and λόγος are opposed to αἴσθησις and μνήμη: the former denote an independent activity of the soul, the latter are two 'experiences' to which reference is made by this activity. Besides Δόξα and λόγος—which were both 'written' in the soul—'pictures' (εἰκόνες) are impressed upon it, which possess truth and falsity in the same degree as the Δόξαι and λόγοι which are their originals. The following argument extends the class of 'speeches and images in the soul' to include the future. It thus becomes possible for Plato to bring hopes and pleasures also into relation with the fundamental contrast of the *Sophist*—the contrast between true and false, 'being' and 'not-being'.

Classification of φύσει ὄντα *the aim of* Διαίρεσις

The key to the mystery is contained, as every one can see, in the precise relation of λόγος to Δόξα. That they are related is now a matter of course for Plato; but how? In the illustration from the *Philebus*, the traveller asks himself the question: 'What is the appearance yonder?' (τί ποτ' ἄρ' ἔστι τὸ . . . φανταζό-μενον; (38 c)). The *Theaetetus* too had, in anticipation, described Δόξα as a form of question and answer; and the fuller detail of the example in the *Philebus* makes this description clear. On the other hand the *Theaetetus*, with its notion of *determining* or *defining*, contributes something essential to the full explanation: ὅταν Δὲ ὁρίσασα, εἴτε βραΔύτερον εἴτε καὶ ὀξύτερον ἐπάξασα, τὸ αὐτὸ ἤΔη φῇ καὶ μὴ Διστά3η, Δόξαν ταύτην τίθεμεν αὐτῆς (190 A).

Instead of taking this example of an image mistaken in perception for a human being, let us consider one of the 'natural' entities, φύσει ὄντα. We know on the evidence of Aristotle that these came in the end to be the chief Ideas; and it was possible for a writer of comedy to single out this aspect of the Academy's activities: περὶ γὰρ φύσεως ἀφοριζόμενοι | Διεχώριζον ζῴων τε βίον | Δένδρων τε φύσιν λαχάνων τε γένη· | κᾆτ' ἐν τούτοις τὸν κολοκύντην | ἐξήταζον τίνος ἐστὶ γένους.[1] Such attempts to classify φύσει ὄντα plainly lie behind the Divisions given in the *Sophist* and *Statesman*. The definitions of some animals given in the *Statesman*, where they are arrived at by Διαίρεσις of the art of tending, show that a systematic zoology had already begun. May we not claim that, on our view of the evolution of the Idea in Plato, an answer to this problem of Δόξα in relation to λόγος lies ready to hand? Λόγος, wherever it appears in this discussion, is *definition*; this is the λόγος οὐσίας in the proper sense, a sense which it definitely receives at *Laws*, 895 D, where a firm distinction is drawn, quite in the spirit of the *Sophist*, between it and a name. A feature common to λέγειν and λόγος is that they require relation to a meaning; even in the sphere of ordinary conversation, λέγειν is 'to mean' (τί λέγεις;). Λόγος then is the concept; and its establishment is, for Plato, a great achievement in philosophy, which should be placed not at the beginning, but at the end of his development. But the visual or intuitive manner of thought survives, even when the earlier Idea has become a concept; the concept being inseparable from Δόξα, which is the 'imagination' of a particular and of its form (εἶδος). In the later phase—as in the earlier one, more typically 'Ideal', when ethics and mathematics provided the central objects—Plato continues to think of the universal as being represented intuitively in an individual.

The intuitive character of the εἶδος *survives*

The εἶδος was originally an ideal *picture*. And Plato continues to suppose that, in knowledge, certain independently existing objects are 'pictured' by the mind, in a vision or intuition. On turning to the study of nature, the department in which he began his work was that of biological types (εἴδη, γένη). Now even if he had wanted, when he practised classification, to suppress the pictorial and intuitive aspect of his thought (and it is hard to see

[1] Epicrates, quoted by Athenaeus, ii. 59 D.

why he should ever have had this intention), still in one way the method of Διαίρεσις must have *strengthened* the element of 'vision' (ἰδέα). It would remain in its true character at the two opposite poles, i.e. the most general and the most particular εἶδος. The intermediate classes had now secured some of those characteristics of the concept which a modern view would take for granted. To Plato these would appear as special activities of the εἶδος.

To take first the *single* most universal Being—a basic idea of Plato's metaphysics—the knowledge of this required a 'vision', in which it would be 'seen' to be the most 'real' of beings, as for Plato it actually was; or the most universal substance, showing the direct union of thought and existence which constitutes the type of all intuition. It is, as Kant observes, a characteristic of things intuited, in contrast to those which are conceived by reason, that variety is got out of them only by limitation. And this applies to Plato's intuition of the highest or most universal Being; he is confident that from it one may descend by systematic determination to the most particular of all beings—beings which admit of no division into 'species' or 'genus'. Hence with them the interest in definition ceases; we are face to face with an entirely new intuition, and with the question of its possibility.

As to the intermediate 'kinds', they also did not cease to be εἴδη. Obviously they possessed some of the functions of concepts—for example, the systematic subordination of lower to higher. And if Plato gave them a part which we find it very difficult to imagine, it was just *because* he inwardly still thought of them as Ideas. They were, he thought, *existent*, and yet only to be comprehended in reasoning (λογισμῷ). Reason, however, did not arbitrarily determine their nature, since this was founded on the higher εἴδη. They were intuited, they were 'original phenomena'; yet they were not empirical, and no immediate datum of sense was their counterpart. 'Patterns' in the strictest sense, they were able to enrich Plato's notion of form with new characteristics, without depriving it of the more essential of those which his earlier interests had given to it.

With the lowest or 'atomic' εἶδος, for which in particular the

method of Division had been designed, the vision of the mind
(εἶδος) had to be supplemented by one of the senses (αἴσθησις).
In the region of natural science, λόγος about the universal required the addition of Δόξα about the particular. It is of vital
importance for one who would understand the views of Plato
that he should make clear to himself how Plato must have
regarded the new development. Must it not, he may ask, have
been distressing to the author of the *Phaedo* to see his εἶδος
wandering into the suspicious vicinity of Δόξα and αἴσθησις?
Nothing could be more wrong than to come with such an expectation to the passages in question. On the contrary, he saw in this
meeting the supreme triumph of logical method, the definitive
solution by thought of the problem of 'participation'; he could
now say that the objects of αἴσθησις were subjected to thought,
the perpetual flux linked up with the intelligible Being of the
Ideas; yet not the least injury had been done to their purity, and
there was now no question of a 'separation'. In the perception
of the 'atomic form', λόγος was certainly reinforced by sense-
perception; but the credit for imparting *truth* to opinion or
αἴσθησις was to be ascribed entirely to λόγος. For this reason
Plato had again proved in the *Theaetetus*, as distinctly as possible,
that αἴσθησις and Δόξα are in themselves a-logical, and neither
can come into any relation with truth. The 'atomic form' had
been found 'in reasoning' (ἐν λόγοις). Αἴσθησις and Δόξα might
deal with the same object, but it was the mind's vision (εἶδος)
which determined truth and falsehood, Being and Not-Being.
It is, at least, only reflection on λόγος which makes it possible
to give an account of truth and falsehood; so that a new meaning
can now be given to the λόγον ἑκάστου Δυνατὸν εἶναι Δοῦναι
καὶ Δέξασθαι (*Statesman*, 286 A).[1] Λόγος οὐσίας now takes the
place of λόγος αἰτίας. The Socratic question about definition
had now at last been really answered. Yet it is no negligible
proof of the entire change in Plato's sphere of interest since the
Socratic Dialogues that now, when the proper method of definition has at last been found, Socrates is dismissed from the leading
part, and given such a modest role. The objects with which the

---

[1] Cf. *Laws*, 895 D: ἓν μὲν τὴν οὐσίαν, ἓν Δὲ τῆς οὐσίας τὸν λόγον, ἓν Δὲ ὄνομα.

young disciples of Socrates had been concerned of old were not capable of definition in the new sense; their place had been taken by an interest in the formation of natural 'types', but such an interest was foreign to the character of Socrates, now fixed in its outlines. Thus he could be made the exponent only of those views which it was possible to connect in some way with the Good, the basic principle of ethics; this was the constant term of reference of all 'inquiry into the cause', λόγος αἰτίας. But this connexion necessarily became looser as time went on. Certainly the Good had from the first been related to knowledge. But then came the development of a conscious theory of knowledge, and Plato found that the principle of teleology could be applied most precisely of all to objects which were entirely remote from the spirit of Socrates—to 'natural objects' (φύσει ὄντα) in the scientific sense of nature.

How far is Plato's theory of Δόξα *and* αἴσθησις *a Psychology?*

At this point we may refer to an axiom fundamental to our whole work; it is now fully plain that Plato never gave up his Socratic assumption that the road to knowledge lay ἐν λόγοις; what happened was that an alteration in the *objects* of his interest led to drastic changes in his means of exposition, i.e. in his method as a philosopher and an artist. He made these changes the more recklessly because, in the last analysis, he always remained true to himself. This is particularly clear at the point we have now reached. A new field of knowledge has been opened up: Plato, with astonishing freedom in regard to his own earlier opinions, has begun a fresh analysis of Δόξα and αἴσθησις and their relation to λόγος. These occupations lead him, though he himself is doubtless unaware of it as a change in method, to Psychology. The Greeks in their notion of Soul (ψυχή) united without distinction two aspects which recent philosophy has learnt to separate as 'mere consciousness' on the one hand, and 'the individual soul' on the other. When Plato's problems carried him in this direction, he formed the doctrine of the World-Soul; it shows the fundamental distance between the ancient and modern views of the Soul. If, then, the discussion upon which

Plato now embarks is termed psychological, it must be in the modern sense; to him the distinction is altogether inessential.

Plato is, at this point in his history as a thinker, trying to make two undoubted facts fit one another: on the one side the negative truth, established in the *Theaetetus*, that sense-perception and mere opinion cannot give rise to knowledge, and so cannot be characterized as false or true; and on the other side the fact that in certain cases mere vision may lead to immediate knowledge of the truth—in other words that we do not need *consciously* and discursively to apply a formula of definition, found by the rules of Division, in order to assign to its εἶδος some object from the realm of nature. After all, there is no doubt that one recognizes many objects for what they are at the first glance. And Plato achieves what, in view of the Psychology of his age, must be con- sidered a remarkable feat: he exposes the discursive method hidden in those inner processes of thought, of which we should say in modern terms that they operate 'behind the threshold of consciousness'. The example quoted from the *Philebus* has shown us how he would bring reflection into our experience of a parti- cular (τόδε τι). By emphasizing the man's distance from the object he is judging, Plato seeks, it should be noticed, to explain the fact of hesitation—he prolongs the process of forming an opinion, in order to bring to full consciousness the dialogue within the soul. In any more complicated case, e.g. in some properly scientific problem, there is no necessity to emphasize the separate stages by which concepts are formed and the εἶδος discovered. They occur automatically in the exercise of Division. Thus Plato comes to see that there is a λόγος immanent within every *true* opinion. But the readiness with which, by the middle term of Διάνοια, he comes to the conclusion that Δόξα and λόγος are completely identical in their content, suggests some more pro- found affinity between them. What was this? In order to dis- cover the historical truth about Plato's notion of λόγος, we must form some estimate of it.

Is Δόξα judgement or imagination?

Our earlier study of the *Theaetetus* had already brought us to this point. At the beginning of the last section of all, the notion of λόξα seemed to waver between judgement and 'imagination', wherein an object is presented to our intuition. Evidently it meant now the one and now the other. The fact is that Plato knows two quite different species of λόξα, and at one time gives this name to something incapable of verification, at another to the λόξα, now verified, which accompanies λόγος. Nevertheless, he must see a much nearer relation between the two species than the translations 'judgement' and 'imagination' suggest; and we have to find a place for λόγος as a third term in the comparison. All these elements, and another which is presently added to them, the εἴδωλον, are in reality different aspects of one thing, i.e. of the single, although highly complex, mode of all Platonic thought, the ἰδέα or intuition. Plato gradually becomes aware of its constitutive elements in their separate nature; but he never succeeds in finding a point outside the complex whole from which he can contemplate it at leisure. Thinking, in terms of the earlier theory of Ideas, had always taken the form of a vision of something determinate in its content, and the key to the new notion of knowledge, as to the old, is the presence of the universal in the particular. (This we have often stressed.) Strong expression is found for this in the statement that the object is visible, although with a new kind of vision. Plato is determined that his new object, which is given to the senses and grasped by αἴσθησις, shall not only be known, but also 'seen' (by the mind) like the earlier Idea. Since, however, it is also visible in the ordinary sense, he naturally finds it a difficult task to define the new 'vision'. For what exactly is the new object? Is it the lowest εἴδος, which cannot be further divided, or is it the sensible thing subordinated to this εἴδος? In a particular scientific problem, can this distinction be made? We must answer yes and no; there are here problems of a most difficult kind, to which modern philosophers are to-day returning in all seriousness. An example may clear up the point which is at issue—With what object are the Academicians dealing in the fragment of Epicrates, when they practise definition on the pumpkin? Are they concerned with *this* pumpkin, or with the εἴδος, the pumpkin in general? Surely

Plato's new notion of 'being' teaches us that the particular only *is* in so far as it is *this*; and to be *this* means to have, or to fall under, this εἶδος. Otherwise it is quite impossible to grasp the object, and even αἴσθησις can only do so in a spurious way. Until we have discovered how the εἶδος and the sensible particular are correlated, the latter remains unknowable; it is not 'one', but 'indefinite' (ἄπειρον). (More will be heard of this in a later reference to the *Philebus*.) If, then, Plato admitted knowledge of particulars to be possible at all—and he was undeniably the founder of the science of nature—it must have been through their close connexion with the εἶδος. And yet it was, in the end, the particular object which was known!

Hence, whereas λόγος comprehends the εἶδος in a systematic definition, δόξα knows the particular object inasmuch as it falls under an εἶδος, and constitutes it in its determinate nature as this or that; but δόξα is likewise—and this is the critical point— the 'end of the thinking process', ἀποτελεύτησις Διανοίας, and, as such, shows how it is possible to 'present' to our minds as a single intuited whole the same λόγος or concept which was formerly a discursive definition. Plato's whole manner of thinking renders this an extremely important point, so much so that when δόξα is *true*, i.e. determined in the way just described, he makes it co-ordinate with the discursive λόγος, and goes so far as to obliterate all difference between them except one of audible expression.

Plato, then, seems to have known that in order to grasp a thing's definition or essence, several distinct acts of thought are required. But it is not this, it is not the power of judgement, that he accentuates; he emphasizes the need for an immediate *vision* of the essence, a 'true presentation' (ἀληθὴς δόξα). Plato still feels an urge towards intuition; the gradual operations of reflection are made to take second place behind the 'ending to the process of thought' (i.e. δόξα), which finally answers the question raised within the soul, Is it this or that? The same question may be stated in terms of the scheme of 'division', which guides Plato throughout his discussion: Which ὄντα must be comprised in a unity to make an 'atomic form'? Such a form is the final ὄν, since it is a 'this', and in it the unity can be 'viewed' by the mind.

Plato's method has a real, not a formal purpose

We have consistently maintained so far that the purpose of Plato's later thought was not really the analysis of judgement, but definition, and, what is more, definition in the sense of immediate knowledge of some Being in its full concreteness. This view has made it possible to explain, and to reconcile among themselves, various contradictions and peculiarities. But the *Sophist* may seem to offer a serious objection to this on account of its first definition of λόγος as a combination of nouns with verbs (ὀνόματα, ῥήματα). And surely the examples which follow ('Theaetetus is seated', 'Theaetetus flies') seem to make it quite clear that Plato is thinking of judgement? But there are certain undeniable facts which we must be careful to bear in mind here: In Plato's day the distinction between ὄνομα and ῥῆμα, in their grammatical sense, was not yet finally settled.[1] Ῥῆμα means any kind of assertion, ὄνομα that of which an assertion is made; there is no idea either of the distinction between subject and predicate, or of that between substantive and verb. Thus Plato, a short time before, had used ῥῆμα of Not-Being (*Sophist*, 257 B), and at *Timaeus*, 49 E, he uses it of τόδε and τοῦτο. There could be no clearer indication of the wide extension of its use. The ὄνομα merely names the subject, the ῥῆμα tells us something about it. If it had been Plato's meaning that all judgement presupposes the union of a substantive with a verb, in the modern sense, he would certainly not in an earlier context (251 A) have tried to answer the question of Antisthenes, whether 'man' and 'Good' can be combined; it is worth noticing how generally he had there introduced the idea of predication:

Λέγομεν ἄνθρωπον δήπου πόλλ' ἄττα ἐπονομάζοντες, τά τε χρώματα ἐπιφέροντες αὐτῷ καὶ τὰ σχήματα καὶ μεγέθη καὶ κακίας καὶ ἀρετάς, ἐν οἶς πᾶσι καὶ ἑτέροις μυρίοις οὐ μόνον ἄνθρωπον αὐτὸν εἶναί φαμεν, ἀλλὰ καὶ

[1] Steinthal, *Gesch. der Sprachwissenschaft bei den Griechen und Römern* (Berlin, 1863), 133 foll.

ἀγαθὸν καὶ ἕτερα ἄπειρα, καὶ τἆλλα δὴ κατὰ τὸν αὐτὸν λόγον οὕτως ἓν
ἕκαστον ὑποθέμενοι πάλιν αὐτὸ πολλὰ καὶ πολλοῖς ὀνόμασι λέγομεν.

But we are obliged to go still further. What sense can there be
in the idea, which is fundamental to the whole Dialogue, of a
combination of 'kinds' (κοινωνία τῶν γενῶν) in the judgement?
'Do *verbs* have Ideas at all?' asks Apelt, and, assuming the usual
interpretation of λόγος, his question is the right one. He is
compelled to answer 'no'. This, then, is the end of the elaborate
doctrine of a κοινωνία τῶν γενῶν—in order to form a judgement,
we need to connect something with an εἶδος which does not exist!
Plainly this cannot be Plato's meaning. Therefore what the
definition of λόγος really shows is that he has no clear notion
of the grammatical verb. Not only is this want of clearness a
feature of ancient thought, but it is also deeply rooted in the
problems with which it was concerned. Is existence a substantive or a verb? Reinhardt (*Parmenides*, 252) appropriately reminds us of the Greek fondness for using a neuter adjective as a
substantive, which has the effect of turning every 'expression'
(ῥῆμα) into a subject. Who can be sure of the difference between
τὸ ἔστι, τὸ ὄν, and τὸ εἶναι in Plato, and even between these and
οὐσία? or κίνησις and τὸ κινεῖσθαι? This brings us back on to
the ground of definition. In a definition a name is combined
with assertions or ῥήματα which might equally find expression
in activities, or be changed by the Greek language, with its
unlimited pliability, into another verbal form, such as κτητική,
μεταβλητική.

The distinction between true and false Δόξα *depends on* Διαίρεσις

The judgement that 'Theaetetus is flying' is false because it
cannot be reconciled with the definition (λόγος οὐσίας) of man,
and attaches to him a μὴ ὄν—a quality from the wrong side of
the Division. The example sounds grotesque; but in order to
see how the assertion and denial here are related to ὄν and μὴ ὄν
respectively, we have to bear in mind the much-ridiculed definition of man as a being without wings, living on land, &c. Whether
the statement concerns the existence of man or one of his activities, is not the main question here. The point is whether the

classes 'man' and 'winged' admit of connexion with each other. The analysis of a thing's essence in 'judgement', showing what predicates it contains, is for Plato a secondary process. The vital thing to him is not the empty form of judgement, but the fact that Διαίρεσις has been proved to give us, by its discovery of class-relationships, a fixed point to which possible true and false judgements can be related.

What does Plato mean at 262 A when he describes each assertion made about the 'name' as a πρᾶξις? This inaccuracy depends on the shifting character of grammatical terms, which we must trace out as best we can. Πράττειν also varies in meaning and can easily denote a *state*; this appears at once from the phrases already discussed in another connexion, εὖ and κακῶς πράττειν. Underlying these changes, there is, no doubt, the original sense of the word as 'to go through with'; Homer's πρήσσειν means 'accomplish a journey'. In view of this original sense, Plato can go further and connect πράττειν with περαίνειν, 262 D. Δηλοῖ γὰρ (ὁ λόγος) ἤδη που τότε περὶ τῶν ὄντων ἢ γιγνο-μένων ἢ γεγονότων ἢ μελλόντων, καὶ οὐκ ὀνομάζει μόνον ἀλλά τι περαίνει, συμπλέκων τὰ ῥήματα τοῖς ὀνόμασι. Πρᾶξις in such a case must be taken to mean 'bringing to fulfilment'. I will mention, merely in passing, that ποιεῖν and πάσχειν in the *Sophist* (247 E) are technical terms with their entire fullness of meaning; for Plato considers that being an object of knowledge is a πάσχειν! Πρᾶξις also, then, must not be taken too strictly and literally.

Why, it may be asked, did Plato ever embrace a definition of λόγος which was liable to so much misunderstanding, and which could surely not demonstrate the truth or falsity of a given λόγος? For this also an explanation may be suggested. In giving his account of κοινωνία, Plato had kept in view the example of letters, some of which can, and others cannot, be combined with each other, whilst a third class, the vowels, runs through them all like a thread (253 A). It was natural in considering the higher grammatical forms, which are even more directly connected with λόγος, to try to find some parallel to this. Because the categories of his day are not sufficiently clear, Plato ends by formulating the task of λόγος in a way which seems far too narrow if modern terminology is introduced,[1] but is extremely wide, and indeed unlimited, if we think what the terms meant in his day. He then at least tries to remove the indefiniteness by a few practical examples, which are merely intended to make some distinctions among words themselves in respect of the possibility of connexion. This distinction has no bearing on his central purpose of deciding whether a λόγος is true or false. This is shown by the fact that it had already been suggested in the *Theaetetus* (206 D) that speech was constituted by the union of ὀνόματα and ῥήματα. In order to accomplish this main purpose, Plato returns to the device of connexion with 'being' and 'not-being'—returns, in fact, to the same idea of Definition which we have been finding everywhere beneath the surface in his later Dialectic.

Such contributions, then, as are made to the theory of judgement in the *Sophist* are elementary in character, and are secondary to Plato's pursuit of his main object. But in saying this, we must not forget to notice that the problems of judgement and definition really are related. As we said at the very beginning, it is true that, in the act of judgement, the Idea performs the same service as a concept—but this does not mean that Plato ever regards it as the proper essence of an Idea to be a mere instrument of logical method. This use of the Idea is well brought out in the term ἐπισφραγίζεσθαι, 'to place a seal upon'; now this is said equally of the Idea in the *Phaedo* and of Definition in the *Statesman* (258 c); so that in this point, at least, Plato's development has altered nothing. It remains Plato's purpose to convert the concept into an Idea *intuited* by the mind and so 'fix' it. (This expression of Rickert's was mentioned at the beginning.) In the *Sophist* the Ideas seem to lose their Eleatic rigidity, and to descend into the flux. But Plato's intention

---

[1] The distinction between ὄνομα and ῥῆμα as substantive and verb respectively is very far from being a settled fact in Aristotle also; but it would lead us too far from our purpose to prove that the above remarks apply equally to him. For the interpretation of λόγος as definition, cf. the philosophical digression in Plato's Seventh Letter, a passage which it is easier to disparage than to understand. We hear of λόγος (which, by the context, must undoubtedly be definition) ἐξ ὀνομάτων καὶ ῥημάτων συγκείμενος (342 B). Some light is shed on the 'copy' mentioned in this place by the *Sophist, Statesman,* and *Philebus;* cf. also *Laws,* 897 E.

remains the same as before: to reach the essence of things, ἐφάπτεσθαι τῶν ὄντων—to secure, once and for all, a hold on reality. The statement that 'life and movement' must pertain to Being signifies that they are qualities pertaining to Being as subject, not 'that Being is constituted by our mind' (Natorp).

Εἴδωλον, εἰκών and φαντασία.

Yet another factor in the notion and definition of the Sophist— the image (εἴδωλον)—provides fresh evidence that the Idea is an *object* which we *intuit*. Εἴδωλα played a part in the *Philebus* passage which we discussed earlier. Since there had been a *rapprochement* between Δόξα and λόγος, the factor of intuition or appearance had been wanting from Plato's scheme. The vacant place was filled by εἰκόνες or εἴδωλα. They give us further evidence that the Greek mode of thought was strongly visual; and just because Plato's interest is now directed upon objects of such a different character, they occupy a place of the highest importance. Recognition of the fact that the soul could create images of its own accord was bound to confirm Plato in his belief that sensation could never be an independent source of knowledge. This is why φαντασία can refer either to the 'appearance' of present sensation (264 A) or to memory-images, and to the imagination of fear and hope which relates to the future (*Philebus*, 39 c foll.). Entirely in agreement with this, we are told that the images and phantasms (εἰκόνες, εἴδωλα) of imagination are not copies of sensations, but of judgements and statements (Δόξαι, λόγοι, *Philebus*, 39 b); or it is from these, at least, that they first receive the character of truth and falsehood. This is, in my view, a new and highly important proof that λόγος (to say nothing of Δόξα) has to some extent inherited the character of a mental intuition from the earlier εἶδος. Knowledge is still supposed to depend on an original 'vision' of the mind, and although λόγος undoubtedly represents its purely logical side, the true and false 'phantasms' provide an element of intuition, and thus restore the balance. Only in this way can subject and object—knowledge on the one side, the εἶδος on the other—be made to correspond. And this completes and rounds off the definition of the

Sophist, which started with the distinction between true and false copies. Our recent sketch has shown us the intimate connexion between αἴσθησις and εἴδωλον, and this finds expression in the word φαντασία at 264 A. Within the digression, it seems to be merely identical with αἴσθησις, but immediately afterwards the qualities of the Sophist are put together, and he is finally defined as an author of deceptive images. It is evident from this that Plato's notion of φαντασία includes, without distinguishing, two factors, two ways of intuiting a particular—namely sense-perception and appearance as a mental image.

Knowledge of the μέγιστα εἴδη *is the ultimate object of* Διαίρεσις (*'Statesman', 285 D*)

In order to confirm this last point once more, and at the same time to advance from the particular question of Δόξα to some wider problems, we may conveniently consult a passage from the *Statesman* (285 D), to which a brief reference has already been made. This passage will show that we have been justified in giving so large a place in this exposition to Δόξα, to the 'atomic form', and to the method of inquiry whereby this form is discovered.

Plato is engaged in illustrating the method of Division (285 B), and its value is made to depend on the improvement of our skill in Dialectic (285 D), just as it was in the *Sophist*. The question may be raised whether such practical illustrations of Division as we have seen are seriously supposed to have this value; and to this a sufficient answer is given at the opening of our passage: 'Surely no sensible man would wish to investigate the definition of the art of weaving for its own sake.' And Plato announces that the objects upon which Division is practised are of two kinds. The first kind consists of those which can be shown to an inquirer in 'perceptible resemblances' (αἰσθητικαί is the traditional reading, but the slight change to αἰσθηταί is obviously required). No special procedure is required; and the person who 'demands an account' (λόγον) can be satisfied χωρὶς λόγου: ἀλλ' οἶμαι τοὺς πλείστους λέληθεν ὅτι τοῖς μὲν τῶν ὄντων ῥᾳδίως καταμαθεῖν αἰσθηταί τινες ὁμοιότητες πεφύκασιν, ἃς οὐδὲν

132 METHOD OF DIALECTIC

χαλεπὸν Δηλοῦν, ὅταν αὐτῶν τις βουληθῇ τῷ λόγον αἰτοῦντι περί του μὴ μετὰ πραγμάτων ἀλλὰ χωρὶς λόγου ῥᾳδίως ἐνδείξασθαι. How the resemblance (ὁμοιότης) here is to be understood we learn from 285 B just above: πρὶν ἂν ἐν αὐτῇ τὰς Διαφορὰς ἴδη πάσας ὁπόσαιπερ ἐν εἴδεσι κεῖνται, τὰς Δὲ αὖ παντοδαπὰς ἀνομοιότητας, ὅταν ἐν πλήθεσιν ὀφθῶσιν, μὴ Δυνατὸν εἶναι Δυσωπούμενον παύεσθαι πρὶν ἂν σύμπαντα τὰ οἰκεῖα ἐντὸς μιᾶς ὁμοιότητος ἔρξας γένους τινὸς οὐσίᾳ περιβάληται.

The 'resemblance', therefore, is in reality the same as the εἶδος, except that it is visible (αἰσθητή). After our recent inquiry we can already guess thát it is the phantasm (εἴδωλον, elsewhere called εἰκών) corresponding to 'sensation'.

We find this view confirmed when we turn to the second kind of objects of Division. These are the greatest and most honourable and beautiful ὄντα, of which there is no obvious 'copy' suited to human comprehension: τοῖς Δ' αὖ μεγίστοις οὖσι καὶ τιμιωτάτοις οὐκ ἔστιν εἴδωλον οὐδὲν πρὸς τοὺς ἀνθρώπους εἰργασμένον ἐναργῶς, οὗ Δειχθέντος τὴν τοῦ πυνθανομένου ψυχὴν ὁ βουλόμενος ἀποπληρῶσαι, πρὸς τῶν αἰσθήσεών τινα προσαρμόττων, ἱκανῶς πληρώσει (tr. 'by showing which he who would satisfy—lit. fill—the soul of an inquirer may do so sufficiently, adapting the image to the sense-perception'). We see from a very similar description at Theaetetus, 194 A, 193 C, what it is that Plato intends by πρὸς τῶν αἰσθήσεών τινα προσαρμόττειν. The idea is that of superimposing one surface upon another.

From the distinction of objects into these two kinds, the following inference is drawn: we need to practise the art of rendering an account of everything, for the greatest and most beautiful realities are incorporeal, and only λόγος can reveal them. But it is with such objects that we are concerned. They determine the correctness of Διαίρεσις; and also in order to establish the 'atomic form', we propose to descend to it by stages of pure thought from the highest εἶδος. Διὸ Δεῖ μελετᾶν λόγον ἑκάστου Δυνατὸν εἶναι Δοῦναι καὶ Δέξασθαι· τὰ γὰρ ἀσώματα, κάλλιστα ὄντα καὶ μέγιστα, λόγῳ μόνον ἄλλῳ Δὲ οὐδενὶ σαφῶς Δείκνυται, τούτων Δὲ ἕνεκα πάντ' ἐστὶ τὰ νῦν λεγόμενα. ῥάων Δ' ἐν τοῖς ἐλάττοσιν ἡ μελέτη παντὸς πέρι μᾶλλον ἢ περὶ τὰ μείζω.

Whilst this passage gives notable confirmation to the 'affinity' between αἴσθησις and εἴδωλον, δόξα and λόγος, which we described, it, on its side, would be scarcely intelligible without our earlier remarks; how, for instance, could one understand the striking contradiction that one who demands λόγος may be satisfied without λόγος? The universal itself is only intelligible through λόγος, but given Plato's fondness for a visual type of thought, it follows at once that he will choose to *represent* the universal in a particular, and this can be 'imagined'; hence it is possible to show or indicate the object which is required without any operations of Dialectic (δηλοῦν, ἐνδείξασθαι, μὴ μετὰ πραγμάτων), by applying its image to a sense-perception, until the one covers the other. And this may mean either that a true 'phantasm' or true 'judgement' is to be brought into being by reference to a true sense-perception, or conversely that a momentary perception is to be raised to a higher degree of clarity, distinctness, and truth; in the latter case there will be a kind of apperception founded upon memory—the remembrance by the Soul of earlier perceptions, imaginations, and λόγοι. As our sketch has shown, Plato's psychological views are peculiarly *a priori*, and it makes no appreciable difference to him on which side of the act of knowledge the stress is laid, for he does not consider it possible that sense-perception can ever be a *source* of knowledge.

Thus the same objects may be dealt with in two ways: they may be represented in a perceptible 'copy', but they may likewise be investigated by a logical method—and in the present context this method can only be the διαίρεσις by which visible objects are 'verified'. (Plato is discussing the Definition of weaving, and immediately before this he has extolled the procedure of Division.) We are instructed to practise this method upon simple objects with a view to the μέγιστα, τιμιώτατα, ἀσώματα and κάλλιστα which have been named. A more definite term for these objects (εἴδη for instance) is not forthcoming, and it is easy to see why—for εἴδη are *always* 'incorporeal', even the εἴδη of things which admit of 'images'. These objects are the μέγιστα εἴδη which we know from the *Sophist*—μέγιστα is twice repeated;

they are, in general, all higher εἴδη which must essentially direct our minds above the sphere of αἴσθησις. We are precluded by 285 E from thinking of such objects as the Statesman, for even here the importance of method prevails over that of the object.

VIII. ΔΙΑΙΡΕΣΙΣ, IDEAS AND PARTICULARS

Διαίρεσις and the self-subsistence of the Idea

A DIRECT result of this study of Διαίρεσις—and one to which we had involuntarily been led in our earlier discussions[1]—is that when Plato has to deal with a case of 'participation' (κοινωνία) he always thinks of the logical relationships found through Διαίρεσις, even though the κοινωνία is of a remote and metaphysical kind, as with the inclusion of Rest and Motion under Being. The fundamental type of *all* κοινωνία is the subordination of species to genus, and the blend of characteristics to constitute a definition which follows directly from it. Thus that 'Motion and Rest *are*' means to Plato that Being is a higher genus under which they fall (*Sophist*, 250 B). Τρίτον ἄρα τι παρὰ ταῦτα τὸ ὂν ἐν τῇ ψυχῇ τιθείς, ὡς ὑπ' ἐκείνου τήν τε στάσιν καὶ τὴν κίνησιν περιεχομένην, συλλαβὼν καὶ ἀπιδὼν αὐτῶν πρὸς τὴν τῆς οὐσίας κοινωνίαν, οὕτως εἶναι προσεῖπας ἀμφότερα; This brings us back to another of the four problems which were a consequence of the evolution of the Platonic doctrine.

The central problem was that of Δόξα; and in discussing it we have had to anticipate the most vital point—the relation of 'being' to 'not-being'. We have now to show more generally that the whole notion of 'being' is dependent on the new dialectical method. The quotation just given from the *Sophist* contains the fundamental fact: 'being' is now thought of as a supreme genus holding together all the other γένη (cf. *Sophist*, 253 B, C), and all things *are* only because they fall under this genus and are comprehended by it. Upon this foundation Plato's Ontology is built; it is, therefore, a direct consequence of his intuitive and objective mode of thought. 'By the predicate of being', says Sigwart, 'nothing is added to the content of an idea as such; the possibility of existential judgement rests on the fact that one may be aware of the same content in either of two forms—as merely imagined, or as presented.' It is because Plato thinks intuitively

[1] See especially that of τὸ μὴ ὄν, pp. 89 and 109 foll.

that he believes he can reach 'being', by inference from concepts, if only he can use Διαίρεσις to secure an unbroken chain leading from the most general Being to the 'atomic form'. We had occasion before, in alluding to Aristotle's criticism of Division, to consider Plato's view of this: he believes that, with every advance in Division, some particular concrete 'being', with an accompanying 'not-being', is constituted by mere logic.

Now Being, in this sense of a generic concept[1] including all the particular forms of being, is neither (1) the being of predication —for it does not provide a link, as the copula does, between the various lower kinds and *subjects*; it is indeed directly contained in these particular determinations, as 'art' is contained in 'art of angling'; nor (2) is it equivalent to mere existing; it is the generic concept of a species of concepts which can easily be transformed into definite existential judgements, because to Plato every operation of thought is an intuition of an object. We find confirmation of this intuitive tendency if we study *Sophist*, 255 B. In this difficult passage, Plato refuses to identify 'being' and 'the same', although the whole Dialogue is founded on the view that 'not-being' coincides with 'the other'. Everything here depends on our understanding 'the same' in the exact sense intended by Plato; if we understand it as *identical*, he would indeed be wrong to dissociate it from 'being': Natorp says that 'Everything that is, is in reality identical with itself', but Plato argues quite differently—he says that if they were equated, all things would be 'the same' (255 B). He appears, then, to understand ταὐτόν here as *equal*. For him the two meanings really coincide. 'To be' means to be an εἶδος. To be, then, is to have a definite character 'this or that', as we often discovered whilst we were analysing Δόξα. Plato can therefore say that everything *is* 'the same' as itself, and yet not be thinking of identity—it is only the possibility of its being in 'this or that' form, through the εἶδος, that he has in mind. If 'identical' were the meaning, we should have to think of 'being' as a concept secured by judgement, but Plato

---

[1] We are entitled to say 'concept', because we are here only concerned with the later Idea on its conceptual side, in so far as it is a member of an ordered class. Plato retains his metaphysical doctrine, and the Idea is never a mere concept.

only recognizes 'being' in some concrete form, in which it can be intuited; and given this supposition, the notion of identity must logically be fused with that of equality. It is at this same point that Διαίρεσις comes to an end; for Plato's interest, in this connexion at least, does not extend further than the 'atomic form'. If we take 'identity' in the strictest logical sense, it assumes that there is a concept of the particular object; but this is wanting in Plato's scheme. As we have now said many times, 'being' does not begin until a thing falls under some εἶδος, and thereby 'is' this or that form. When something is said to be equal, Plato at once associates this statement with the εἶδος in his mind at the time,[1] hence 'equal' is a 'narrower' concept than 'being'; being includes *all* the ways of being equal, or, to think in terms of the εἶδος: all the ways of being self-identical. That which is equal to itself '*is*'—falls under the generic concept of being; but that which 'is' is not necessarily equal to itself.[2] This may be proved by conversion; everything which is not 'this'—i.e. some εἶδος—must be 'the other'. Upon this Plato's theory of true and false assertion and denial was founded.

The problems of μέθεξις *and of the One and the Many*

To turn now to our two remaining problems: how, in the end, did Plato think that the method of Division helped him to over-

---

[1] We shall return to this problem later, in casting a rapid glance at the Aristotelian system. Apelt rightly raises the objection that Plato, in his doctrine of 'being' and 'not-being', has not explained the existence of judgements proper, but only of ' formulae of comparison'. From our standpoint we can offer this solution: Plato's Διαίρεσις does in fact enable him to discover relationships of class inclusion, but since he is seeking to define, and to define the 'atomic form', there is no need for him to consider the difference of judgements according to quantity. It does not matter whether it is *the* angler, or all anglers or some anglers, who have the qualities enumerated—this difference is foreign to Plato's particular problem of definition. It is always *the* angler as one of a class, the particular as representative of the universal, that Plato has in mind. If Plato had not prepared the way, Aristotle, lacking that visible display of the range and meaning of concepts which a Διαίρεσις gives, could never have brought his doctrine of the syllogism to such perfection; even his examples, which so often arise from Διαιρέσεις in the Platonic Dialogues, give evidence of this continuity.

[2] It would be a special task, and one worth undertaking, to consider from the point here reached the proper sense of ὅμοιον, and its change of meaning. This would be a considerable help in our understanding of the Eleatic notion of Being (*Parmenides*, 127 E).

come the problems of μέθεξις, and of the One and the Many? The *Philebus* answers this question very clearly. It is the function of this Dialogue to solve the problems stated in the *Parmenides* with the help of the doctrines of the *Sophist*. It has been the custom in interpreting the earliest Dialogues to read all the later problems into them, when the truth is that they were only there potentially. Reference to 'the One and the Many' is thus found as early as the *Euthyphro*, and it is forgotten that the essential thing is the emphasis, the manner in which the question is actually asked. To take the example from the *Euthyphro*: Plato is interested in the Idea of 'the pious itself', the cause of all piety in other things, whereas Euthyphro, in the manner typical of the early Dialogues, mentions a few of the many pious acts. Does this give the least indication that Plato sees any difficulty whatever in the participation of many things in One? A clearer instance of this contrast is in the *Meno*, where indeed the terms One and Many themselves occur: παῦσαι πολλὰ ποιῶν ἐκ τοῦ ἑνός, 77 A, and, later in the Dialogue, we are even warned against 'breaking up Virtue into fragments', μὴ καταγνύναι μηΔὲ κερματίζειν τὴν ἀρετήν, 79 A. However, Plato as yet looks only in one direction—towards unity; and he never raises the question how the 'many' instances receive their character from the one εἶΔος, e.g. that of piety. We saw above how the earlier Dialectic, owing to its essential nature, must aim at unity.

What a difference there is between the method of Socrates there and in the *Philebus*! Here it is Socrates who points out, and insists upon, the great diversity of pleasures, and Protarchus replies to him: 'Surely a thing must be most like itself, and pleasure must be of all things most like to pleasure?' (12 D):

πῶς γὰρ ἡΔονῇ γε ἡΔονὴ [μὴ] οὐχ ὁμοιότατον ἂν εἴη, τοῦτο αὐτὸ ἑαυτῷ, πάντων χρημάτων;

And Socrates answers: Καὶ γὰρ χρῶμα, ὦ Δαιμόνιε, χρώματι· κατά γε αὐτὸ τοῦτο οὐΔὲν Διοίσει τὸ χρῶμα εἶναι πᾶν, τό γε μὴν μέλαν τῷ λευκῷ πάντες γιγνώσκομεν ὡς πρὸς τῷ Διάφορον εἶναι καὶ ἐναντιώτατον ὂν τυγχάνει. καὶ Δὴ καὶ σχῆμα σχήματι κατὰ ταὐτόν· γένει μέν ἐστι πᾶν ἕν, τὰ Δὲ μέρη τοῖς μέρεσιν αὐτοῦ τὰ μὲν ἐναντιώτατα ἀλλήλοις, τὰ Δὲ Διαφορότητ' ἔχοντα μυρίαν που τυγχάνει, καὶ πολλὰ ἕτερα οὕτως ἔχονθ' εὑρήσομεν. ὥστε τούτῳ γε τῷ λόγῳ μὴ πίστευε, τῷ πάντα τὰ ἐναντιώτατα ἐν ποιοῦντι. φοβοῦμαι δὲ μή τινας ἡδονὰς ἡδοναῖς εὑρήσομεν ἐναντίας.

Exactly the same examples, colour and shape, had been used by Socrates in the *Meno* (73 E, 74 C), but with an opposite intention. Instead of contrasting their species, he had formed them into a unity. 'Perhaps in the *Philebus* we have an exception, arising from the special nature of the subject, pleasure.' But this is disproved by Plato's method (and by the results he reaches) in the remainder of the Dialogue. He has travelled far from the point of view of *Republic*, 505 C, where the bare fact that pleasures are both good and bad, and that therefore pleasure belongs to the changing world (τὰ μεταπίπτοντα), suffices to condemn it. And more: the same treatment is at once extended to varieties of knowledge (13 E). We know from the *Sophist* and *Statesman*, and from Plato's very similar expressions in *Phaedrus*, 262 A, that it is the special task of Διαίρεσις to recognize the finer shades of 'difference' and 'similarity' in a thing before we decide to discard it root and branch.

Having shown in the *Philebus* the need for a Διαίρεσις of pleasures, Plato is definitely faced with the problem of the One and the Many; and once more he gives a clear outline of the position of the *Parmenides*, which we already know. He says he is not thinking of the 'hackneyed paradoxes concerning the One and the Many' (τὰ δεδημευμένα τῶν θαυμαστῶν περὶ τὸ ἓν καὶ πολλά, 14 D)—the paradox, for instance, that Protarchus may be both one and many, both great and small—although this was the meaning first attached by the young Socrates to Parmenides' doctrine in the Dialogue called by his name; the serious problem is whether ideal unities themselves have 'many' aspects: ὅταν δέ τις ἕνα ἄνθρωπον ἐπιχειρῇ τίθεσθαι καὶ βοῦν ἕνα καὶ τὸ καλὸν ἓν καὶ τὸ ἀγαθὸν ἕν, περὶ τούτων τῶν ἑνάδων καὶ τῶν τοιούτων ἡ πολλὴ σπουδὴ μετὰ Διαιρέσεως ἀμφισβήτησις γίγνεται. Notice here, first that there is a definite allusion to the important part of Διαίρεσις in this question of the One and the Many, and secondly the wide range of εἴδη, as shown by the instances; there is a contrast with *Parmenides*, 130 C, where the assumption of an εἶδος of Man still seemed unsafe.

The two resulting problems are clearly indicated: Are we justified in assuming such 'unities' at all? (This problem is expressed in a phrase which is probably corrupt; ὅμως is doubtful.) And how are the difficulties of 'participation', or of χωρισμός, to be explained? The latter problem is eventually identified with that of the One and the Many, as it is in the closely parallel passage, *Parmenides*, 131 A.

Πρῶτον μὲν εἴ τινας 2εῖ τοιαύτας εἶναι μονά2ας ὑπολαμβάνειν ἀληθῶς οὔσας· εἶτα πῶς αὖ ταύτας, μίαν ἑκάστην οὖσαν ἀεὶ τὴν αὐτὴν καὶ μήτε γένεσιν μήτε ὄλεθρον προσ2εχομένην, ὅμως εἶναι βεβαιότατα μίαν ταύτην; μετὰ 2ὲ τοῦτ' ἐν τοῖς γιγνομένοις αὖ καὶ ἀπείροις εἴτε 2ιεσπασμένην καὶ πολλὰ γεγονυῖαν θετέον, εἴθ' ὅλην αὐτὴν αὐτῆς χωρίς, ὃ 2ὴ πάντων ἀ2υνατώτατον φαίνοιτ' ἄν, ταὐτὸν καὶ ἐν ἅμα ἐν ἑνί τε καὶ πολλοῖς γίγνεσθαι.

We are told (15 c) that this situation may either be the source of all our 'perplexity', or, if we have the right method, of all our 'success' (ἀπορία, εὐπορία). In the *Parmenides* Socrates had not this right method, but he has it now; in the *Parmenides* Plato had represented the apparent contrast of the One and the Many in λόγοι as the ground of all 'perplexity'; now, in the *Philebus*, he calls it 'an eternal and never-changing property inherent in all our λόγοι' (τῶν λόγων αὐτῶν ἀθάνατόν τι καὶ ἀγήρων πάθος ἐν ἡμῖν, 15 D)—an arena indeed for the display of all the arts of sophists and eristics, which give such delight to inexperienced youth. Plato had depicted such sophistries long ago in the *Euthydemus*, where he had found a solution to them not through logic, but through the doctrine that there is an End to which knowledge in all its forms is subordinate. To study this End was the business of the 'kingly art', and this art in its turn was closely reminiscent of Dialectic as understood in the *Republic* (see above, p. 35).

Now, although the *Philebus* also treats of the Good, the whole situation is changed. The logical issues are disputed, and a solution found without the least reference to the Good, just as they were in the Dialectic explained in the *Sophist*; a purely logical procedure is described. But what is its nature? If we continue to follow the text of the *Philebus*, repetition will become unavoidable, and I would prefer at present to pass over the decisive passage (16 c). However, a theoretical account of Dialectic is given, and then (17 A), as often happens in Plato, the person giving the answers replies that he has not fully understood. Thereupon the thing is explained by a practical example. This example leaves us in no doubt that Plato still founds his entire hope of an escape upon the method of Division, which is the more significant since he here leaves in the background the obtaining of definitions, which elsewhere strikes us immediately as the principal aim of this method. The example chosen is that of letters, which serves Plato in the *Sophist* also as an illustration of class relationships; and he amplifies it by another, that of tones. Is the specialist the man who knows what a letter and a tone are, and knows also that there are many letters and many tones? No doubt such a man knows the unity of speech—μία φωνή, 17 B—and knows moreover that this same speech is 'infinite', inasmuch as there are an infinite number of sounds. But neither the knowledge that sounds are infinite, nor the knowledge that they are one, is enough to make a man a specialist and give him possession of the τέχνη. In order to be an expert in the science of speech, one must know *how many* kinds it has, and which they are: Καὶ οὐδὲν ἑτέρῳ γε τούτων ἐσμέν πω σοφοί, οὔτε ὅτι τὸ ἄπειρον αὐτῆς (sc. φωνῆς) ἴσμεν οὔθ᾽ ὅτι τὸ ἕν· ἀλλ᾽ ὅτι πόσα τ᾽ ἐστὶ καὶ ὁποῖα, τοῦτό ἐστι τὸ γραμματικὸν ἕκαστον ποιοῦν ἡμῶν. This is now explained with great precision, beginning with the kinds of tone, which are all distinguished in strict accordance with the rules of the sciences of harmony and rhythm. So far, then, we have an example of the transition from 'the One' to 'the Infinite', showing how it is mediated by the lower kinds. But the converse is also possible; one may be faced at the outset with an 'infinite', and it would then be a mistake to ascend to the unity; the attempt should first have been made to determine the intervening stages, the lower kinds of the 'one' (18 A). Plato takes as an instance the discovery of letters by the person also named in the *Phaedrus*, Theuth. This man was confronted by sound as yet undetermined, φωνὴν ἄπειρον. He first noticed the vowels in the 'undetermined', and then recognized these again in their lower species, οὐχ ἓν ὄντα, ἀλλὰ πλείω (18 B). Next he distinguished the 'half-vowels', and finally a third εἶδος of letters, the consonants. The next passage is especially remarkable for a terminology which is reminiscent of the well-known sentence in the *Sophist*, 253 D, and likewise of the phrase μετιέναι καθ' ἕκαστά τε καὶ ἐπὶ πάντα, 235 C. It runs (18 c): 'After this he divided the letters which are without voice and sound (ἄφθογγα καὶ ἄφωνα) until the individuals were reached (μέχρι ἑνὸς ἑκάστου), and the vowels and the intermediate class in like manner, until, having learnt the whole number of them, he gave to each and to all the name of letters (ἑνί τε ἑκάστῳ καὶ σύμπασι στοιχεῖον ἐπωνόμασε)'. From the purely logical standpoint, one might ask why the inquiry here began from 'undetermined sound', φωνὴ ἄπειρος, if in the previous case it began from 'sound as a unity', μία φωνή, and if the eventual procedure in both cases is Division. (In the passage from the *Sophist* also, we remember, it was Division which was distinguished as the true and fundamental method.) But when we consider the actual example given, we see that the method is, in fact, correctly portrayed. Every language had at one time to face the great task of imposing order upon the undetermined mass of sounds by the distinction of definite types, and thus making it possible to write and read. It may really have been the example of Egypt which made Plato especially conscious of this achievement—for Egypt still possessed a second form of script, as a reminder of the time before that separation was made.

Having given a satisfactory explanation of the method of εἰδῶν Διαίρεσις—as he calls it, 20 c—Plato has next to apply this method to Pleasure and Knowledge. Before these illustrations which we have been considering, he gave an abstract discussion of its nature (16 B–17 A), and that he was talking there also of the classification of concepts will, I hope, scarcely now be doubted. Let us turn to this discussion. With a delicate blend of respect and gentle irony, Plato refers to the law that contraries are naturally coupled with each other, and says that it is a piece of wisdom preserved from old, a new fire brought from heaven by a second Prometheus. It has been handed down to us from the men of old, who stood nearer to the Gods. Plato gives us a clear hint of the person whom he has in mind,[1] for he uses the terms πέρας and ἀπειρία in place of One and Many; the light, but definite touch of irony shows that he does not really suppose himself to be merely borrowing the wisdom of the ancients. The essential thing is therefore to determine, if we can, at what point he is aware of adding something essentially new to the old doctrine of contraries—of improving it by a contribution of his own. And this point is clearly indicated. Since, says Plato, all things are a compound of One with Many—and it has now been decided that thought is akin to the One or Limit—such being the order of nature, obviously it is our task to search for the Unity among things that are many; since by hypothesis all things are compounded, it must be present in them. Δεῖν οὖν ἡμᾶς τούτων οὕτω διακεκοσμημένων ἀεὶ μίαν ἰδέαν περὶ παντὸς ἑκάστοτε θεμένους ζητεῖν—εὑρήσειν γὰρ ἐνοῦσαν—

I interrupt the sentence here in order to call attention to the full accord which exists, so far, between this method and the one which Plato has in view in his earliest Dialogues, for example the *Euthyphro*; only whereas the problem in the *Meno* is to derive essential shape and colour from the many instances of each, here at the opening of the *Philebus* we have the same problem reversed. Plato in his statement of the problem makes an unambiguous reference to his earlier doctrine of Ideas. The earlier εἶδος was without qualification μονοειδές. Until the *Republic*, no passage can be found in which the divisibility of such an 'indivisible Idea' (ἀμέριστος ἰδέα) into further εἴδη is suggested. (The *Parmenides* refers to the ὅλον εἶδος.) We may remind ourselves again that he had given definite consideration to the problem of 'the One and the Many' in the *Republic* (525 E: this passage has been previously discussed). He there makes everything depend on our securing a Unity in which no 'manyness' at all will be present. Here we see the great advance in knowledge which distinguishes the later phase of Plato's Dialectic from the earlier: it is now recognized that the 'unchanging and eternal fact' of contrariety must apply *both* to our λόγοι ('reasonings') and to the things of the world of sense—the two series must run parallel; for otherwise they cannot

_____
[1] [i.e. that it is Pythagoras.]

enter into a relation with mutual give and take, and knowledge is a clear example of such a relation. It is for this reason that in the *Parmenides* and *Philebus* the greatest stress is laid upon our being able to demonstrate that concepts themselves are not free from 'manyness'. The manner of approach to this problem is our only criterion for deciding whether a Dialogue belongs to the same dialectical group as the *Sophist*. If we make the distinctive achievement consist in its 'ordering the manifold by the concept', we miss the true course of Plato's development; for in a sense the earlier Idea had always done this—its function had been to represent the universal. And on the other hand, as must presently be shown, it was even now not identical with the concept. Plato now recognizes that the Idea in its earlier shape— what he had called μονοειδὲς εἶδος, with εἶδος in its full etymological sense of intuition—cannot solve even the problems for which he had first designed it, except on certain conditions. (We have seen that in the earlier phase he ignored these conditions, and why he did so.) In the process of extending his notion of knowledge, and bringing it into direct contact with the world of becoming, he had added new characteristics to the Idea; and naturally these are such that its earlier success as a mode of explanation is not withdrawn. Hence we can understand why Plato feels it to be so essential to ensure that his doctrine shall remain continuous in its outlines—to connect the new with the old, and establish the old more firmly with the aid of the new. So long as this tendency in him is not recognized, what we call the Platonic question, i.e. the question as to the chronology of his works and the course of his philosophical development, is hopelessly complicated.

The number of Divisions

But what precisely is 'the new'? Let us see how the interrupted sentence of the *Philebus* continues: 'After the one form we must search for two,[1] if we can find them—if not, for three or some other number—and we must divide each one of the new units again in the same way, until we not only see that the original One

[1] Μεταλάβωμεν may be corrupt, but the sense is not doubtful.

is both one and many and infinite, but also learn *how many* it is.' The traditional text is, I believe, correct: Plato needs a plural for ἕν; in the *Sophist* he had, for this purpose, substituted ὅλον for ἕν (p. 101), and elsewhere in the *Philebus* ἑνάς or μονάς. The predicative use of ἕκαστον, depending on the phrase τῶν ἓν ἐκείνων, which forms a single notion, is understandable, although in order to explain the use of the plural, we should perhaps prefer to see ἕν between inverted commas. However, the addition of ἕκαστον makes it clear that only a distributive plural is intended. We need not think that transposition is necessary, although it may be true that the association with ἓν ἕκαστον emboldens Plato to his rather drastic terminology. After the explanations of the *Sophist*, and in view of all that follows in the *Philebus*, the sense is unambiguous.

In the *Sophist* and *Statesman*, where the predominant form of Διαίρεσις had been dichotomous, its demonstrative force was founded on the certainty that the number of possibilities was only two, and hence that the section was really made at a natural 'joint' (Διαφυή, *Statesman*, 259 D). Thus there also it was the *number* of subordinate kinds which decided the issue, and made it possible for Διαίρεσις to yield knowledge of fact. But in the *Statesman* there had already been departures from twofold division, and in the *Philebus* Plato goes still further. (It is true that, here also, Division into two sections comes first—μετὰ μίαν Δύο, εἴ πως εἰσίν—but then it is natural that it should.) And indeed it is no essential part of Plato's doctrine that every ὄν should have *only one* μὴ ὄν opposed to it. (It will be remembered that we previously connected ὄν and μὴ ὄν with twofold Division.) Now, in the *Philebus*, the principal emphasis falls on the precise number of the sections, and this is entirely logical; only a division known to be exhaustive can lead to true knowledge of the 'unities' in their higher and lower classes, and this fact is confirmed as soon as we consider the examples of letters and tones; if, for instance, I had only made the distinction between vowels and consonants I should have misunderstood the Διαφοραί ... ὁπόσαιπερ ἐν εἴδεσι κεῖνται (*Statesman*, 285 B)—I should inevitably find myself in confusion not only about the half-vowels, but also about the vowels and consonants from which I had failed to distinguish them.

Plato says that, when we have rightly divided the first 'unity', we must apply the same procedure to each of the newly found unities, τῶν ἐν ἐκείνων ἕκαστον, until we not only see that the original unity is 'one and many and infinite', but also learn how many it is. We have now seen that in one sense this is the truth —the importance of the method of Διαίρεσις does depend on the precise number of higher and lower species. It is not enough merely to comprehend the manifold in a unity; and Διαίρεσις is, in this point, unlike the earlier Dialectic. Plato's next words (16 D) show that it is really this that he intends to emphasize:[1] 'But the form of the infinite must not be brought near to the many until one has observed its full number, the number between the one and the infinite; when this has been learnt, each several individual may be forgotten and dismissed into the infinite.' We are warned not to apply the ἰδέα τοῦ ἀπείρου to the plurality (πλῆθος) of concepts before we have fully surveyed the number of this plurality—the number of classes situated between the infinite and the (highest) unity. When this number has been learnt, but not before, the particulars of this whole class may be dismissed into the 'undetermined'.[2] (The ἄπειρον is, for Plato, both undetermined and undeterminable.) Such is the heaven-sent method, and such its true use; but the wise men of to-day are arbitrary in establishing 'the one and the many', finding them either too quickly or too slowly, and applying the infinite directly to the One. (Οἱ Δὲ νῦν τῶν ἀνθρώπων σοφοὶ ἓν μέν, ὅπως ἂν τύχωσι, καὶ πολλὰ θᾶττον καὶ βραδύτερον ποιοῦσι τοῦ Δέοντος, μετὰ Δὲ τὸ ἓν ἄπειρα εὐθύς, τὰ Δὲ μέσα αὐτοὺς ἐκφεύγει —οἷς Διακεχώρισται τό τε Διαλεκτικῶς πάλιν καὶ τὸ ἐριστικῶς ἡμᾶς ποιεῖσθαι πρὸς ἀλλήλους τοὺς λόγους.) The allusion in 'too quickly or too slowly' must be to inaccurate division—on overhasty divisions, cf. *Statesman*, 261 A, 266 D, 277 A, 285 A; more-

---

[1] Τὴν Δὲ τοῦ ἀπείρου ἰδέαν πρὸς τὸ πλῆθος μὴ προσφέρειν πρὶν ἄν τις τὸν ἀριθμὸν αὐτοῦ πάντα κατίδῃ τὸν μεταξὺ τοῦ ἀπείρου τε καὶ τοῦ ἑνός, τότε Δ' ἤδη τὸ ἓν ἕκαστον τῶν πάντων εἰς τὸ ἄπειρον μεθέντα χαίρειν ἐᾶν.

[2] Ἓν ἕκαστον τῶν πάντων. By πάντα is meant the πλῆθος, the number of intermediate unities, 18 B.

over, shortly before our passage Socrates says that this method is easy to describe, but hard to employ rightly in a particular case—and if so, καὶ πολλά in the text is necessary. Alternatively, Plato may be hinting at what follows, and thinking of those who immediately confront the one with the many. To this mistake the passage as a whole refers. Either alternative may be right; it makes no essential difference to the general result. The important thing is the existence of intermediate classes (μέσα), and therefore the science of accurate division. As in the *Sophist*, accurate division is what distinguishes Dialectic from 'eristic'.

Εἰς ἄπειρον μεθιέναι

The essential thing now is to find what is meant by 'dismissing into the infinite' and 'applying the idea of the infinite'. After what has been said, everything down to this point should be now clear: the radical 'separation' between the two worlds of λόγος and of becoming has vanished. No longer is absolute Unity dominant in the world of Ideas, and absolute multiplicity in the world of sense; instead of a contrast, there is now a parallel. The Idea, divided in its turn, has accepted the qualifications of one and many, and displays its properties in the form of a system of classes (see above, pp. 90 foll.). It was shown in the *Sophist* how the Idea, by being divided as long as division could continue, obtained individual content and thereby descended into the region of δόξα and αἴσθησις where, in the form of accurate definition, it established their truth and correctness. And the fact is undeniable; λόγος determines the 'undetermined' given to our senses, making it not simply an object of apprehension, but an individual or atomic 'form'. For this purpose also it is essential, according to the *Philebus*, that we should be able to bring our division to an end; how else could we determine the exact number of kinds, and set a limit (πέρας) to division in the form of an ultimate unity (ἕν)? The *Philebus* here only teaches in outspoken terms a result which was reached in the *Sophist*, and which we have seen confirmed in our discussion of ταὐτόν and ἕτερον (p. 136): viz. that in the present line of argument, Plato deliberately restrains his interest from proceeding beyond the lowest εἶδος. He recognizes no *sensible* objects, except as included under the last, indivisible εἶδος; the objects given to our senses as particulars are not genuine objects until they are 'comprehended' within their class. The lowest εἶδος is attained by reasoning, λόγος, the sensible object by δόξα; but it is only by being related to this εἶδος that δόξα can become true. Thus in so far as the particulars of our sense-experience are not included under the lowest εἴδη, they are 'undetermined'—they 'are not', in the sense of the verb 'to be' which we expounded above. What is called γένεσις εἰς οὐσίαν, 'the process of coming *to be*', is made possible by the unity derived from the εἶδος. Beyond the lowest εἶδος begins the kingdom of the ἄπειρον, and this is the meaning of the phrase τὸ ἓν ἕκαστον τῶν πάντων εἰς τὸ ἄπειρον μεθέντα χαίρειν ἐᾶν. For Plato's purpose the remaining problems also, those of 'separation' and of 'the one and the many', are consequently solved.

IX. THE *PHAEDRUS*

WE shall return later to what has been said in the last section; but some more general questions first demand our attention. In attempting to view the Dialectic of Plato from his own assumptions, we are obliged to face the shibboleth of Platonic scholarship—the question what place to assign to the *Phaedrus* in the order of time and of system; fortunately this will give us a chance to collect and reinforce some essential points of interpretation. In a Dialogue abounding in puzzles, not the least puzzling feature is the view of Dialectic. This can be seen from the latest discussion of its nature, between H. von Arnim[1] and Pohlenz.[2] There is an obvious correspondence between the sketch of dialectical procedure in the second part of the *Phaedrus* and the information given in the *Sophist* and *Statesman*. Accordingly any scholar who, like von Arnim and H. Maier,[3] favours a late date for the composition of the *Phaedrus*, seizes upon this as a sure foundation for his view. We ourselves, in expounding *Sophist*, 253 D (above, p. 96), agreed that *Phaedrus*, 265 D, was a near enough parallel to be used provisionally for confirmation. On the other hand we must entirely admit the claim of Pohlenz that on the view which has always prevailed, whereby the method of Division is a mere exercise in formal logic, this argument could scarcely be decisive enough to count against contradictory instances. It is also easily shown that Plato had always employed divisions wherever his subjects required them, like those of the arts and sciences (*Gorgias, Euthydemus, Republic*).[4] The ἀνάμνησις of the *Phaedrus* myth would certainly direct us back to Plato's earliest period; and we have tried to connect the absence of ἀνάμνησις from the later, dialectical Dialogues with his more careful attention to the realm of becoming (above, p. 63). Our own history of Dialectic also, which has led to an entirely different estimate of Division, must therefore face the final test of the *Phaedrus*. Two undeniable facts stand in contrast:

(*a*) In the latter half of the Dialogue, Plato makes clear refer-

---

[1] *Plat. Jugenddialoge*, 197 foll.   [2] *G.G.A.* 1916, 268.   [3] *Sokrates*, 556.
[4] See the work of Lukas to which allusion was made on p. 81.

ence to the ultimate term or ἄτομον, the last (or first) term which is inseparable from the method of Division, and makes it a very important contribution not only to formal logic, but also to positive philosophy, 277 B: 'Until a man knows the truth of the several particulars of which he is writing or speaking, and is able to define them as they are, and having defined them again to divide them into their kinds until the indivisible is reached.'

(b) On the other hand the Myth refers to ἀνάμνησις, 249 B: 'For a man must have intelligence of universals, and be able to proceed from the many sense-perceptions to one conception of reason; this is the recollection of those things which our soul once saw while following God, when regardless of that which we now call being, she raised her head up towards the true being.'

The contradiction which lies beneath the surface here is clearly exposed by von Arnim (op. cit. 198). Certainly we nowhere find, in such clear and definite contrast, the view that the class-concept is formed by 'abstraction' from many perceptions, and the view which bases it on Recollection—an apriorist view, diametrically opposed to the other. It may be granted that the former view is a return to the doctrines of pre-Socratic sages (Alcmaeon B 1 a Diels); this makes no difference to the substantial problem. Of the prevailing views, I am inclined to think that the judgement of Natorp is still relatively the best founded (pp. 65 foll.)—that the *Phaedrus* shows us Dialectic in an unclear and immature form. But if we apply to the *Phaedrus* the insight which we have gained into the history and philosophy of 'division', we may be led to quite a different result.

The second part of the *Phaedrus*, then, arrives at the ἄτομον εἶδος, whereas the first part lays strong emphasis on the *a priori* factor, 'recollection', mentioning sensation in the same context. There is a special connexion between the ἄτομον εἶδος and sensation; on this ground the 'divisions' and the theoretical digression in the *Sophist* form one philosophical and artistic whole; and on the same ground this Dialogue is connected with the *Theaetetus*, whose problem it solves. Our examination of the *Philebus* brought us to the same point, and in our interpretation of *Sophist*, 253 D, it was once again the problem of the 'individual' which had to be left as an unsolved remainder. The passage from the *Phaedrus* obliges us specially to consider the question of abstraction from the data of sense. Our whole exposition has aimed at discovering what place in systematic philosophy Plato attributes to the Idea. We have examined the nature of the universal and of the discursive class-concept, and the clear result has been that it would be impossible to understand the development of Plato if his Idea were a concept. Had it been so, none of the difficulties, of which he himself gives so clear an account, would ever have arisen. Now it appears that in the beginning these difficulties were indeed not contemplated. Are we to think that they had already been solved? or simply that they had not yet been framed? We have also done our best to answer these questions. But we are now faced with a new point, of which some brief indication has already been given. It is of great importance here to understand the relation between literary form and philosophical content in the Dialogues. Suppose that, when Plato looked back from a later stage in his development, he realized that the new features, which had been grafted on to the Ideas by his later Dialectic, were likewise fundamentally and substantially necessary for a complete solution of his earlier problems, would not this set a special problem for him as an artist? He would then see, as any modern reader does, that when he made Socrates in the *Meno* say: 'Do not disperse and divide Virtue, but seek to discover it in its entirety', he had really assumed an answer to the problem of the *Parmenides*, viz. how can Virtue be at the same time one and many? He would see, moreover, that the hard thinking of the dialectical Dialogues had left the sense of the 'Idea' essentially unaltered; for the last and lowest unit of Division, which can comprehend the objects of sense, possesses the same characteristic which had belonged to the original Ideas, viz. that of being an indivisible whole. He would find that every test had confirmed his first assumption that knowledge can be attained only ἐν λόγοις (in reasoning), and that even the objects of Nature as presented to our senses are only to be grasped through reasoning; by 'reasoning' alone can 'opinion' become true. Here it may be well to emphasize once more that in basing our argument on the hypothesis of two contrasted stages in the development of Dialectic, we do not wish to deny that the meaning of 'Idea' evolved without a sudden break. Plato's thought, being of a very objective kind, followed the gradual changes in its objects; new methods were fashioned in conformity to the objects, and these methods are quite sharply distinguishable; and yet Plato could think that he had always remained true to one view of method. Now would not Plato, as an artist, be attracted by the idea of giving a picture of his system in this final unity—of taking the old problems in hand once more, but at the same time allowing the newly found assumptions and methods to play a subdued part, thus obeying his own principle of 'reminding those who already know' (*Phaedrus*, 275 D)? In his dogmatic writings—in those which offer solutions to problems—Plato could not assign the leading role to Socrates, and he had no wish to do so. But there could be no better way of representing the continuity of his own development than to revive the mysterious figure of Socrates, and invest him again with all the glory in which he personally imagined him.[1]

Since Socrates had formerly been allowed to pronounce upon so many problems whose full difficulty Plato did not realize at the time, and this in spite of his profession of ignorance, it was reasonable for Plato in retrospect to attribute to him the solutions which a fuller understanding of the same problems required. The brilliant argument of the *Phaedrus* turns to ridicule all our ideas of chronology. Although an authentic Socratic Dialogue, it gives us reminiscences of Aristotle's *Rhetoric*, and of the doctrine of motion in the *Laws*—of the World-Soul, and the

---

[1] I have here renounced all attempt to determine the sequence of Plato's writings in detail. If the general trend of his development is still as uncertain as the controversy about the *Phaedrus* and *Theaetetus* proves it to be, we must in future be more modest, and for the moment be satisfied with the alternatives 'before and after the *Republic*'. Above all we must allow for the artist in Plato, and leave him free to see certain problems with a special breadth and depth of view. We can scarcely expect every Dialogue simply to be the reflection of his knowledge at the time of writing, and show a point beyond which he had 'not yet' advanced. The example of the *Theaetetus* teaches us this. That the *Phaedrus* also was written after the *Republic*, and at a time when Plato was in conscious command of the method described in the *Sophist*, *Statesman*, and *Philebus*, seems to me beyond doubt. On this basis, we may hope that it is possible for more precise results yet to be obtained.

political theories of the *Statesman*. Here we must select for examination the relatively small section on Dialectic. If it was his purpose to relate the old to the new, Plato would be faced by one principal task—to explain the·'inductive method' of Socrates who, in the early Dialogues, had always started his inquiry from particular cases. Such attention to particulars was quite reconcilable with Plato's earlier ideal theory of ἀρετή and with its *a priori* point of view, modelled on the pure intuitions of Mathematics; it was even a natural consequence of the characteristic way in which he had at first combined the universal with the particular; we showed this in our analysis of the εἶδος in the first Chapter. In the second Chapter we depicted the change in his intellectual interest, and saw how its effect was to attach to the εἶδος some of the characteristics of concepts, such as the subordination of a lower rank to a higher. In consequence of this, genuine 'abstraction' was one of the latest phenomena in Platonic Dialectic, which only appeared above the horizon at the very end; i.e. Plato was at last compelled to allow to αἴσθησις upon careful conditions, a certain degree of importance in the constitution of objects. The treatment of Δόξα in the *Philebus* taught us this. True, the passage from the *Philebus* could only be understood when we amplified it by evidence from the *Sophist* showing the method of verification of αἴσθησις; i.e. when it was assumed that the αἴσθησις had already been 'apperceived' as a unity (ἕν). The *Philebus* also assumed that the difficult problem stated in the *Parmenides*—namely, how the εἶδος can be 'parcelled out'—had been solved and was beyond question answerable. So it was indeed declared to be in the last passage which we took from the *Philebus* (16 c); and its solution is likewise treated as the presupposition of Dialectic in the *Sophist*, 257 c: 'The nature of the different seems to me to be cut into small sections, as knowledge is.—In what way?—Knowledge also is, I imagine, one; but any part of it which presides over some definite object is separated from the rest, and given a name of its own.' 258 d: 'We showed that the nature of the different was divided, and that it belonged to all existing things in respect of each other.' 260 b: 'We made the discovery that not-being was a single definite kind, scattered among all existing things.' What is especially noticeable in the *Philebus* is Plato's insistence that what was scattered and disjoined is to be unified—the many are made one. 23 E: 'Since we find each class torn apart and scattered, let us attempt to reunite them, and see how each was both one and many.' 25 A: 'All these terms must be included in the class of the infinite, as their unity, in accordance with our avowed purpose of bringing together all that was divided and dispersed, and setting the seal of one nature upon it as far as possible.' In the *Meno*, opposite advice had been given: do not break Virtue into pieces, look for the single Virtue; if it is broken into fragments, it is not Virtue at all. In the *Phaedo* also the contribution of the senses had been very differently estimated (75 A, B). No doubt it was mentioned as an important fact that only experience can lead us to 'equality' and other Ideas; but 'the Equal' was emphatically *not* divided among particular instances, in such a way that it could be extracted from them by Induction, or even by collection into a unity. Far from it; for what we experience as equal is not equal at all in comparison with the self-subsistent, single Idea of Equality, which is of an essentially higher order. But the newer view of the Idea as the 'universal' which is torn asunder in its instances, and yet always remains itself, is taken for granted throughout the *Phaedrus*, 265 D: 'first, the comprehension of scattered particulars in one idea; the speaker should define his several notions and make his meaning clear.'

If we now return to the *Phaedrus* and think especially of the factor of 'collection' in Dialectic, we may begin to see meaning even in the obvious contradiction of the difficult passage from the myth. Plato enlarges upon the phrase of Alcmaeon; he says that something is to be collected from many perceptions,[1] formed by thought into a unity, and predicated as an εἶδος. He is plainly aware of the danger that this formulation may easily be misinterpreted in support of a sensationalist view of knowledge; fortunately the passage occurs in a myth, which is designed to depict pre-existence; and so he has ready to hand his strongest

---

[1] Συναιρούμενον occurs only in this passage, and the term is chosen in order to indicate the contrast with διαιρεῖν.

piece of evidence against any empiricism—the fact of ἀνάμνησις. In the *Phaedo* the Ideas had depended on ἀνάμνησις; in the *Sophist* they had become allied to sensation, but had not in any way submitted to its supremacy; it was, indeed, their function to determine sensation, and make it capable of truth. The εἶδος throughout its history had comprised a 'one' and a 'many', and the *Phaedrus* only brings a much clearer understanding of their alliance. It thus succeeds in combining, without contradiction, the old and the new; we shall soon see what was 'new', or at least in what direction it was to be found; meanwhile the apparently 'old' remains in a dim light, as though we were meant to be blinded by the brilliant light of the vision of ἀνάμνησις, and not see clearly the object to which it points. No hint of any particular Ideas is given either in this, or in the earlier context, 247 D. We hear nothing in the *Phaedrus* of a celestial abode of the Ideas.

There remains one obscurity in the treatment of Dialectic in the *Phaedrus*, which is scarcely perceived by Plato, but seems much graver to Aristotle. When it is said that a unity is derived from many sensations, to what sensations does this refer? They cannot be sensations which are already true in the sense of the *Philebus* and *Sophist*, since in that case the unity has already been applied to them. They cannot, on the other hand, still be part of the 'undetermined' (ἄπειρον), since they would be unnecessary to the discovery of 'unity'; or, at least, it is quite an inessential point that there are 'many' of them. The *Phaedo* showed how the Idea can be abstracted and contemplated by itself without our taking account of all perceptions—nowhere is a complete enumeration required. But the same dilemma applies, in precisely the same way, to the later passage in the *Phaedrus*, where, without reference to ἀνάμνησις, Plato uses the formula: 'to comprise in one view and collect under one Idea the many scattered instances'. If that which is scattered is really 'many', it is in separate parts, related as are the instances of 'being' and 'not-being' according to the doctrine of the *Sophist*.[1] This is to say that individual things must first have been brought under the unity of one of the Ideas thus divided and 'scattered'. Failing

---

[1] See the examples given above, p. 153 fol.

this interpretation, how and where is the Idea divided and 'scattered' at all?

Let us briefly recall the definition of the dialectician given at *Sophist*, 253 D. In the first section we learn that μίαν ἰδέαν διὰ πολλῶν, ἑνὸς ἑκάστου κειμένου χωρίς, πάντῃ διατεταμένην ἱκανῶς διαισθάνεται, i.e. according to Natorp's version, 'he combines together a number of objects given individually and separately to the senses (ἑνὸς ἑκάστου κειμένου χωρίς) in a single concept extending throughout them all, such as "red", and including the indefinite "many" in a definite whole'. Previously we had to allow that Apelt and others were right in holding that the allusion here is to a κοινωνία τῶν γενῶν, and in understanding the units (ἑνὸς ἑκάστου κειμένου χωρίς) to be single concepts, which have already been separated by definition. But Natorp could appeal to the version of Dialectic in the *Phaedrus* (which, however, he held to be early) or in the *Philebus*, and interpret all three passages as describing an abstraction from the sensible on the ground of a unity given to it by the mind. The answer to the problem will be seen if we recall to mind what was said earlier of 'opinion' and the 'atomic form'. The interpretations both of Natorp and of other scholars reveal a peculiar assumption on the part of Plato, which we have found again and again in this study: the only 'individual' recognized by him is the 'atomic form', the object of true opinion. Hence 'abstraction' for him is indeed coincident with the subordination of lower *kinds* under a higher one. In examining the disputed passage from the *Sophist*, we arrived before at this result; and we found that the combining process is not mentioned at all in the first clause, but only in the second. Consequently the 'division' of form becomes all the more important for Plato; and so at *Phaedrus*, 265 E, likewise, the art of correct division is mentioned side by side with that of combination, as its necessary complement. Plato remained in the most literal sense an Idealist. To him the universal was represented in the particular, while the particular could only be grasped in the Idea; in intuition both elements were united. The problem of the individual *thing* remained unsolved; Plato has here reached the point at which Aristotle opposes him.

X. DEMOCRITUS

ONE last task remains before we touch upon Plato's relation to Aristotle. What of the school of professed 'atomists'? Our view of division has brought Plato into a nearer relationship to them. Hitherto his attitude to the most important physical hypothesis of the ancients has been a dark mystery, and perhaps it says something for our view that we can make it a little clearer. It is worth noticing that Plato's doctrine of 'not-being'—that it is no less real than 'being'—has always suggested to his readers the famous antitheses of Democritus: μὴ μᾶλλον τὸ ᾿δὲν ἢ τὸ μη᾿δὲν εἶναι, 'something is not more real than nothing'.[1] Every one sees that in the *Sophist* the 'One' of the Eleatics gives place to a new idea of unity which does not exclude plurality; but no one thinks of the new indivisible unity of Leucippus and Democritus, whose philosophy was also an answer to the Eleatics. This is because the exercises in Division are regarded as a tissue of hollow platitudes. Yet the fact is beyond doubt: in so far as Eleatic problems of some kind played a part in the formation of Plato's thought—and the Idea's own spontaneous development brought it up against such problems—not the least important influence on Plato was the bold inspiration of the Atomists who, converting a mere problem into a postulate, had been able to oppose all sophistical objections. The 'divisions' and the 'atomic form' survive in the work of the later Academy; we must think not only of the rather insignificant surviving treatise on Divisions, but also especially of the atomistic theory in Mathematics.

And yet since the time of Aristoxenus [2] the relation of Plato's philosophy to that of Democritus has appeared to be one of diametrical opposition and hopeless conflict. Scholars have failed to understand that Plato, far from 'avoiding a contest with the best of philosophers' (Diogenes, l.c.), was very deeply and clearly conscious that it was his duty to confront his brilliant predecessor before his own interpretation of nature could claim to be established. It will be agreed by those who know the conventions of

---

[1] Diels, B 156: cf. Cohen's *Platons Ideenlehre und die Mathematik*, 14.
[2] Diog. ix. 40, fr. Diels, A 1.

ancient literature that the avoidance of any overt mention of a man is anything but a sign of pure negation and conflict. In order to grasp the peculiar relation between Plato and Democritus, we should start from the point at which they are both Atomists. Plato takes over from Democritus his principle of a division repeated until the 'atomic form' is reached; like Democritus he overcomes rigid and absolute Eleaticism by denying the principle on which it rests, that 'not-being' is incomprehensible. Many modern scholars attribute a form of 'idealism' to Democritus, but this is certainly untrue to the spirit of his doctrine; the fact is that Plato, in deliberate antithesis to him, transforms his doctrine into a logical idealism; his 'atom' is the 'atomic form', and his 'not-being' is the principle which separates such 'atoms' from each other, namely logical difference, just as in the system of Democritus 'not-being' is a void separating *material* atoms from one another. Everything in Plato's writing on this subject which remains in the twilight of figurative expression finds its explanation through this parallel; 'not-being' is the 'cause of division' and lesser Ideas are described as 'parts' (μέρη) of the higher one which includes them.[1] Of the direction of Plato's Logic there can be no doubt. But it is also beyond question that the constant infiltration of mathematical ideas, whilst it serves to confirm Plato's thinking in the objective and intuitive character it already had, at the same time modifies its logical character in a way which increases, when we look closely, the similarity to Democritus. For geometrical shape was also an important feature of the atoms, ἰδέαι, of Democritus. Let us go back to Socrates' historical survey in the *Phaedo*; here Plato had shown the main intention of his philosophy in its earlier period; and the same intention is now reaffirmed. Pure knowledge and the practical interest of ethics are to Plato inseparable; the former is not secure until it appears to us in the shape of the Good. In order to establish Idealism and refute materialism Plato must have a teleological view of Nature, and this view has now become far clearer to him than it ever was before. His method of Divi-

---

[1] [Stenzel probably alludes to *Phileb.* 23 D, where Plato hints that it is necessary to postulate a cause of division: see L. Robin, *Platon*, p. 160.]

sion leads him straight to the same two main varieties of cause
which he had distinguished in the *Phaedo*. Mind and matter are
causes, but causes sharply contrasted in essence.

The method of Division had been applied most fruitfully to
biological types. Here it could show its proper essence, and give
the richest display of its power. But Plato saw in it something
more than a mode of definition for the purposes of natural
science. Its use in science taught him certain new characteristics of the Ideas. Each concept in science had a definite meaning, and was placed in a higher or lower rank according to the
definiteness of its content and the number of its instances. He
now transferred the same scheme to 'immaterial' forms,[1] to the
most abstract concepts and their relations. We found proof of
this in our analysis of the passage in which 'Being' was represented
as a general class including particular beings (*Statesman*, 285 D).
But we postponed until the present moment the final stage in
that analysis, because it can help to show us how Plato's metaphysical view is related, on the one side to the materialism of
Democritus, and on the other to Aristotle's natural philosophy.
Our former concern was with the effect on Plato's *logic* of the
notion of a Being including particular beings as its species. We
have now to describe briefly how the same idea of Being—which
Plato in his peculiar way regards not as a concept but as an existing essence—comes to dominate his teleology and theology. The
fact that particular 'beings' are species of Being is the connecting
link. 'Being' immediately suggests to Plato the kingdom of biological classes, because that is the most natural subject for 'division'; he understands it as the generic form of all living creatures,
in the wider sense of 'life'. Then, by applying too conscientiously
the logic of the theory of Division, Plato reaches a remarkable
result: this form must itself have the specific property which
belongs to the types it includes, i.e. life. In this way a logical
method becomes the source of the mystical idea of a highest
Being, which is the essence of all that is. We must demonstrate
the immediate connexion of this mysticism with the logic of
the *Sophist*, before we can follow out its result in the peculiar

[1] ἀσώματα.

doctrines of the *Timaeus*. The question at issue, which at first sight is purely logical, is whether movement 'is', and so shares in Being. 'Can we ever be made to believe that motion and life and soul and mind are not present with perfect Being? Can we imagine that Being is devoid of life and mind, and exists in awful un-meaningness an everlasting fixture?' Belief in such a rigid and lifeless Being would place us in company with the Eleatics, and, we may say, with the Atomists as well, since their Being was equally material and lifeless. 'That would be a dreadful thing to admit, Stranger.—But shall we say that Being has mind, and not life?—How is that possible?—Or shall we say that both inhere in perfect Being, but that it has no soul which contains them?—And in what other way can it contain them?—Or that Being has mind and life and soul, but although endowed with soul remains absolutely unmoved?—All three suppositions appear to me to be irrational.—Under Being, then, we must include motion, and that which is moved' (248-9, tr. Jowett). Thus a proof of the existence of the World-Soul is fitted into a logical discussion of the possibility of communion between Being, rest, and move-ment. In *Philebus*, 30 A foll., Plato proves in a very similar way that the World-Soul must be assumed to exist if the Universe is governed by rational law and not by chance. And in another outstanding passage of the *Sophist* he argues that there can be no teleology unless the cosmos is animated by soul; where the proof is once more connected with 'division' of the forms of universal life. In this passage (265 c foll.) Plato is once more on the defensive against the 'violent man'[1] who asserts that the state of the world is one of disorder. The Eleatic Stranger has just made the acquaintance of Theaetetus, and is allowed to express Plato's personal feelings about him; and it is in this highly per-sonal context that Plato reveals something near to admiration for the complete and coherent view of his great opponent,[2] al-though it is repugnant to his inner nature and, as he hopes, to that of Theaetetus.

[1] For this frequent thought, cf. *Philebus*, 29 A: ὅταν ἀνὴρ Δεινὸς φῇ μὴ οὕτως ἀλλ' ἀτάκτως ἔχειν, and compare Aristotle *de gen. anim.* 789ᵇ 2: Δημόκριτος Δὲ τὸ οὗ ἕνεκα ἀφεὶς λέγειν πάντα ἀνάγει εἰς ἀνάγκην οἷς χρῆται ἡ φύσις (Diels, *Vorsokratiker*, A 66).

[2] i.e. Democritus.

'*Str.* Looking, now, at the world and all the animals and plants, at things which grow upon the earth from seeds and roots, as well as at inanimate substances which are formed within the earth, fusile or non-fusile, shall we say that they come into existence—not having existed previously—by the creation of God, or shall we agree with vulgar opinion about them?

Theaet. What is it?

Str. The opinion that nature brings them into being from some spontaneous and unintelligent cause. Or shall we say that they are created by a divine reason and a knowledge which comes from God?

Theaet. I dare say that, owing to my youth, I may often waver in my view, but now when I look at you and see that you incline to refer them to God, I defer to your authority.

Str. Nobly said, Theaetetus, and if I thought that you were one of those who would hereafter change your mind, I would have gently argued with you, and forced you to assent; but as I perceive that you will come of yourself and without any argument of mine, to that belief which, as you say, attracts you, I will not forestall the work of time. Let me suppose, then, that things which are said to be made by nature are the work of divine art, and that things which are made by man out of these are works of human art. And so there are two kinds of making and production, the one human and the other divine' (tr. Jowett).

Thus the method of division has to assume the permanence of natural types; this permanence is associated with 'divine craftsmanship', θεία τέχνη, and thus it becomes a vital part of the proof that our world displays a divine purpose. We learn this from the *Timaeus*. In explaining his view of the Idea as a pattern (παράδειγμα) Plato had always used the analogy of human arts and crafts, in which a purpose conceived by the mind is brought to realization in matter. The fact that, in *Republic* 596 A, he explains the function of the Idea as a pattern by the much-ridiculed examples of the 'essential' table and bed, is an excellent proof of our point that what he visualized in his earlier period was not so much a number of definite Ideas, as a wider notion in which these Ideas were comprehended, viz. that of an End or purpose. This notion was never far from the earlier doctrine, which was concerned with Virtue. Now the examples in *Republic* 596 A are really very instructive. Greek thought never admits that there may be unending development. 'Tragedy,' says Aristotle in the *Poetics*, 1449^a 14, 'eventually secured its true nature.' The various arts are not invented, but 'found'. The idea of an undetermined choice never enters the ordinary Greek mind, and Democritus is here, as in other respects, in advance of his time. All higher activity is therefore guided by permanent and real standards. And the association of a productive art with an End is so regular, that when Plato's interest was turned in the direction of 'natural' objects, and he discovered there a realm of eternal Forms always reappearing in fresh instances, he made the converse inference: namely that, if there is orderly change behind the manifold appearances of nature, if these appearances are not the play of mechanical forces, this can only proceed from an intelligence which is at work in Nature. The remarkable thing is that in describing how this intelligence operates, Plato goes back to human craftsmanship for his analogy: the idea that all thinking starts with intuition of an object is so firmly implanted in him that he cannot allow even the divine mind to create the Idea of the world 'by a spontaneous act of consciousness'. Still less can this be admitted as an explanation of human knowledge.[1] Even God creates the world after a pattern, and that pattern is the 'intelligible living creature', Being as the most abstract class of which all living creatures are members. The world is 'one living thing having in itself all living things both mortal and immortal'[2] (69 c), cf. the description of its pattern (30 c).

The correspondence between the order of Nature as discovered to our thought by logical division, and as realized in the cosmos, has further consequences. The 'not-being' of Democritus had been converted by Plato into its logical equivalent, the

[1] [Stenzel quotes from Windelband, *Logos*, i. 194 : to the ancients the human understanding, no less than the senses, was a mirror in which a given object could be reflected: it is the modern spirit which, from long experience, dares to pronounce the proud words, 'the laws of Nature are prescribed for her by the understanding'.]

[2] Certain touches in Plato's description of this 'unique' world, ἓν ὅλον (32 D), this 'being including all beings' (33 B), distinctly recall the doctrine of the historical Parmenides. Since Aristotle also in his description of the πρῶτος οὐρανός (*de Caelo*, 279^a 6 foll.) expresses himself in very similar terms, we may regard it as definite that the οὐρανός is the 'sphere' mentioned at *Phaedrus* 247 c.

principle of 'difference'. He now restored it to its proper place
in the order of Nature. Thus there are two contrasted principles—the 'other', accounting for perpetual change and individuality, and the 'same', the constant element in the world, due
to the thought of the World-Soul. Plato's new proof of the Immortality of the Soul as an eternal principle of both thought and
movement, is derived from cosmology and not from ethics.

The prominent point in this brief survey has been Plato's determination to employ the atomistic doctrine of 'division' as the
basis for a teleological account of Nature, and thus deliberately
to reverse the intention of its author, Democritus. But the similarity of the two philosophies is seen in one strange application
of 'division'. The central problem is again that which faced us
in our interpretation of the *Phaedrus*—viz. what is the nature of
the 'atomic form'? We found that, when the division of concepts
came to an end, there was still a remainder which the mind could
not grasp. Now we owe to Xenocrates (fr. 53 Heinze, cf. p. 68 in
his work) the information that, when Plato had divided living
beings into classes and these into individual animals, he continued his division until he reached the five material elements.
(The number of these need not detain us here.) He abandons,
in fact, the division of concepts—takes a sudden plunge down
from the world of Ideas and its 'atomic' members. He passes
over the problem, recognized in the *Philebus*, of the relation
between the Idea, or unity, and the 'unlimited' which it determines. Now if Plato thus introduces a physical division, he must,
as we have shown before, be simply identifying the 'atomic form'
with the concrete object of experience, and evading the real
problem, which he had already expressed in its mathematical
form in the *Philebus*. One form of unity, the 'Idea', is being replaced by another, the mathematical 'shape'. And it is probably
in this direction that we must look for the well-attested mathe-
matization of the Ideas in their last phase. If so, Plato is one
stage nearer to the ἰδέαι of Democritus, which were only dif-
ferentiated from each other by shape. He now emphasizes the
mathematical element more strongly than before; he is content to
think of form as πέρας, the 'boundary' of the real; he can ignore

the void. What was the reason for the conformity of things to mathematical limits? Plato, from his teleological point of view, could give an explanation where Democritus had none, viz. that regular figures were beautiful.[1] 'Division' was important also in the solution of some purely mathematical problems (though contemporaries scarcely saw them to be thus limited)—constancy, incommensurability, and the whole theory of indivisible magnitudes. Here we have intentionally passed over a new and important variety of division. But a comprehensive new work on 'the Platonic bodies'[2] (i.e. the five regular solids) is announced; such a work would enable us to proceed further with the questions we have examined here.

[1] Natorp, p. 357.
[2] [Stenzel alludes to the work of Eva Sachs, *Die fünf Platonische Körper*, which appeared in 1918.]

XI. ARISTOTLE

THUS Plato, when he reached the 'atomic form', had violently cut the Gordian knot; he had obliterated the boundary between organic and inorganic. This led his immediate successors to inferences which, we may hope, would never have won his approval. It was at the same point that his greatest disciple took leave of him and created the science of organic life—biology—which was a natural sequel to the doctrine of 'atomic forms'. It was not Aristotle who 'substituted an ideal atom for the material one of Democritus';[1] what he did was to carry on the doctrine of Plato in a direction of his own. He employs 'division' probably on a larger scale than Plato, making it serve the special purposes of botany and zoology. He studies with its help the relative extent of logical classes; and he thus arrives at an elaborate doctrine of concepts and at syllogism.[2] But the problem left unsolved by 'division'—the nature of the 'atomic form', and its relation to the world of sense—becomes the central problem in his metaphysical theory, the kernel of his much-misunderstood criticism of his master's doctrine.

Plato had recognized the problem of 'separation', and had appreciated and described all the problems associated therewith. But he came to regard the question of 'separation', and in the last resort also that of abstraction, as one which affected the relation of Ideas to one another; and by showing how Ideas were united and interwoven in the 'atomic form', he thought he had brought down the Ideas to the borders of experience and enabled them to unite with 'opinion' and 'sensation'. The two worlds were interconnected through gradual stages, 'middle terms', as they are called in the *Philebus* (μέσα); these were destined to acquire an unexpected importance in the theological speculations of the later Platonists. But in the end his gaze returns to the topmost Idea; it is at the apex of the 'division' that he finds his lasting interest. He has no interest in the lowest differentia-

---

[1] Charles Werner, *Aristote et l'idéalisme platonicien*, Geneva, 1909, p. 61.
[2] H. Maier, *op. cit.*, ii. B 56.

tions. With his characteristic blend of jest and earnest, he professes to discover, in the highest regions of the cosmos, another sphere of 'intuition', which lies beyond and above that of 'true opinion' (*Timaeus*, 51 D). In such intuition, no doubt, the human race has but a small share, ἀνθρώπων δὲ γένος βραχύ τι (51 E). The formation and re-formation of the 'patterns of all creation' was to him indeed the 'eternal diversion of the eternal mind'; and the Ideas may be thought of as forces active in a uniform and animate Universe, a Universe which he 'could not believe to be devoid of life, soul, and thought'. But if the Ideas were active forces, then there must be a single Idea of Nature as an active organism, from which Nature herself must have been copied by 'divine craftsmanship'. That Plato should draw this inference shows how profound and clear was his understanding of the logical nature of intuition.

Aristotle was interested in the other extreme of the scale of 'division'. With all his power he continued to advance the study of Nature, of which this method had been the favourite instrument in the Platonic school; and he continued the work of his master from the exact point where he had turned aside to a new method.[1] In Aristotle's view the transition to a mathematical 'form' left the problem of the 'atomic form' unsolved. It seemed to him that Plato had vaulted over an essential stage in his inference; that he had only revealed once more his original problem about the Ideas and their intuition: how were the particular and the universal related? With an increasing obstinacy, therefore (which is psychologically understandable when we notice how little interest Plato's favourite pupils were prepared to devote to the question), he insisted again and again that the *real* 'separation' had not been overcome by Plato's solutions. Thus it was that he came to state and emphasize, over and over again, the very arguments which the master had invented and used, in the confident hope of having answered them.

What judgement philosophy, as a systematic science, must pass on the solution which Aristotle himself found and established on every side with an acuteness and penetration which

---

[1] [i.e. where Plato had deserted logical in favour of mathematical division.]

never grew tired—this question, although its great significance must not for a moment be overlooked, we shall here put aside. It suffices for us to show here that that solution is natural and understandable in view of the philosophy of Plato, of the intellectual situation at the time, and of Aristotle's own quite personal scientific interests. Plato had done homage to the shade of Democritus, had made the bold descent from 'form' (εἶδος) to Matter; by means of mathematical shape, he hoped to raise matter at least to a 'spurious' ideality. When Aristotle, determined to do justice to matter, brought about a *rapprochement* between the Platonic ὕλη and the 'atom' of Democritus, i.e. concrete reality, he was merely following an example set by Plato. Aristotle, however, believed that he could retain 'form' in its proper nature as an intellectual concept, and still couple it with matter. Plato, because his manner of thought was intuitional, had returned again and again to the problem of the relation between universal and particular. Aristotle, whose thinking also was intuitional to an eminent degree, drew the final inference from that problem—that εἶδος and matter, form and formed, were bound by nature in an inseparable connexion with each other. On the one hand, he takes the intuitable aspect of the εἶδος, and gives it the most definite objective existence in a sensible individual; on the other hand, he sets free at the same time the remaining aspect of 'form' as an intellectual concept, which had been obtaining more and more prominence in Plato; now that the universal is not bound to the particular, Aristotle is able to give it its proper nature as an abstract concept. 'Form', εἶδος, inheres in the individual object, but the *universal* is only an object of thought. Now if he tried to equate Plato's εἶδος with either of these, Aristotle was faced with the fact of 'separation'. By comparison with his immanent 'form' it existed 'apart'; by comparison with *his* 'universal', it naturally seemed to have a substantial existence to which it had no right. This is the burden of his whole criticism of the theory of Ideas. How, we may ask, did he himself imagine that 'form' exerted its effect in the concrete σύνολον, the λόγος μετὰ ὕλης? Here we may find support in Aristotle for the view on which our work has been entirely founded. He shows how, even when a thinker feels his thought to be entirely abstract, and claims that it is so, he must after all take his bearings from a determinate class of objects. Plato, when the objects of Nature had become the centre of his speculation, had applied the method of division to biological types; and this had confirmed his belief in the Ideas, and added new characteristics to them. And it is in the particular processes of the living world that Aristotle finds the prototype of form and matter, and sees the inseparable union of universal and particular constantly illustrated. As the oak is contained in the acorn, so is form in matter; either it is fully developed, or it is there in potentiality; and so Aristotle was convinced that he had finally overcome the difficulties of 'separation' by situating the End *in* the individual (ἐντελέχεια). It is significant that he should have thought this, for it shows how much more a thinker is influenced by the vital effect of the objects in which he is interested than by logical distinctions. Plato had drawn a distinction between the mechanical and the final cause, and it was this which had brought him into conflict with Democritus (*Timaeus*, 46 D); but he had gone on to construct a 'theodicy', in which he showed that we must assume an intelligent design in Nature. The same forces which Plato sees displayed in the macrocosm, are located by Aristotle in the individual; he attributes a motive force to the End (τέλος), in spite of *Metaphysics*, 983ᵃ 30. And here the Aristotelian doctrine brings us back to the significance of ἀρετή in the doctrine of Ideas which we explained in the earlier part of this work. A reference to his 'entelechy' in fact occurred there on p. 9, footnote 4. The circle is now completed: Plato's experiments in 'division' had carried him down to the 'atomic form', and this leads Aristotle to make 'form' a property of the individual; but he conceives the operation of this 'form' in a way which shows that the original intention of the Ideal Theory, in its connexion with ἀρετή, was preserved: from imperfection a thing strives to realize its real being—to become what it truly *is*. In this sense we may consider Aristotle the authentic heir of Plato.

INDEX

Alcmaeon, fr. B 1 a Diels: 150, 154.
Antisthenes, 27, 72, 94, 126.
Aristotle, 165 ff.
  An. pr. 46ᵃ 30: 91.
  de Caelo, 279ᵃ 6: 162.
  de gen. anim. 789ᵇ 2: 160.
  metaph. 983ᵃ 30: 168; 1021ᵇ 20: 33;
    1039ᵇ 33: 50; 1050ᵃ 21: 33;
    1086ᵇ 5: 52.
  phys. 246ᵃ 13: 33.
  poetics, 1447ᵇ 11: 2; 1449ᵃ 14: 162.
Aristoxenus, fr. A 1 Diels: 157.

Democritus and Plato: 157 ff.

Eleaticism, 36, 59 ff., 64, 137, 157 ff.
Epicrates, 119, 124.

Heraclitus and self-knowledge, 34.
Heraclitus and the flux, 64.

Isocrates, *ep.* i. 2. 3: 21.

PLATO:
  Apol. 22 B: 18.
  Charm. 164 C: 34; 165 E, 166 B: 36;
    166 C: 34; 169 B D, 172 B C: 35.
  Crat. 440 B: 65.
  Epist. vii, 342 B: 129 *n.* 1.
  Euthyd. 291 B: 35.
  Euthyphro, 6 D: 138.
  Gorgias, 468 D: 31; 477 B: 33; 480 ff.:
    35; 503 E: 33; 504 A B: 32; 523 A,
    524 A B: 14.
  Laws, 803 B: 22; 895 D: 121; 897 E:
    129.
  Meno, 71 E: 33; 73 E, 74 C: 139; 77 A:
    98, 138; 79 A: 138; 81 A: 13;
    86 B: 9; 88 E: 35; 98 A: 48.
  Parmenides, 127 E: 137; 129 B: 60;
    E: 94; 130 B: 54; C: 139; 131 A ff.:
    59; 132 A B D: 57–9; E: 45; 135 D:
    19; 137 C: 100.
  Phaedo, 75 A B: 40, 154; D: 129; 76 B:
    48; 78 D: 48, 73; 80 B, 83 E: 73;
    99 C: 11, 43; E: 7, 12; 100 A: 7;
    B C: 8; D: 47; 101 C: 101; D: 7;
    E: 43; 102 D: 59; 105 C: 101;
    114 D E: 9.
  Phaedrus, 229 D: 20; 245 A: 18; 247 C:
    162; 247 D: 155; 249 B: 150; 262 A:
    36, 114, 139; 265 B: 17; C D: 96,
    150; E: 91, 156; 266 A: 18; B: 96;
    270 A: 19; 275 D: 20; E: 21; 276 E:
    20; 277 B C: 90, 114, 150; 278 B:
    17; C: 20.

PLATO (*cont.*)
  Philebus, 11 B: 114; 12 D: 138; B E,
    14 D, 15 A: 139; 15 B C D: 140;
    16 B: 146; D: 142–8; 17 B: 141;
    18 A B C: 141; 20 C: 142; 23 E,
    25 A: 154; 29 A, 30 A: 160; 38 A,
    39 A: 113–17; 39 B C: 130; 58 C:
    55.
  Republic, 353 B: 32; 454 A B: 80;
    476 A: 48, 81; D: 81, 87; 478 B:
    53, 70; 491 D: 31; 505 A: 15;
    C: 139; D: 39; 506 C: 15, 48;
    509 B: 10, 43; 511 C: 51, 82;
    517 B: 15; 523 B: 59; 525 D E: 60;
    530 B: 46; 531 B C: 82; E: 48;
    533 A: 15; 534 A: 48; 537 B C: 31,
    46, 83, 107; 596 A: 161; 601 D: 32,
    35; 609 A, 610 E: 33; 613 A: 44.
  Sophist, 216 B: 97; 217 D: 77; 218
    A B C D: 77, 84; 221 A, 224 C: 93;
    227 B: 55; 229 D: 90; 235 C: 104;
    246 B: 89; 247 E: 128; 248 E: 160;
    250 B: 98, 102; 251 A: 126; 253 A:
    100, 128; B: 135; C: 98, 100;
    D: 96–106; E: 106, 107 ff.; 254 B C:
    97, 104; 255 B: 136 ff.; E: 97, 103;
    256 B: 98; 257 B: 126; C: 92, 110;
    258 D: 153; E: 98; 260 B: 153;
    C: 110; 262 A: 128; D: 128; 263 D
    E: 69, 111 ff., 114; 264 A: 109, 130;
    B: 69; D E: 94, 99, 105; 265 C D:
    77; 266 E: 112; 268 C: 93.
  Statesman, 258 C: 95, 129; 259 D: 145;
    261 A: 147; 262 B ff.: 92; 266 D:
    55, 147; 268 C: 95; 277 A: 147;
    279 A: 95; 281 C: 94; 285 A: 36,
    84, 147; B: 91, 94, 131, 145;
    D: 84, 131, 159; 287 A: 78; C: 91,
    96; 295 E, 296 B: 21; 304 A: 19;
    D: 20.
  Symposium, 202 A: 48; 205 E: 39;
    210 A: 4; 211 A E: 73; C: 56.
  Theaetetus, 153 B C: 64 ff.; 157 D: 52,
    65; 163 D: 70; 169 D: 52; 172 A B:
    52, 65; 174 A B: 100; 176 A ff.: 52,
    65; 177 B: 65; D: 39, 65; 179 C:
    62, 70; 184 A: 64, 68; D: 68, 69;
    185 C E: 68; 186 A–D: 67, 68;
    187 A: 69 ff.; 188 E: 70; 189 A B:
    53; E: 112, 114; 190 A: 69, 118;
    193 C, 194 A: 132; 195 E: 70;
    200 C, 201 B: 71; 203 E: 73; 204 E:
    100; 205 C: 73, 100; D: 73; 206 D:
    70, 72, 129; 208 C D: 73, 74, 95;
    E: 74, 83; 210 B: 75.
  Timaeus, 29 C: 22; 30 C, 32 D, 33 B: